CW01161188

Teaching Assistants, Inclusion and Special Educational Needs

This book offers the first collection of international academic writing on the topic of teaching assistants. It serves as an indicative summary of current research and thinking in this field and as a point of departure for future research and development.

With contributions from leading researchers, the book draws together empirical work on the deployment and impact of teaching assistants from various perspectives and from a range of methodological approaches. It highlights and celebrates the vital everyday contributions teaching assistants make to their schools and their communities: from their role within classrooms to their moment-by-moment interactions with pupils and teachers. The book examines the effect that teaching assistants can have on pupils' learning and well-being, and considers issues of over-dependence on classroom paraprofessionals and the unintended consequences to which this can lead. Bringing together work from a journal special issue with brand-new and updated chapters, the contributions offer insight into the liminal space between educator, caregiver, behaviour manager, and facilitator of learning and of peer relations, which characterizes the teaching assistant role.

This timely and important book will be essential reading for academics, researchers, and students interested in special educational needs, disability, and inclusion, and those interested in the wider topic of paraprofessionals in labour markets.

Rob Webster is a reader in Education and Director of the Education Research, Innovation and Consultancy unit at the University of Portsmouth, UK.

Anke A. de Boer is an associate professor at the Inclusive and Special Educational Needs unit, University of Groningen, the Netherlands.

Routledge Research in Special Educational Needs

This series provides a forum for established and emerging scholars to discuss the latest debates, research, and practice in the evolving field of Special Educational Needs.

Books in the series include:

Inclusive Teamwork for Pupils with Speech, Language and Communication Needs
Rosalind Merrick

Social and Dialogic Thinking and Learning in Special Education
Radical Insights from a Post-Critical Ethnography in a Special School
Karen A. Erickson, Charna D'Ardenne, Nitasha M. Clark, David A. Koppenhaver, and George W. Noblit

Policy, Provision and Practice for Special Educational Needs and Disability
Perspectives across countries
Edited by Peter Wood

Technology Use by Adults with Learning Disabilities
Past, Present and Future Design and Support Practices
Jane Seale

International Issues in SEND and Inclusion
Perspectives Across Six Continents
Edited by Alan Hodkinson and Zeta Williams-Brown

Teaching Assistants, Inclusion and Special Educational Needs
International Perspectives on the Role of Paraprofessionals in Schools
Edited by Rob Webster and Anke A. de Boer

For more information about this series, please visit: www.routledge.com/Routledge-Research-in-Special-Educational-Needs/book-series/RRSEN

Teaching Assistants, Inclusion and Special Educational Needs

International Perspectives on the Role of Paraprofessionals in Schools

Edited by
Rob Webster and Anke A. de Boer

Routledge
Taylor & Francis Group

LONDON AND NEW YORK

First published 2023
by Routledge
4 Park Square, Milton Park, Abingdon, Oxon OX14 4RN

and by Routledge
605 Third Avenue, New York, NY 10158

Routledge is an imprint of the Taylor & Francis Group, an informa business

© 2023 selection and editorial matter, Rob Webster and Anke A. de Boer; individual chapters, the contributors

The right of Rob Webster and Anke A. de Boer to be identified as the authors of the editorial material, and of the authors for their individual chapters, has been asserted in accordance with sections 77 and 78 of the Copyright, Designs and Patents Act 1988.

All rights reserved. No part of this book may be reprinted or reproduced or utilised in any form or by any electronic, mechanical, or other means, now known or hereafter invented, including photocopying and recording, or in any information storage or retrieval system, without permission in writing from the publishers.

Trademark notice: Product or corporate names may be trademarks or registered trademarks, and are used only for identification and explanation without intent to infringe.

British Library Cataloguing-in-Publication Data
A catalogue record for this book is available from the British Library

Library of Congress Cataloging-in-Publication Data
A catalog record has been requested for this book

ISBN: 978-1-032-20859-6 (hbk)
ISBN: 978-1-032-20862-6 (pbk)
ISBN: 978-1-003-26558-0 (ebk)

DOI: 10.4324/9781003265580

Typeset in Galliard
by SPi Technologies India Pvt Ltd (Straive)

Contents

List of figures vii
List of tables viii
List of contributors ix
Acknowledgements xiv

Introduction 1
ROB WEBSTER AND ANKE A. DE BOER

PART I
Teaching assistants and schools 9

1 Paraprofessional support in Irish schools: From special needs assistants to inclusion support assistants 11
YU ZHAO, RICHARD ROSE AND MICHAEL SHEVLIN

2 In-between special needs teachers and students: Paraprofessionals' work in self-contained classrooms for students with intellectual disabilities in Sweden 29
DANIEL ÖSTLUND, THOMAS BAROW, KAJSA DAHLBERG AND ANETTE JOHANSSON

3 The ambiguous role of paraprofessionals in inclusive education in Germany 46
ANIKA LÜBECK AND CHRISTINE DEMMER

PART II
Teaching assistants and pupils 59

4 Inclusion moments for students with profound intellectual and multiple disabilities in mainstream schools: The teacher assistant's role in supporting peer interactions 61
INEKE HAAKMA, ANKE A. DE BOER, SANNE VAN ESCH, ALEXANDER E. M. G. MINNAERT AND ANNETTE A. J. VAN DER PUTTEN

5 Give them wings to fly: Critiquing the special needs
   assistants scheme through the lens of pupil independence   85
   CLAIRE GRIFFIN AND PETER BLATCHFORD

6 The perspectives and experiences of children with special
   educational needs in mainstream primary schools regarding
   their individual teaching assistant support   104
   HAYLEY PINKARD

PART III
Teaching assistants and teachers   123

7 Teaching assistants and teachers providing instructional
   support for pupils with SEN: Results from a video study
   in Swiss classrooms   125
   FRANZISKA VOGT, ANNETTE KOECHLIN, ANNINA TRUNIGER
   AND BEA ZUMWALD

8 The role of teaching assistants in managing behaviour
   in inclusive Catalan schools   143
   ANDREA JARDÍ, IGNASI PUIGDELLÍVOL, CRISTINA PETREÑAS
   AND DORYS SABANDO

9 Secondary teachers' perspectives on their work with
   teacher assistants   158
   CLAIRE JACKSON, UMESH SHARMA AND DELPHINE ODIER-GUEDJ

PART IV
The past, present and future of research on
teaching assistants   175

10 Maslow's Hammer: Teacher assistant research and
   inclusive practices at a crossroads   177
   MICHAEL F. GIANGRECO

11 Conclusion: Researching teaching assistants: What have
   we learned and where do we go next?   194
   ROB WEBSTER

   Index   208

Figures

2.1	Paraprofessionals self-reported knowledge about special needs teachers' educational planning for a school week (N = 60)	35
2.2	Paraprofessionals self-reported knowledge about content in the curriculum (N = 60)	37
4.1	Initiatives by students with profound intellectual and multiple disabilities	71
4.2	An example of student initiations (student 3)	72
4.3	Initiatives by peers	73
4.4	An example of peer initiations (student 5)	75
4.5	Initiatives by teaching assistants	76
4.6	An example of TA initiations (student 6)	77
6.1	Thematic analysis themes and sub-themes	110
6.2	'What is my TA like' 1	111
6.3	'What is my TA like' 2	112
6.4	'My ideal TA'	114
10.1	On the brink	180
10.2	Island in the mainstream	183

Tables

1.1	Individuals interviewed in each case study school (N = 538)	16
4.1	Students' characteristics	65
4.2	Coding scheme	66
4.3	Description of inclusion moments	68
5.1	Total special needs assistants classroom context across all cases	90
5.2	Total frequency of interaction data across all cases, comparing target pupil interactions with comparison pupil interactions	91
5.3	OPTIC schedule observation data for target pupils across all cases, as sourced from Griffin (2018, 198)	92
5.4	Type of academic task undertaken by target pupils across all observed lessons (n = 77)	92
6.1	Participant information	107
7.1	Types of individual support, coding scheme and examples	132
7.2	Content of instructional support, coding scheme and examples	133
7.3	Individual support distinguished in minutes by type and TA versus teacher in the two models and in total	134
7.4	Content of instructional support for pupils with SEN, descriptives and differences	135
7.5	Instructional support provided by TA and teacher for different attainment groups during individual seatwork in classes where TAs are employed for the whole class	136
8.1	Coding categories and sub-codes	147

Contributors

Thomas Barow is an associate professor of Education in the Department of Education and Special Education, University of Gothenburg, Sweden. In his research, he examines questions of inclusion in education in international and historical dimensions.

Peter Blatchford is an emeritus professor in Psychology and Education at the UCL Faculty of Education and Society, directed research programmes on the deployment and impact of support staff in schools (DISS), the educational effects of class size differences and pupil adult ratios (CSPAR), collaborative group work (SPRinG) and projects on grouping practices in schools, school recess/breaktimes, and the educational experiences of children with Special Educational Needs in primary and secondary schools. He has recently completed a three-year Leverhulme-funded Major Research Fellowship. His publications include *Rethinking Class Size* (2020) and *The Child at School: Interactions with Peers and Teachers* (2016).

Anke A. de Boer works as an associate professor at the University of Groningen, at the Inclusive and Special Needs Education unit. Besides this, she works for the Regional Expertise Centre for Northern Netherlands, an organisation for special education. Her work focuses on special educational needs and influencing factors on policy, teacher, and student level.

Kajsa Dahlberg is a special needs teacher for students with intellectual disabilities. She is a postgraduate in special needs training with specialization in learning disabilities. She holds a degree of master of science with a major in education with specialization in special education at Gothenburg University, Sweden.

Dr. Christine Demmer holds a junior professorship in Qualitative Research Methods and School Inclusion in Educational Science at Bielefeld University. Her research interests include methodologies and methods of qualitative educational and biographical research, pedagogical action in the context of inclusion and heterogeneity, and inclusive teacher training.

x   *Contributors*

Sanne van Esch works as a behavioural scientist at Vanboeijen, an organisation for people with disabilities. She was involved in the study on inclusive education for students with profound intellectual and multiple disabilities.

Michael F. Giangreco, PhD, is University Distinguished Professor Emeritus of Special Education at the University of Vermont. Prior to joining the faculty in 1988 he served in a variety of capacities (e.g. community residence counsellor, special education teacher, special education administrator). His work focuses on various aspects of education for students with developmental disabilities within general education classrooms such as curriculum planning, support services decision-making and coordination, alternatives to over-reliance on teacher assistants, and inclusive educational service delivery. Beyond his more traditional scholarship, he is known for his cartoons lampooning the absurdities and realities of special education.

Claire Griffin is a chartered educational psychologist and lecturer in educational and developmental psychology at Mary Immaculate College, Limerick, Ireland. She is programme leader of the BEd in Education and Psychology programme and supervisor of trainee educational psychologists. Claire originally worked within primary and special education settings. Thereafter, Claire engaged in postgraduate training in special education and Educational Psychology, qualifying as an Educational Psychologist in 2012. Claire undertook PhD studies through University College London and successfully graduated in 2018. Claire has worked on a number of national research projects in Ireland and has been recipient of a range of awards and grants.

Ineke Haakma holds a PhD degree in special needs education and youth care. She conducted various studies, amongst others on inclusive education and students with profound intellectual and multiple disabilities.

Claire Jackson is a PhD candidate in the Faculty of Education at Monash University, Australia. She is a teacher, school leader, and education consultant, providing support for students with disability and building the capacity of teachers and teacher assistants to make adjustments to support the inclusion of students with diverse learning needs. She also works on national projects relating to inclusive education and school funding for students with disability, and has co-authored professional learning materials and digital resources for Australian schools and teachers. Her doctoral research is investigating how teachers and teacher assistants collaborate to facilitate inclusive practice.

Andrea Jardí is a PhD student from the University of Barcelona in the Department of Teaching and Learning and Educational Organization. She is a member of the research group 'Learning, Media & Social Interactions' (LMI) and a member of the Educational Support to Inclusive

Education group belonging to the Educational Sciences Institute (ICE) of the University of Barcelona. She has a FPU PhD fellowship from the Ministry of Education and Vocational Training. Her research is focused on inclusive education and ways of improving the educational support offered by different stakeholders to vulnerable children.

Anette Johansson is a special needs teacher for students with intellectual disabilities. She has experience from working as a paraprofessional. She is a postgraduate in special needs training with specialization in learning disabilities at Gothenburg University, Sweden.

Annette Koechlin is a lecturer at the Institute for Professionalization and System Development, University of Teacher Education in Special Needs in Zurich, Switzerland. Her general interest concerns research on professionalisation of special needs teachers with a particular focus on cooperative educational practices in inclusion-oriented schools and classrooms.

Dr. Anika Lübeck conducted research on inclusive schooling at Bielefeld University and completed her doctorate on paraprofessionals. Still dedicated to this topic, she now advises paraprofessionals, teachers, and parents at an independent organization.

Alexander E. M. G. Minnaert is Full Professor of Special Needs Education and Clinical Educational Sciences at the University of Groningen and Scientific Advisory Board member of the Academy of Finland. Students' motivational, social-emotional, and learning processes are his three main focus areas of research within different levels and contexts of more inclusive and equitable quality education. Moreover, innovations, transformations, and interventions in education and youth care constitute a focus point in his research as well.

Delphine Odier Guedj is Adjunct Senior Lecturer at Monash. She is currently a professor at the Haute Ecole Pédagogique du Canton de Vaud in Switzerland and manages a research laboratory, lasalé (https://lasale.hepl.ch/). Delphine's research is grounded on human rights principles in order to transform lives. Drawing on a wide range of research and theory at the nexus between didactics, sociolinguistics, and body movement studies, her work aims to promote social justice, collaborations, and inclusion. She has been conducting research on interactional teaching pedagogies, parental advocacy, collaborations, and the activities of parents in schools.

Daniel Östlund is an associate professor at Kristianstad University, Sweden. He has experience from working as a paraprofessional, as SENCO, and as special needs teacher for students with intellectual disabilities. His area of research interest includes inclusive education, relations in education, and education for students with intellectual.

Cristina Petreñas is a lecturer (tenure-track) at the Department of Psychology in the area of Development and Educational Psychology at the University of Lleida. She is a member of the research group 'Language and Education' and a member of a Seminar about Inclusive Education Research. Her work is concentrated on inclusive education and the educational support in multilingual and multicultural educational contexts, considering topics as cultural identity, attitudes, acculturation process, among others.

Hayley Pinkard is an educational psychologist working for Southampton City Council. Her role involves working collaboratively with children and their families, and members of school staff, to promote more positive academic and social-emotional outcomes. She has a particular interest in empowering young people with special educational needs to share their views and to become more involved in decisions about the provision that they receive. She completed a doctorate in Educational Psychology at the University of Southampton in 2016 and an undergraduate degree in Psychology at the University of Exeter in 2009.

Ignasi Puigdellívol holds a doctorate in educational sciences from the University of Barcelona, where he is a professor in the Department of Teaching and Learning and Educational Organization. He was the dean in the Teacher Training Faculty at this University. He is a member of the Learning, Media & Social Interactions (LMI) research group. His field of research is focused on inclusive education, particularly in special education needs and minority groups.

Richard Rose is Emeritus Professor in Inclusive Education at the University of Northampton, UK. His current research is in the area of inclusion and children's rights, with some of this work being undertaken in India and Cambodia. He has previously worked as a teacher in schools in England and his research has been published widely in international academic journals and books.

Dorys Sabando has a PhD in Education from the University of Barcelona, where she is a lecturer (tenure-track) in the Department of Teaching and Learning and Educational Organization. She is a member of the research group Learning, Media & Social Interactions (LMI) at the University of Barcelona. Her field of research focuses on inclusive education, pre-service teacher training in behaviour self-regulation, and educational apps for early childhood. Her main publications include articles related to the role of support teachers, community support network in inclusive education, and the profile of inclusive schools in Catalonia.

Umesh Sharma is a professor in the Faculty of Education at Monash University, Australia, where he is the associate dean (Equity and Inclusion). Umesh's research programmes in the area of disability and inclusive education span India, Pakistan, China, Bangladesh, Fiji, Solomon Islands,

Vanuatu, and Samoa as well as Australia, Canada, the United States, and New Zealand. He is the chief co-editor of the *Australasian Journal of Special Education* and the *Oxford Encyclopedia of Inclusive and Special Education*.. He has authored over 175 academic articles, book chapters, and edited books that focus on various aspects of inclusive education.

Michael Shevlin is professor in Inclusive Education and Director of the Trinity Centre for People with Intellectual Disabilities in Trinity College Dublin (www.tcd.ie/tcpid). His teaching and research has focused on promoting the voice of marginalised people within decision making processes that affect their lives.

Annina Truniger is a PhD candidate at the University of Tubingen, Germany, and the St Gallen University of Teacher Education. Her main research interests include research on heterogeneity and inclusion as far as inequality in and through educational institutions.

Annette A. J. Van Der Putten is Professor at the University of Groningen, at the unit of Inclusive and Special Needs Education. Her research focuses on the support of persons with profound intellectual and multiple disabilities and their families. Annette is also chair of the academic collaborative center related to people with PIMD.

Franziska Vogt leads the Institute of Research in Teaching and Learning and the Centre of Early Childhood Education at St.Gallen University of Teacher Education, Switzerland. She received her PhD in 2002 at Lancaster University, United Kingdom, researching teachers' teamwork. Her research interests encompass professionalisation and teacher collaboration, as well as quality in early childhood education and care. Projects focus on learning through play, early literacy and numeracy, and gender.

Rob Webster is a reader in Education at the University of Portsmouth, UK, where he is also the Director of the Education Research, Innovation and Consultancy (ERIC) Unit. Between 2011 and 2017, Rob led a landmark research study of the everyday educational experiences of pupils with SEN. Prior to this, he was a researcher on the world's largest study of TA deployment and impact: the ground-breaking DISS project. Based on this work, Rob developed the award-winning Maximising the Impact of Teaching Assistants (MITA) programme, which has been accessed by over 1,000 UK schools.

Dr. Yu Zhao has been working as a researcher in education since 2011. She has been involved in different research projects regarding inclusive education and special needs education nationally and internationally.

Bea Zumwald is a professor at the St.Gallen University of Teacher Education. Her research interest concerns multiprofessional collaboration in inclusive schools, special education, inclusive teaching, and qualitative research methods.

Acknowledgements

This book builds on and contains papers that were originally included in a special issue of the *European Journal of Special Needs Education*, published in May 2021, which we co-edited. In addition to thanking all the contributors to this collection, we would like to thank the journal editor, Seamus Hegarty, and the members of the editorial board for suggesting and supporting our curation of the special issue. We are indebted to a team of reviewers for their time and dedication in reading and commenting on manuscripts. They are:

- Elias Avramidis – University of Thessaly, Greece
- Dianne Chambers – University of Notre Dame Australia, Australia
- Emma Clarke – Bishop Grosseteste University, UK
- Jennifer Doran – National Council for Special Education, Ireland
- Mary Beth Doyle – Saint Michael's College, USA
- Alexander Minnaert – University of Groningen, The Netherlands
- Melanie Nind – University of Southampton, UK
- Julie Radford – UCL Institute of Education, UK
- Elke Struyf – University of Antwerp, Belgium
- Klaus Wedell – UCL Institute of Education, UK
- Christian Wendelborg – Norwegian University of Science and Technology, Social Research, Norway
- Mara Westling Allodi – Stockholm University, Sweden.

Introduction

Rob Webster and Anke A. de Boer

The drive towards the inclusion of pupils with special educational needs (SEN) in mainstream schools has been accompanied and enabled by an increase in the employment and deployment of a relatively new kind of paraprofessional educator, most commonly defined as teaching assistants, teacher aides and paraeducators. Education systems in many developed countries have seen sizable and sustained increases in this section of their school workforce (Giangreco, Doyle and Suter 2014; Masdeu Navarro 2015). In many cases, this growth has been part of a broader and longer-term trend in the rise of paraprofessionals in other sectors – notably health, social work, law and the police – to assist the delivery of public services.

The origin of the paraprofessional role in schools can be found in the parent-helper model. During the 1980s, the trend for this in the UK saw some schools, mainly infants and primaries, have as many as 50 parents helping a week (Caudrey 1985), providing a much-needed extra pair of hands for activities such as school trips and art. Parent-helpers also assisted teachers with the particularly time-consuming task of listening to pupils read, which they typically did outside the bustling classroom. Good reading skills improved children's access to the curriculum, and as this was something that parents routinely did at home, schools not unreasonably surmised that this task could be safely delegated to willing volunteers.

Soon, additional adults were working more frequently alongside teachers *inside* the classroom. Throughout the 1980s and 1990s, mainstream schools began educating greater numbers of children and young people who might have previously attended a specialist setting. Parent-helpers were quickly co-opted to the inclusion cause. Voluntary arrangements were formalised into salaried positions as 'welfare assistants' and 'special needs assistants', as school leaders took the pragmatic decision to reappoint some of their parent-helper capacity to support pupils with the greatest need of adult attention. Other parent-helper roles evolved into more general 'classroom assistant' or 'teaching assistant' posts. In all cases, the teaching assistant (or TAs, as we collectively refer to them hereon[1]) role was classed as a 'non-teaching' role. This largely remains the case today, though it leaves the precise purpose and function of the TA role in a state of perpetual ambiguity.

DOI: 10.4324/9781003265580-1

It is now claimed that policies of inclusion and provision for pupils with SEN in mainstream schools in many countries would be impossible to implement without TAs (Blatchford et al. 2012). Its relative intuitiveness – more individualised support for pupils that struggle most – is arguably why it is *the* model of choice for education systems and schools striving for inclusion, and why it has replicated itself more successfully than just about any other approach. In a comparatively short space of time, in many schools and classrooms across the world, TAs have, quite quietly, become 'the mortar in the brickwork … hold[ing] schools together in numerous and sometimes unnoticed ways' (Webster et al. 2021).

The essentialness of TAs to schools was revealed during the Covid pandemic. A survey of over 9,000 UK TAs revealed just how pivotal they were to allowing schools to keep functioning and to supporting pupils and families during successive lockdowns (when schools were partially open) (Moss et al. 2021). While teachers delivered lessons remotely from home to children who were also housebound, TAs were in school, managing small classes and groups of vulnerable children and those whose parents were keyworkers (e.g. health professionals). Many TAs reported that they continued to provide bespoke support to individuals with SEN (who were included in the vulnerable group) and deliver targeted interventions. Meanwhile, out in the community, TAs shuttled between homes to check in on families, deliver food parcels and drop off resources to ensure that children without devices or internet access could carry on learning remotely.

While this book reports research that was completed before the Covid pandemic hit, it brings into the light the similar and vital everyday contributions TAs make to their school community. It is, in one sense, a celebration of the role and value of TAs, but it also offers up an important and timely critique of the wider systems and cultures, which seem to exist globally, that have led to the curious situation whereby the inclusion and education of some of the disadvantaged children in our schools has become almost entirely contingent on a workforce of 'non-teachers'.

Research on and involving TAs

Invoking Abraham Maslow's famous analogy to describe the 'human tendency to be over-reliant on a familiar tool to the exclusion of other potentially more appropriate tools', Professor Michael Giangreco sums up the predicament in Chapter 10 of this volume, thus:

> In schools where TAs are treated as Maslow's Hammer, they are a primary, sometimes nearly exclusive, tool to educationally and socially include students with certain [SEN and] disabilities. A student needs more instructional time or support – assign a TA. A new student with a disability (e.g., intellectual disability, autism) will be attending the school – assign a TA. A student exhibits behavioural challenges – assign a TA. A teacher expresses the need for support…, a parent wants to

ensure their child is not lost in the shuffle..., a team wants to protect a student from bullying or facilitate peer interactions – assign a TA.

As one of the foremost researchers on issues relating to TAs, Giangreco's papers were among the first to appear on this topic in peer-reviewed journals in the 1990s. Ever since, as the prevalence and prominence of TAs in schools and classrooms has grown, researchers have been keen to characterise effective models of TA deployment and to identify and measure their impact in various forms (Blatchford, Russell and Webster 2012; Sharma and Salend 2016). On the one hand, positive effects of having TAs in schools have been found in terms of teacher workload and reduced stress (Blatchford, Russell and Webster 2012). Yet when it comes to TAs having an impact on pupil outcomes, the direction of that effect appears to vary depending on exactly how TAs are utilised.

Large-scale research examining the impact of TAs providing general classroom support suggests that pupils, particularly those with SEN and/or with low prior attainment, perform worse, relative to their peers, in classes with a TA present (Blatchford, Russell and Webster 2012). However, results from well-designed trials where TAs are trained to deliver structured curriculum intervention programmes to individual pupils or small groups show, on average, moderate, but consistently positive, benefits (Alborz et al. 2009; Sharples 2016; Slavin 2016, 2018; Nickow, Oreopoulos and Quan 2020).

The evidence that TAs can improve pupils' so-called soft skills and well-being is also mixed, though this particular area of research is comparatively less mature than that which majors on academic outcomes. For example, facilitating the inclusion of pupils with learning difficulties has unintended consequences in terms of reducing interactions with teachers and peers, and creating dependencies on TA support (Webster, 2022). Yet, when TAs are trained to have constructive interactions with pupils that are designed to help them become more independent, there is evidence that pupil engagement improves (Dimova et al. 2021).

It is worth noting that there are some roles carried out by some TAs and other support staff in some schools that are explicitly non-teaching in nature, and these are often incorporated into the descriptive ambit of the TA title. These include the delivery of therapies to support pupils with emotional and/or behavioural difficulties, supporting personal care needs and parent liaison (see Alborz et al. 2009). In such cases, the task of mapping the evidence on, for example, the TAs' role in delivering speech and language therapies and/or occupational therapies, is compounded by loose conceptualisations of 'support' and the extremely limited number of research studies (McAnuff et al. 2022).

Returning to the impact of the learning support function that represents the mainstay of TAs' everyday role, two recurring and related themes arise from the literature that are associated with the variability in pupil outcomes. Firstly, the nature and quality of preparation and training teachers receive to plan for and deploy TAs, and (as noted already) the nature and quality of training TAs receive to be effective in their role (Webster et al. 2011); and, secondly, the availability of opportunities for teachers and TAs to plan and prepare together effectively. While such opportunities seem rare, the absence of liaison time is heavily implicated in reports – including some contained in this book – of why TA support in the classroom tends to be ineffective. This is a crucial point in the wider debate about TAs, because it shows the lack of agency and control that they have over improving their own skill levels and performance. It is the decisions made – or not made – *about* TAs by school leaders and teachers, not decisions made *by* TAs, that best explains their lack of impact in classrooms.

Policymakers claim that there is a clear demarcation between the role and function of teachers and TAs: teachers teach and TAs support (Blatchford, Russell and Webster 2012). School leaders and teachers, plus the professional associations and trade unions that represent them, also have an interest in maintaining this distinction and the stance that TAs are 'non-teachers'. Yet a consistent feature of the picture painted by over three decades of research on and involving TAs is that the model of inclusion to which many education systems have drifted – or, for those currently introducing their first cadres of TAs into classrooms, could yet drift – inevitably cast TAs in a pedagogical role (Webster et al. 2011). TAs tend to default to 'teaching' because their very presence and purpose in the classroom – to provide individualised support to pupils with SEN – results in the teacher providing *less* pedagogical support to those same children (Webster 2022). TAs often feel obligated to make up the shortfall.

Simple claims, therefore, that TAs are 'not teachers' or are 'non-teaching' staff not only depart from reality, but offer little in the way of clarity in response to questions about what they actually *do* and what they are actually *for*. Likewise, it provides inadequate cover for the fact that pupils with SEN have not been particularly well served by a model of inclusion that relies so heavily on TAs and, as Giangreco says, 'to the exclusion of other potentially more appropriate tools'; in this case, a teacher who is confident and competent to teach children with additional needs.

The lack of common agreement and clarity about the specific purpose of TAs in the education machine means that teachers and school leaders often overlook and undervalue their contributions. In the UK at least, many TAs felt that they had been forgotten about in the political and media discourse, despite having had a more visible than usual frontline role during the most disruptive phases of the pandemic (Moss et al. 2021).

It also leads to this vital part of the school workforce not being utilised in potentially more effective ways. Resolving the persistent problem of role ambiguity requires addressing two questions that have been repeatedly sidestepped. Firstly, how do we characterise the 'support' that TAs provide? If, as the dichotomisation implies, what TAs do is *not* teaching, then what *is* it and how is it distinct from teaching? How, in other words, do we define this nebulous concept of 'support'? The second and more fundamental question – the one within which the attention-absorbing debates about TAs roil – is:

how can we best include and educate pupils with SEN in mainstream schools? To be clear, addressing this question is not about replacing TAs, but about expanding our range of options and approaches to achieving this aim.

The purpose and structure of this book

It is with such vital and unresolved questions in mind that we invite the reader to consider this collection of international writing on the role, purpose and contribution of TAs in inclusive education. With a growing number of jurisdictions developing their own paraprofessional education workforce – together with the increasing amount of research interest and activity this attracts – the time is right to reflect on experiences and practices from territories where TAs are comparatively more established. This book draws together empirical research and perspectives on the function, deployment and impact of TAs. It intends to serve as both an indicative summary of research and thinking in the field to date, and as a point of departure for future research and development.

This book contains papers that were originally included in a special issue of the *European Journal of Special Needs Education*, published in May 2021. The call for papers, made in early 2019, generated a truly international response. As co-editors of the special issue, we received 48 abstracts from authors in 17 countries, across five continents. The peer-review process resulted in the publication of seven papers, which describe findings from original studies conducted in six European territories. These articles are republished in this volume, together with two papers by researchers from Germany and Australia. Each chapter offers insight into the liminal space between educator, caregiver, behaviour manager and facilitator of learning and of peer relations, which characterises the TA role.

The chapters are organised in terms of four overarching themes. The first theme describes the role of the TA with regard to inclusion and provision for pupils with SEN in three different European systems. Zhao, Rose and Shevlin draw on data from a longitudinal study to track the evolution of the special needs assistant role in Ireland, and the attempts at policy level to exclude from it 'any teaching activity'. The study by Östlund, Barow, Dahlberg and Johansson, meanwhile, reveals that the 'complexity of being both an educator … and a caregiver' to pupils with intellectual disabilities who are educated in self-contained classrooms in Sweden is upheld in part by a lack of support for TAs' professional development and opportunities to collaborate with special needs teachers. In the third chapter, Lübeck and Demmer discuss the ambiguity associated with the TA role in Germany. They identify the 'great challenges' stakeholders face in operationalising the TA role within classrooms, when their employment arrangements mean they sit outside managerial the jurisdiction of the school.

The second trio of chapters explore the pupil experience and what is like to work with a TA. Firstly, Haakma, De Boer, Van Esch, Minnaert and Van Der Puttena report on a project from the Netherlands, in which TAs supported and mediated verbal and non-verbal interactions between pupils with profound intellectual and multiple disabilities and their typically developing peers, as they engaged in a shared activity. Then, returning to Ireland, Griffin and Blatchford examine 'the complex relationship between paraprofessional support and pupils' development of independence'. They report on the constructs of TA support and highlight the more and less effective practices that support pupils' independence, captured via their large-scale, mixed methods study. Similarly, in the chapter that follows, Pinkard describes findings from innovative, child-friendly interviews with primary-aged pupils with SEN in England on their perspectives and experiences of TA support. While pupils emphasise the positive effects of TAs' 'nurturing characteristics', the hidden cost of high amounts of individualised support are revealed in terms of 'a significant degree of separation from teachers'.

The reliance on TAs to facilitate inclusion is a theme that bridges us to Part III of the book, which compares and contrasts the role of the TA and the role of the teacher. The piece by Vogt, Koechlin, Truniger and Zumwald reports on the instructional support for pupils with SEN provided by TAs and teachers in Swiss classrooms. Data from their video study found that, compared with teachers, TAs not only have longer one-to-one interactions with lower attaining pupils and those with SEN, but that the nature of TAs' instructional support tends towards 'telling pupils what to do', rather than 'co-constructive support, such as scaffolding'. Next, Jardí, Puigdellívol, Petreñas and Sabando explore how TA and teacher teams manage disruptive behaviour in schools in Catalonia, Spain. Semi-structured interviews with TAs and teachers describe how they coordinate their roles and the proactive strategies they use to de-escalate problematic behaviours in the classroom. Finally, Jackson, Sharma and Odier-Guedj report on the experiences secondary school teachers in Australia have of working with TAs, and the factors that facilitate and impede practice. Their contribution, and indeed several of the others included in this book, reminds us of the need to adequately prepare pre-service and in-service teachers to work effectively with TAs.

Two chapters comprise the concluding thematic section of this book, which considers the past, present and future of research on TAs. The first is the republished article by Michael Giangreco we commissioned for the *European Journal of Special Needs Education* special issue. Drawing on more than 40 years' experience of working with TAs and their colleagues, principally in the US, Giangreco provides a worldly perspective on the state of the field. In particular, he reflects on the persistent predicament regarding the systemic reliance on TAs to facilitate inclusion, and what school leaders and classroom practitioners can do to address this. In the final chapter, Webster adds to the recommendations for future research listed by Giangreco in his chapter and returns to the two unresolved questions we raised above concerning the characterisation of TA 'support', and how pupils with SEN can be best included and educated in mainstream schools, in ways that are less reliant on TAs.

While it cannot claim to represent the totality of topics, perspectives and provenances in what is a maturing field of study and thought in education, this compilation showcases a range of recent international empirical research conducted on the topic of TAs. Our collection is admittedly Euro-centric, but the essential themes and messages from the research are highly relatable and transferable to other contexts. In this sense, this book is particularly timely for and relevant to policymakers and educators in parts of the world that are beginning to build their TA workforces at the same time as rebuilding from the effects of the pandemic. Firstly, in terms of learning the lessons from places like the UK and the US, where the rapid acceleration of the employment and deployment of TAs in schools proceeded on the basis of assumption rather than evidence, and resulted in unintended and troubling consequences. Such exemplars provide a salutary reminder of the importance of instituting cultures and processes *from the start* that do not undermine inclusion or the educational experiences of and outcomes for pupils with SEN in disproportionately negative ways. And secondly, in terms of designing policies and practices, again *from the start*, which maximise the role and contribution of TAs and harness their capacity and potential. The final chapter of this book offers a blueprint for effective TA deployment that could be used as the basis for an impactful, long-term strategy. This will be of interest to ambitious leaders and legislators who seek to use this moment to fundamentally reset aspects of their education infrastructure for the post-pandemic world.

A theme that weaves its way through the contributions to this book is that the research community is at its most effective and impactful when researchers work directly and in partnership with schools to address the strategic and operational challenges connected to TA deployment and the inclusion and participation of pupils with SEN. A positive message from this book, therefore, is that the responses to the challenges of the current decade, and beyond, lie in researcher-practitioner collaboration. In all, we hope this book inspires interest and innovation, and contributes to the generation of ideas and activities that ensure TAs, and the children and young people they dedicate themselves to nurturing and developing, both thrive.

Note

1 For the purposes of this book, the commonly understood term 'teaching assistants' (TAs) is used to refer to school staff in pupil-based and classroom-based support roles who work mainly with pupils with SEN. Included in this definition are school staff known, among other titles, as teacher assistants, teacher aides, teaching aides, classroom assistants, learning support assistants, special needs assistants, paraeducators, paraprofessionals and pedagogue assistants. This definition excludes teachers.

References

Alborz, A., Pearson, D., Farrell, P. and Howes, A. 2009. *The Impact of Adult Support Staff on Pupils and Mainstream Schools*. London: EPPI-Centre, Social Science Research Unit, Institute of Education. Accessed 25 October 2021. http://eppi.ioe.ac.uk/cms/Portals/0/PDF%20reviews%20and%20summaries/Support%20staff%20Rpt.pdf?ver=2009-05-05-165528-197

Blatchford, P., Russell, A. and Webster, R. 2012. *Reassessing the Impact of Teaching Assistants: How Research Challenges Practice and Policy.* Oxon: Routledge.

Caudrey, A. (1985) 'Growing role of parents in class causes alarm', TES, 12 April.

Dimova, S., Culora, A., Brown, E.R., Ilie, S., Sutherland, A. and Curran, S. 2021. *Maximising the Impact of Teaching Assistants. Evaluation Report.* London: Education Endowment Foundation. Accessed 7 October 2021. https://educationendowmentfoundation.org.uk/projects-and-evaluation/projects/maximising-the-impact-of-teaching-assistants

Giangreco, M.F., Doyle, M-B and Suter, J.C. 2014. 'Teacher Assistants in Inclusive Schools.' In *The SAGE Handbook of Special Education*, edited by L. Florian, 691–702. 2nd ed. London: SAGE Publications.

Masdeu Navarro, F. 2015. Learning Support Staff: A Literature Review. OECD Education Working Papers. No. 125. Paris: OECD. https://doi.org/10.1787/19939019

McAnuff, J., Gibson, J., Webster, R., Kaur-Bola, K., Crombie, S., Grayston, A. and Pennington, L. 2022. School-Based Allied Health Interventions for Children and Young People Affected by Neurodisability: A Systematic Evidence Map Disability and Rehabilitation, http://dx.doi.org/10.1080/09638288.2022.2059113.

Moss, G., Webster, R., Bradbury, A. and Harmey, S. 2021. *Unsung Heroes: The Role of Teaching Assistants and Classroom Assistants in Keeping Schools Functioning During Lockdown.* London: UCL. Accessed 1 April 2021. https://discovery.ucl.ac.uk/id/eprint/10125467/

Nickow, A., Oreopoulos, P. and Quan, V. 2020. The Impressive Effects of Tutoring on PreK–12 Learning: A Systematic Review and Meta-Analysis of the Experimental Evidence. NBER Working Paper No. 27476. Accessed 1 August 2020. https://www.nber.org/papers/w27476

Sharma, U. and Salend, S.J. 2016. 'Teaching Assistants in Inclusive Classrooms: A Systematic Analysis of the International Research', *Australian Journal of Teacher Education* 41 (8): 118–134. Accessed 11 February 2021. http://ro.ecu.edu.au/ajte/vol41/iss8/7

Sharples, J. 2016. *EEF Blog: Six of the Best – How our latest Reports Can Help You Support Teaching Assistants to Get Results.* Accessed 17 April 2020. https://educationendowmentfoundation.org.uk/news/six-of-the-best-how-our-latest-reports-can-help-you-support-teaching-assist/

Slavin, R. 2016. *Trans-Atlantic Concord: Tutoring by Paraprofessionals Works.* Accessed 17 April 2020. https://robertslavinsblog.wordpress.com/2016/03/03/trans-atlantic-concord-tutoring-by-paraprofessionals-works/

Slavin, R. 2018. *New Findings on Tutoring: Four Shockers.* Accessed 17 April 2020. https://robertslavinsblog.wordpress.com/2018/04/05/new-findings-on-tutoring-four-shockers/

Webster, R. 2022. *The Inclusion Illusion: How Children with Special Educational Needs Experience Mainstream Schools.* London: UCL Press.

Webster, R., Blatchford, P., Bassett, P., Brown, P., Martin, C. and Russell, A. 2011. 'The Wider Pedagogical Role of Teaching Assistants', *School Leadership and Management* 31 (1): 3–20. http://dx.doi.org/10.1080/13632434.2010.540562

Webster, R. Bosanquet, P., Franklin, S. and Parker, M. 2021. *Maximising the Impact of Teaching Assistants in Primary Schools: Guidance for School Leaders.* Oxon: Routledge.

Part I
Teaching assistants and schools

1 Paraprofessional support in Irish schools

From special needs assistants to inclusion support assistants

Yu Zhao, Richard Rose and Michael Shevlin

Introduction

Internationally policymakers and administrators concerned to improve learning opportunities for students with special educational needs have endorsed models advocating the use of paraprofessional support in schools. Whilst these paraprofessionals are to be found under a broad range of titles, including teaching assistants, learning support assistants, classroom aides, paraeducators and special needs assistants, they are considered to be essential to the management of classrooms where students of diverse needs are educated together (Giangreco and Doyle 2007; Giangreco, Doyle and Suter 2013; Takala 2007).

Within Ireland, the use of special needs assistants (SNA) is sanctioned by the National Council for Special Education (NCSE), a semi-autonomous body established by the Education for Persons with Special Educational Needs Act (Oireachtas 2004) to oversee support provision in mainstream and special schools for children and young people who have disabilities and/or special educational needs. The SNA scheme emphasised the provision of support for the additional care needs of children and young people who otherwise might not be able to attend school. It was stated that the role of the SNA is to provide personal care support as distinct from having a teaching role Department of Education and Science Circulars (07/2002; 30/2014).

SNA provision is explicitly targeted at enabling students with additional care needs to attend school. Care needs are many and varied and include personal care, mobility, respiratory difficulties, complex medical and/or physical needs. In addition, other students may also be supported by SNAs, including those who are deaf/hard of hearing, those who are blind/visually impaired and those who have challenging behaviour or severe communication difficulties (National Council for Special Education 2018).

Background to SNA provision in Ireland

Current Irish policy for children with special educational needs is based on principles of inclusion that have been developed from the 1990s through the first decades of the current century. Educational provision and support for children with disabilities and/or special educational needs rapidly expanded

DOI: 10.4324/9781003265580-3

from the late 1990s onwards, and this expansion was mandated through enabling legislation (Education for Persons with Special Educational Needs, Oireachtas 2004). This landmark legislation and subsequent policy initiatives were clearly underpinned by a state commitment to establishing inclusive learning environments in mainstream schools. The role of the Special Needs Assistant was considered crucial as Irish mainstream schools adapted to delivering more inclusive learning environments. However, the rapid expansion of support provision (resource teachers/special needs assistants) often outpaced government efforts to regulate how this provision should be conceptualised and effectively delivered to benefit children with disabilities and/or special educational needs. Special Needs Assistants were often perceived as a panacea to address the many and complex needs experienced by the children of concern. As a result, at school level many practices emerged such as special needs assistants engaging in pedagogical activity which was explicitly prohibited in Department of Education Circulars on the role of Special Needs Assistants.

The Department of Education and Skills in Circular 30/2014 provided much needed clarity about the role and functions of SNAs. The Circular stipulates that while the SNA can assist the teacher in enabling students to access education the role of the SNA does not encompass additional tuition which is the remit of qualified teachers, whether classroom, subject or support teachers.

The SNA scheme forms an essential component in this support infrastructure alongside support teachers, therapeutic professionals and increased training for prospective and current teachers. SNA provision has expanded rapidly in recent decades, with 23% growth from 2006 (8,390) to 2011 (10,320); 35% increase from 2011 (10,320) to 2017 (13,969). Consequently, the number of students receiving SNA support increased by 56% over the time period 2011–2017 from 2011 (22,284) to 2017 (34,670). The number of students supported by SNAs as a percentage of the overall school population increased from 2.5% (2011) to 3.7% (2017) (National Council for Special Education 2018).

At government level, it is recognised that SNA provision has been effective in enabling pupils with special educational needs to attend school and has been particularly successful in meeting the additional care needs of younger pupils (National Council for Special Education 2018). The consultation process on the role revealed that SNA support is highly valued by pupils, parents and schools (National Council for Special Education 2018). Recent policy advice and implementation have focused on addressing significant gaps in existing support provision by creating a resourced continuum of support including regional support services comprising therapeutic professionals, nursing staff and educational psychologists (National Council for Special Education 2018). Within this reconceptualised model of support special needs assistants are now designated as Inclusion Support Assistants assigned to attending to additional care needs and not straying into any pedagogical or therapeutic activity as had occurred in the past.

Irish research

Irish research on the role of paraprofessionals in supporting children with special educational needs has been relatively limited when compared to jurisdictions where the paraprofessional role has been an established feature over many decades. Irish research has tended to focus on the parameters of the SNA role as defined in government policy in contrast to the actual role as it operated in schools.

Kerins and McDonagh (2015) suggest that confusion caused by a lack of clarity in the role and purpose of the position of SNAs is a matter of some concern as Ireland embraces an agenda intended to support the development of inclusion. Their survey of 318 SNAs found that SNAs were engaged in three distinctive forms of student support related to care needs; school planning and collaboration; and pedagogical/teaching duties. However, a clear departure from the original intention of the SNA scheme and defined by Kerins and McDonagh (2015) as providing support of a pedagogical/teaching nature included tasks such as planning work for pupils to do in class, teaching small groups of students with SEN and correcting students' work.

The research reported by Kerins and McDonagh (2015) reinforces the findings from Rose and O'Neill (2009) and Keating and O'Connor (2012), who observed that the interpretation of the role of the SNA was a matter of inconsistencies and that there are important questions to be asked about the professional boundaries between SNAs and teachers. The authors of both these research studies suggest that the perception of the role of the SNA varies from school to school and this has an impact upon both the perception of paraprofessional duties and the relationships established between teachers and support staff. Keating and O'Connor (2012) propose that SNAs have a critical role to play in assisting with the appropriate participation of pupils with SEN in all school activity in mainstream settings. Furthermore, the close relationship established by many SNAs with individual pupils places them in a strong position to ensure effective support (Giangreco, Doyle and Suter 2013). Continuing professional development for SNAs is recognised as essential for delivering high-quality support for pupils who have special educational needs (National Council for Special Education 2018). This professional development was regarded as critical when SNAs were working with pupils who had behavioural difficulties or pupils on the ASD spectrum (Kerins et al. 2018).

Project IRIS

Project IRIS (Inclusive Research in Irish Schools) was a four-year longitudinal study of the provision made for children and young people with special educational needs. Data were collected to ascertain the quality of provision made by schools and support services; the effectiveness of policy; the experiences of students, teachers and families; and the learning outcomes for students in schools across the country (Rose et al. 2015).

Methods

Adopting a mixed methods approach, a national survey gained an overview of how special educational needs issues were being addressed across the country. This was followed by the development of focused case studies utilising qualitative data obtained through interviews, focus groups, document scrutiny and observation, which enabled a more detailed analysis of how educational policy and school provision impacted on the learning experiences and outcomes for children with special educational needs. This chapter reports mainly on the findings obtained from interviews conducted with primary school principals, teachers, SNAs, students and their parents. A detailed discussion of the methods and analysis of the quantitative data has been reported elsewhere (Rose and Shevlin 2014).

Identifying research questions, establishing research instruments and selecting a sample

The National Council for Special Education (NCSE) identified seven research questions to be addressed through the study. Two of these questions demanded insights into the ways in which the curriculum was delivered and support provided to pupils with special educational needs, these being:

- How is the curriculum applied and delivered to these pupils/students?
- How does the school use special educational resources and other support services to provide an inclusive education?

The specific research questions adopted for this study comprised:

- What is the contribution of special needs assistants to including children with disabilities and/or SEN in mainstream classrooms?
- How do education stakeholders perceive the role of special needs assistants in supporting children who have disabilities and/or SEN?

An initial review of Irish and international literature (Rose et al. 2010), enabled the research team to identify four themes (Policy, Provision, Experience and Outcomes) which were used throughout the research process in order to ensure coverage of issues related to these research questions and to inform the development of case studies (Rose and Shevlin 2014).

A case study model was developed based upon a multi-respondent approach collecting data through interviews, focus groups, observation, document scrutiny and a national survey that sought to ensure that the views of stakeholders and providers of provision would be respected and compared, in order to ensure a trustworthy and in-depth understanding of the phenomena being investigated (Bassey 1999). At the centre of the model is the school and around this the four areas investigated by the researchers in order to gain a holistic view of how each school was responding to the needs of pupils with special educational needs. By interrogating these areas using data collected from respondents identified in the vertical boxes to the sides of the model, the researchers were able to gain an understanding of the influences of policy and provision upon the sample population and to understand the experiences of children and families and the outcomes of the procedures deployed in schools. The model allows for fair comparison across data providers (e.g. parents, teachers, therapists) and across schools. It is further strengthened through multi-source triangulation and multiple methods triangulation as advocated by Patton (2001).

Flyybjerg (2006) asserts that case studies can provide illuminative narratives giving unique insights into the complexities and contradictions of real-life situations. This, he suggests, is a method that has advantages over many others used in social sciences research when the cases generated are based upon well-structured and transparent systems of data collection and analysis. The approaches to data collection and interpretation within Project Iris were piloted prior to implementing the field work pathway described below.

During field work the research team visited ten primary schools, ten post-primary schools and four special schools. As SNAs have been involved in primary school education for a considerable period it was decided that this chapter should focus on this sample of schools in order to trace the evolution of the role more succinctly. All ten schools were selected randomly, using national databases to identify school variables from DES and NCSE. Within each case study school, a group of students were identified with the assistance of school principal and resource teachers, to ensure representative coverage of all categories of SEN identified within national assessment documentation. These sample students ($N = 77$) were followed throughout the project's duration.

All ten case study schools were visited twice, in order to gain a picture of how SEN provision was allocated to support children with special educational needs and to understand the sample students' learning experiences and outcomes.

The case study approach provided a framework throughout the research process for data collection during different phases of school visits. Using this approach, data were collected through classroom observation, school document scrutiny and semi-structured interviews with a full range of service users and providers. This chapter is primarily concerned with the support provided by primary school SNAs in addressing learning needs for children with special educational needs within case study schools.

The conduct of the research was monitored by the University of Northampton ethics committee which scrutinised examples of data collection instruments and other documentation to ensure the work adhered to clear ethical guidelines. All researchers involved had completed Garda clearance or, in the case of UK-based researchers, Criminal Records Bureau (CRB) clearance.

Semi-structured interviews

A pilot study was conducted with a sample of service users and providers, to verify the appropriateness of research instruments and establishing interview

16 Yu Zhao et al.

schedules (Malmqvist et al. 2019). Semi-structured interviews were conducted with a broad range of professionals, sample pupils and their parents in each case study school over the course of two school visits. The project code of ethics and an information sheet describing the purpose of the research was given to all participants, including students, who were also asked to complete an interview consent form. All interviews with students took place in the company of a known adult. The pupils appeared to engage very freely with the researcher and did not refer to the known adult for clarifications, so the influence of the known adult on pupil responses appears to have been minimal.

A total of 251 interviews (see Table 1.1) were conducted in ten case study primary schools over the course of the two school visits.

Table 1.1 Individuals interviewed in each case study school (N = 538)

	Parents	Pupils	Teachers	Resource/ Support teachers	Principal/ Deputy principal	SNAs	Other professionals
Primary schools							
1	18	2	3	6	1	3	0
2	5	7	7	2	2	3	0
3	7	6	5	3	1	5	0
4	6	7	8	5	1	6	0
5	8	8	12	1	2	4	0
6	3	4	3	4	1	3	0
7	4	2	4	4	1	2	0
8	2	6	3	0	1	2	0
9	6	4	6	4	1	5	0
10	6	6	4	1	1	3	1
Total	65	52	55	30	12	36	1
Special schools							
11	4	3	6	2	2	4	2
12	6	6	5	4	1	0	1
13	4	4	1	3	1	2	1
14	6	7	4	2	2	1	0
Totals	20	20	16	11	6	7	4
Post-primary schools							
15	5	7	4	3	2	2	2
16	3	5	5	4	2	3	4
17	3	3	3	1	1	2	0
18	6	6	5	5	1	2	0
19	4	5	3	5	1	1	2
20	4	5	2	1	1	2	2
21	7	1	4	0	2	4	3
22	5	5	3	0	2	4	1
23	1	5	3	1	1	4	2
24	3	6	4	0	1	4	0
Total	41	48	36	20	14	28	16
Total – all schools	126	120	107	61	32	71	21

Coding and analysis

All data were analysed by research team members. Data from interviews conducted with all professionals, students and parents were coded using criteria established under three of the four themes to allow the research team to make comparison of school provision, learning experiences and outcomes for individuals with special educational needs across schools. For the purpose of data collection to answer the two specific questions being addressed in this chapter, questions related to policy were not asked as the focus was upon work at school level, rather than national level. These codes were established based on an early scrutiny of data from previously conducted focus groups, survey and interviews with a range of professional and parent groups and of school documentation. An analysis of transcripts from the early data collected as part of the larger project enabled codes to be derived and refined. Transcripts were blind-coded by two or, sometimes, three researchers who initially devised codes related to each research question. These analysts then compared the codes and looked for areas of common agreement before applying them definitively as part of the analysis process. Where there were disagreements regarding the allocation of codes, these were discussed. If consensus was not achieved after these discussions, it was agreed that the allocated code may not be secure and this part of the data was therefore discarded.

A system of code management established a framework of commonalities, whereby recurrent themes that were representative of a majority of responses obtained across the full sample of respondents (service users and providers) were regarded as trustworthy (Bassey 1999) and a fair indication of the tenor of the data obtained. Where a majority of the overall sample had not provided evidence of a common response, these were considered to be exceptionalities (Rose and Shevlin 2014) and were therefore deemed unrepresentative as indicators of typical support provision. While exceptionalities can at times be useful in the identification of innovative or unusual practices in providing classroom support, in this instance, the researchers had been asked to provide evidence of those strategies and approaches commonly used in providing classroom support.

This process of multi-researcher triangulation achieved through a process of blind coding has been commonly used when conducting research of this nature (Patton 2001) where an extensive data set is to be analysed.

Findings

Findings were defined according to themes that arose whilst clustering codes related to the research questions. The researchers then returned to the transcripts to identify examples of what had been said during interviews. It was decided that quotations from these would only be used if they were verifiable across interviews from each of the respondent groups (parents, pupils, SNAs, teachers). In this way, the researchers were able to provide examples that may be described as typical of the responses obtained.

The interview data from SNAs, parents and pupils indicated that the role of the SNA was complex and multidimensional. The findings are reported under two key components of the case study model: Provision and Experience. The Provision section comprises physical caretaking, organisational support, managing behaviour, promoting independence, collaboration between SNAs and teachers and perspectives of school professionals about SNA role. The Experiences component includes pupils' attitudes towards SNA support and parents' attitudes towards SNA support.

Provision

Physical caretaking

Physical caretaking, the original rationale for the SNA role, was deemed essential, especially for pupils who had severe physical disabilities. One eight-year-old pupil, for example, is totally reliant on SNA support for basic daily living activities such as toileting and eating as recounted by his SNA:

> …when he came to school he had never eaten anything at all, whereas now he has a small lunch … he has to do mouth exercises, for biting, because his food at the moment is pureed and now, we're trying to introduce lumps, so he has to kind of practice, to build up the muscles.

Furthermore, a Deputy Principal from a case study primary school evaluated the contribution from SNAs regarding daily caretaking for children with SEN:

> If you have a child that has toileting needs as part of a disability that can be very difficult, you can rely very much on an SNA who is comfortable with that sort of thing,

Likewise, another principal from a case study primary school indicated that SNAs provided care support for children in their school, which made the school run successfully:

> I think that the SNAs we have are very good and very caring towards the children, and I would hope that they would see the role as pastoral as much as anything else.

Organisational support

Organisational support for specific pupils was evident enabling an eight-year-old pupil with Down syndrome to get ready for his schoolday:

> Well it's really to keep him on task and to sort him out in the morning when he arrives here, make sure he hangs his coat up … and get him to get himself sorted and get his books organised out of his bag and his pencil case out of his bag.

Furthermore, a class teacher of an eight-year-old boy on the autism spectrum indicated that support from his SNA helped in keeping him on task:

> So when he's on his own doing the test he could daydream there for ever, if he got stuck on one, he wouldn't cop on to go on the next one, you know, he'd stay stuck and he wouldn't even ask me, the SNA is generally there for O, to keep him on task.

Likewise, a principal from another case study primary school mentioned that she coped well with students and her work because of SNAs' organisational support:

> The SNA is an integral part of the set-up, because with that amount of children in the class with needs ... she would always keep me tuned in to what was happening, I mean without an SNA in the room, it would be very difficult to cope.

Managing behaviour

A ten-year-old boy with behavioural difficulties was offered support in a discreet fashion to avoid embarrassing him as one parent observed:

> Now we're lucky we got an SNA, that made an absolute huge difference ... the school, they didn't make it out that this is C.'s SNA, they incorporated it into the classroom, like he doesn't think that he has 'oh I have a special helper.

This approach to support was evident in another primary school as the SNA assigned to a ten-year-old girl who had behaviour difficulties commented:

> I'm the SNA with R. for years, and R. I would say still doesn't even know I'm her SNA ... I just keep a distance, always keep a distance from her, that she would never be aware that she has a minder or whatever!

Promoting independence

SNAs were aware that pupils should not become over-dependent on their support and conscious that support should not become overpowering as reported by an SNA in a primary school:

> I don't think any of the kids here in the school mind having SNA's, like, we're kind of part of the room, and we don't sit and make them feel that

> I'm here to help you … you go away and let them do it and if they're doing it wrong you give them a hand, rather than sit beside him and make him feel uncomfortable, you know. You'd kind of move and go back and move and go back.

A resource teacher from another case study primary school believed that too much support would hinder the pupil's attempts to become more independent:

> Particularly because if you have a child with a lot of needs, the SNA is nearly like an extra mum, and they nearly anticipate too much, and they, we don't want the Velcro system, they all work under that policy to let the kids be as independent as possible, so we kind of feel that if you chop and change a little bit, maybe twice, or three times through their school life, it works to their advantage.

Collaboration between SNAs and teachers

Collaboration between SNAs and teachers in supporting children experiencing difficulties was dependent on the teacher perspective on the role of the SNA. The SNA who supports John, an 11-year-old who has severe dyslexia, observed that her role could be expansive or restricted depending on the attitude of the classroom teacher:

> I've found, my job is, it's the strengths and skills of SNA's are only incorporated into a class as much as a teacher will allow…. I think the SNA even just with paired reading, going over maths lessons that they've done already with the teacher, I think the SNA should be utilised a lot more than they are, rather than, I've been in other classes where you sit. And it's an awful waste of resource.

School professionals' perspectives regarding SNAs' support

Enabling pupils to engage in positive social interactions was considered a vital element in the SNA role as demonstrated in the seating plan intervention designed by a teacher and SNA to include a ten-year-old pupil who was on the ASD spectrum:

> …she (teacher) kept changing who she sat next to, until there was a combination where there was a group of kids around her that would be chatty in a nice way, and one day teacher almost had to tell her to be quiet, which would have been a first, it was lovely.

Her SNA encouraged this type of interaction and was able to: '...step back and see her enjoying herself and starting to mix'. In another primary school, playground activities were adapted to include everyone: '...we had a few different break time problems, so we made up loads of different playground games, so there's a different game every break time, the whole classroom has to play, and they all love it, and the children who found it difficult to join in, there's a few of them in the classroom, are all joining in, and they've come on heaps'.

A primary school principal indicated that SNA support was necessary for children with special educational needs in helping and encouraging them in positive social interactions at school, especially when they experienced transition between year groups:

> ...because I see the bond that is built up with putting a child with the SNA, I thought that would help the child to relax, the children are very nervous, very, very tense children ...when the SNA could move on with the child, and she would know somebody in the school up along.

Likewise, a support teacher from another primary school mentioned that SNA support was essential during the transition progress for children with SEN, and transition could be less stressful in social interactions with the continuous SNA support:

> Well what we've just changed recently now is that our SNA's would have maybe changed in September when the teacher changes, but now this year that we have brought in that the SNA will change at mid-term in February, so that when they go to their new class, at least they'll be bringing their SNA with them, and they'll be able to give you an overview on what the child's like.

Experiences

Pupils' attitudes towards having SNA support

The experiences of pupils and parents in relation to the support afforded to them by SNAs provide insights into the efficacy of this provision and the perceptions of service users. It was evident from the observations conducted in schools that SNAs were allocated tasks by teachers that aimed to provide support for pupils in a number of areas.

Pupils often spoke positively about the support that they received, as was the case of a pupil with social, emotional and behavioural difficulties in a post primary school:

> I have an SNA that definitely helps, especially in like the big class, you know. Because like you could just ask the SNA like, instead of always asking the teacher.

Others were able to discriminate when they needed SNA support, stating, for example, that they may need assistance in maths lessons, but not at other times.

However, pupils did not always appreciate the support offered by an SNA and some resisted support as reported by an SNA regarding a nine-year-old boy who had difficulties in learning:

> …they don't want to be singled out and made different, so you have to be very careful how you approach them. Because that's why I make it so obvious that I'm helping others, … I can see he gives me looks sometimes, so I have to pretend that I'm working with A. beside him as well!

A 12-year-old boy appeared to resent having to rely on SNA:

> He, J. is a challenge in a way, in that he does not want an SNA. He doesn't like the fact that he needs one, because he's a very bright boy, but he's very severely dyslexic, and doesn't like others to know that he finds things difficult, because he likes to be very good, and he likes to be the best at everything.

J.'s class teacher describes how support can be diversified to minimise J.'s discomfort:

> …he (J) hates having the SNA sitting beside him … and other days then, she'll just go round and say, 'are you sure you have your capital letters', and she'll do it to several of them all around him, so that he doesn't feel too particular, because he's at an age now where he doesn't want her he recognises that P. (SNA) makes him different.

Parents' attitude towards SNA support for their children

From the interviews with SNAs and parents, it was apparent that while SNAs carried out traditional caretaking there was increased emphasis on adopting a pedagogical role. The delivery of the curriculum and the support provided by SNAs are closely interlinked, with suggestions that curriculum access and the progress made by pupils are often dependent upon the interventions of paraprofessionals in the class. Evidence from the interviews with both parents and pupils suggests that the work undertaken by SNAs includes support for academic activity. The comment from one primary school pupil (ten-year-old boy who had specific speech and language difficulties) was typical of many responses.

> She helps me with my writing, and, she helps me with my speech and my work.

Parents were aware that their child could require specific SNA supports for maths instruction to enable learning to occur as illustrated by the following comment from the parent of an eight-year-old boy who has ASD:

> …his SNA comes up and sits beside him, mainly during maths I think … not for the whole of the classes, it's mainly maths that would be a struggle.

This point was reinforced by the parent of a nine-year-old girl who has ASD:

> …she has a helper in the classroom now, C. (SNA), and she's there, she helps her, and even C. says how she's coming on well with the maths.

This structured SNA support was directed by the class teachers. Parents appeared to be content that SNAs adopted a role in the specific planning of specialist interventions. The SNA took responsibility for employing social stories (which requires a degree of pedagogical understanding) to support a child on the autism spectrum focused on improving his personal and social skills. His parent commented that

> Yes, we've done social stories and I know his previous SNA used to actually write them for him, she was brilliant. On one occasion again, he didn't want to get his hair cut, and she wrote a lovely social story about getting your hair cut, … it's trying to tap into ones that would be appropriate to the stage he's at.

Another parent reported that her child who has a hearing impairment had benefitted from the structured SNA support for developing language skills:

> I mean she struggled in junior infants with, they were doing phonics, and she was struggling with the hearing and the pronunciation, that's all come together this year, so we can see a massive difference to last year … her SNA, the resource teacher, they've just been brilliant … and like she's doing fantastic in school and every report we've had has been good.

Emotional reassurance

Providing reassurance to pupils constituted another critical aspect of SNA work as recounted by one parent whose child had ADHD and required focused emotional support as he tackled classroom tasks:

> …if there's something that involves him reading and then doing a little bit of writing, he has a tendency to get frustrated and start actually

huffing and puffing in the class, and she's also trying to reassure him that, just take a deep breath, you'll be fine, let's work on one and see how we get on, and then we'll move on to the next one, and sure if you don't get them all today, at least you tried your best and so on.

A class teacher of a five-year-old boy with physical disabilities reflected that he normally could not cope alone when she dealt with other children in class; however, his SNA provides emotional support:

> …well the Special Needs Assistants are a great support because you know, they would have been with R. from the beginning, so I suppose she has a special relationship with him, and I actually found it quite difficult to teach R. myself, as in to do the exercises, because he might tend to push me away, whereas he knows that E. (SNA) will help him through

Another class teacher of an eight-year-old boy with emotional and behavioural difficulties observed that the SNA was able to understand and manage this boy, and provide him with emotional support, enabling him to work well at school:

> Sometimes he has to put his head down on the table mid-way through an assignment, but I have an excellent classroom assistant, and she is very good at knowing when she can put pressure on him to lift up his head and pushing him on.

Discussion

It is worth noting that there was consistent agreement across the respondent groups (parents, pupils, SNAs, teachers) about the impact of SNA provision on the school lives of the pupils being supported. The findings from this research strongly support the contention that the special needs assistant role is an essential element in ensuring that children and young people with disabilities and/or SEN can meaningfully participate in the school environment.

The findings clearly indicate that the core elements of the SNA role continue to be focused on physical caretaking and organisational support, which are essential prerequisites for the meaningful participation of these children in ordinary classroom activities. To some extent, the significance of this core SNA activity has been overlooked in the debate about the quasi-pedagogical activities often observed in classrooms (Kerins and McDonagh 2015). While inconsistencies in how the SNA role was implemented across schools have been reported (Keating and O'Connor 2012; Rose and O'Neill 2009), there was a high level of consistency among the case study schools in their emphasis on the importance of physical caretaking and organisational support offered by special needs assistants in their schools.

Enabling pupils to manage their behaviour in classrooms was considered an essential element of the SNA role and was highly valued by teachers, school principals and families. Supporting pupils to manage their behaviour is a complex activity requiring high levels of expertise. SNAs were very aware that they had received comparatively limited training in how to effectively manage pupil behaviour and were concerned that this limited their ability to fully support the pupils they supported. This finding aligns with recommendations from the National Council for Special Education (National Council for Special Education 2018) review and research from Kerins et al. (2018) that emphasised the urgency of providing appropriate training for SNAs to undertake the newly conceptualised Inclusion Support Assistant role (National Council for Special Education 2018).

The findings indicate that there were high levels of collaboration between SNAs and teachers, and this is considered essential in ensuring consistent support for pupils. However, research has indicated that even where there are clear lines of management, it is not unusual for paraprofessionals to be operating autonomously, making decisions about instruction, delivering pedagogical support and recording pupil performance (Giangreco, Suter and Doyle 2010). There was strong evidence in this study that SNAs were perceived to be an essential element in the school support team and collaboration in designing appropriate classroom support was highly valued.

School professionals perceived that SNA support was essential in enabling pupils to engage in appropriate social interactions with their peers and their teachers. This support was deemed to be critical in ensuring that pupils could manage the many transitions experienced in primary schools. The importance of SNA supporting transitions was also highlighted in recent research on transition processes in Ireland (Scanlon et al. 2019).

The findings related to the experiences of pupils, parents and teachers in respect of the support provided by SNAs reveal a number of important issues.

There appears to be an element of security on the part of parents who believe that their children will be better included in learning when SNA support is present. While this perception is reinforced by both teachers and pupils, there are occasions when SNA support is seen by pupils in particular to inhibit social interaction with their peers and be a cause of anxiety that they may be singled out as different. Many pupils within the study valued the support provided by SNAs but were also concerned that this should be delivered in as unobtrusive a manner as possible.

Both parents and pupils valued the support provided by SNAs not only in terms of support for personal needs but also for that related to curriculum content. This support focus differs from that expected by paraprofessionals whose brief is one of a caregiver rather than an educational professional and is an indication of the changing role of the SNA status. This situation, far from raising concerns on the part of parents, is generally regarded as a positive development through which pupils are more readily enabled to access learning and be maintained in classrooms alongside their peers.

Teachers acknowledge the changing role of SNAs and regard them as essential partners in pedagogical enterprise. For those pupils who have physical needs, the care role continues to be an important focus of the SNAs' work. However, teachers recognise that the support provided for pupils with more general learning difficulties, being able to utilise their skills in working on curriculum activities under their direction, is a critical means of ensuring pupil inclusion in learning.

Conclusion

It is very evident from this study that SNAs are viewed as an essential element in establishing inclusive learning environments by all the major participants in the education system. Participants particularly valued the quality of the SNA commitment to supporting students to be fully included in classroom learning and social interaction. Policymakers have attempted to narrowly define their role as caretaking, though this policy stance has shifted and there is an implicit recognition that SNAs are involved in supporting pedagogical activity, though under the direction of the class teacher. The recent re-designation of SNAs as Inclusion Support Assistants is a clear indicator that their role is highly valued in creating inclusive schools, though with the caveat that their role does not encompass an explicit teaching dimension. Perhaps, it can be argued that this approach avoids the pitfalls experienced in other jurisdictions where teaching assistants were increasingly expected to cater to the learning needs of students with special educational needs.

Acknowledgements

The authors wish to thank the National Council for Special Education, Ireland, who funded the research discussed in this chapter.

Originally published as Yu Zhao, Richard Rose & Michael Shevlin (2021) Paraprofessional support in Irish schools: from special needs assistants to inclusion support assistants, European Journal of Special Needs Education, 36:2, 183-197, DOI: 10.1080/08856257.2021.1901371.

© Taylor & Francis Ltd (2021), reprinted by permission of the publisher.

References

Bassey, M. 1999. *Case Study Research in Educational Settings*. Buckingham: Open University.
Flyybjerg, B. 2006. "Five Misunderstandings about Case-study Research." *Qualitative Inquiry* 12 (2): 219–245. doi:10.1177/1077800405284363.

Giangreco, M. F., and M. B. Doyle. 2007. "Teacher Assistants in Inclusive Schools." In *The Sage Handbook of Special Education*, edited by L. Florian, 429–439. 1st ed. London: Sage.

Giangreco, M. F., M. B. Doyle, and J. C. Suter. 2013. "Teaching Assistants in Inclusive Classrooms." In *The Sage Handbook of Special Education*, edited by L. Florian, 691–701. 2nd ed. London: Sage.

Giangreco, M. F., J. C. Suter, and M. B. Doyle. 2010. "Paraprofessionals in Inclusive Schools: A Review of Recent Research." *Journal of Educational and Psychological Consultation* 20 (1): 41–57. doi:10.1080/10474410903535356.

Keating, S., and U. O'Connor. 2012. "The Shifting Role of the Special Needs Assistant in Irish Classrooms: A Time for Change?." *European Journal of Special Needs Education* 27 (4): 533–544. doi:10.1080/08856257.2012.711960.

Kerins, P., A. M. Casserly, E. Deacy, D. Harvey, D. McDonagh, and B. Tiernan. 2018. "The Professional Development Needs of Special Needs Assistants in Irish Post-primary Schools." *European Journal of Special Needs Education* 33 (1): 31–46. doi:10.1080/08856257.2017.1297572.

Kerins, P., and D. McDonagh. 2015. "The Special Needs Assistant Scheme to Support Teachers in Meeting the Care Needs of Some Children with Special Educational Needs Arising from a Disability: Potential Implications for Post-primary Schools." *REACH: Journal of Special Needs Education in Ireland* 28: 31–42.

Malmqvist, J., K. Hellberg, G. Möllås, R. Rose, and M. Shevlin. 2019. "Conducting the Pilot Study: A Neglected Part of the Research Process? Methodological Findings Supporting the Importance of Piloting in Qualitative Research Studies." *International Journal of Qualitative Methods* 18: 1–11. doi:10.1177/1609406919878341.

National Council for Special Education. 2018. "*Comprehensive Review of the Special Needs Assistant Scheme: NCSE Policy Advice Paper No. 6.*" Trim, Co. Meath: National Council for Special Education. (NCSE) Ireland.

Oireachtas 2004. *Education for Persons with Special Educational Needs Act (EPSEN)*. Dublin: Stationary Office.

Patton, M. Q. 2001. *Qualitative Evaluation and Research Methods*. 2nd ed. Thousand Oaks, CA: Sage Publications.

Rose, R., and A. O'Neill. 2009. "Classroom Support for Inclusion in England and Ireland. An Evaluation of Contrasting Models." *Research in Comparative and International Education* 4 (3): 250–261. doi:10.2304/rcie.2009.4.3.250.

Rose, R., and M. Shevlin. 2014. "The Development of Case Studies as a Method within a Longitudinal Study of Special Educational Needs Provision in the Republic of Ireland." *Journal of Research in Special Educational Needs* 16 (2): 113–121. doi:10.1111/1471-3802.12066.

Rose, R., M. Shevlin, E. Winter, and P. O'Raw. 2010. "Special and Inclusive Education in the Republic of Ireland: Reviewing the Literature from 2000 to 2009." *European Journal of Special Needs Education* 25 (4): 359–373. doi:10.1080/08856257.2010.513540.

Rose, R., M. Shevlin, E. Winter, and P. O'Raw. 2015. "Project IRIS-Inclusive Research in Irish Schools. A Longitudinal Study of the Experiences of and Outcomes for Children with Special Educational Needs (SEN) in Irish Schools." *Research Report Number 20 Trim*. Co. Meath: National Council for Special Education (NCSE) Ireland.

Scanlon, G., Y. Barnes-Holmes, M. Shevlin, and C. McGuckin. 2019. *Transition for Pupils with Special Educational Needs: Implications for Inclusion Practice and Policy.* Oxford: Peter Lang.

Takala, M. 2007. "The Work of Classroom Assistants in Special and Mainstream Education in Finland." *British Journal of Special Education* 34 (1): 50–57. doi:10.1111/j.1467-8578.2007.00453.x.

2 In-between special needs teachers and students

Paraprofessionals' work in self-contained classrooms for students with intellectual disabilities in Sweden

Daniel Östlund, Thomas Barow, Kajsa Dahlberg and Anette Johansson

Introduction

In international educational research, the role of paraprofessionals has been debated for some time. However, in education for students with an intellectual disability (ID) in Sweden, the practice of paraprofessionals has not received much attention, even though questions have been raised about their function, training and professional development. In this chapter, we explore questions tied to paraprofessionals' roles and assignments with the purpose to investigate their cooperation with special needs teachers (SNT), their specific assignments in self-contained classrooms for students with ID, and the support given for their further education.

For students with ID in Sweden, different educational pathways exist from being fully included in general education settings to belonging to a special school with its own campus. This school setting, often in the form of self-contained classrooms, is a compulsory school for students with an intellectual disability and an upper secondary school for students with an intellectual disability, offering students adapted curricula. In Sweden, about 88% of students with ID in compulsory school are in such self-contained classrooms with high staff density. The other 12% attend general education classrooms (Swedish National Agency for Education 2018). For students with ID, an adapted curriculum exists and is orientated towards general education. Paraprofessionals are generally employed by the school – and in some cases by an assistance service company – as a special educational effort and are expected to work with a student in need of special support. In a study by Lindqvist et al. (2011, p.) a majority (82.3%) stated that they had 'nine years of compulsory school or upper secondary school as their highest education' (p. 147). The other 17.7% had a university education. Regarding SNTs for students with ID, Klang et al. (2019) found that teachers working in a mainstream setting had higher expectations on students' academic performance, but lower focus on students' social participation. Anderson and Östlund (2019) demonstrate that SNTs work primarily with teaching and, to a lesser extent, with supervision and school development. The study pinpoints

DOI: 10.4324/9781003265580-4

the importance of collaboration with paraprofessionals and co-planning. Therefore, this chapter addresses a neglected occupational group and aims to provide knowledge on the working conditions of paraprofessionals in self-contained classrooms for students with ID.

Issues concerning paraprofessionals working with students with ID

Up until the 1990s, and similar to other school systems (Thompson et al. 2018), education for students with ID in Sweden was embedded in social welfare, often promoting care rather than education. For many years, this tradition gained criticism (National Agency for Education 2001; Swedish National Audit Office 2019). Due to curriculum reforms (National Agency for Education 2001; Swedish National Agency for Education 2011), education for students with ID gained clearer focus on academic achievement, not least with an increased focus on both formative and summative assessment. For paraprofessionals, this resulted in the need to work more extensively on students' academic performance and not just the tasks related to care and well-being (Anderson and Östlund 2017).

Parallel to curriculum implementation, the formal qualification demands for teachers working within curricula for students with ID increased, but without corresponding requirements for these paraprofessionals. In current education policy, there are no national guidelines on the work of paraprofessionals. At the same time, studies on education for students with ID in Sweden (Anderson and Östlund 2017, 2019; Östlund 2015) report that it is common for SNTs and paraprofessionals to work in teams with joint responsibility for the students' academic progress, social development and well-being.

Paraprofessionals working in teams

International research (Biggs, Gilson and Carter 2016; Cipriano et al. 2016; Symes and Humphrey 2011) shows that collaboration between teachers and paraprofessionals is crucial to special educational needs students' success in school. Previous studies have also shown that caregivers and professionals have a central role in supporting students with ID in their capability to address social relationships (Mason et al. 2013). Mitchell (2008) describes collaboration as a process that allows staff groups with different occupations to combine their resources to solve problems that occur in teaching practice. Teaching students in need of support often requires collaboration and coordination between staff members. Martin and Alborz (2014) find that information between teachers and paraprofessionals is often exchanged in recess or other spontaneous occasions – an obstacle for deeper cooperation. According to Saufley Brown and Stanton Chapman (2017), this depends on a paraprofessional showing an interest in increasing their opportunity to participate. There is a risk that hierarchical structures in the work team damage the collaborative climate unless paraprofessionals' participation and influence are encouraged (Balshaw 2010). Adaptations of learning activities are often made spontaneous, so it is sometimes difficult to formally determine or evaluate the contribution of paraprofessionals (Haycock and Smith 2011). However, it has been noted that paraprofessionals carry out instructions and make educational decisions – tasks that should be carried out by teachers (Brock and Carter 2013; Broer, Doyle and Giangreco 2005; Giangreco 2021; Sharma and Salend 2016).

In all Nordic countries, paraprofessionals have been an important role working closely with students, especially for those with different types of disabilities (Egilson and Traustadottir 2009; Hedegaard-Sørensen and Langager 2012; Hemmingsson, Borell and Gustavsson 2003; Takala 2007). This research (Anderson and Östlund 2019; Hedegaard-Sørensen and Langager 2012; Takala 2007) shows that collaboration between paraprofessionals and teachers is emphasised as a basic prerequisite for teaching to work effectively in the schools. Finnish research (Takala 2007) shows that work teams consisting of teachers and paraprofessionals have very limited opportunities for educational and didactic discussions and supervision, indicating shortcomings in the cooperation between SNTs and paraprofessionals. Östlund (2015) demonstrates that the provision of one-on-one instruction for students with ID is common for paraprofessionals. In another Swedish study, Anderson and Östlund (2017) show that schools that consciously work with school development can progress, such as favouring the paraprofessionals in their role and practice. Hedegaard-Sørensen and Langager (2012) highlight that close collaboration between SNTs and paraprofessionals increases an awareness of SNTs regarding their responsibility towards students and paraprofessionals. It was also clear that the paraprofessionals felt more appreciated, valued and more confident in their role, their assignment and their abilities when they had equal and non-hierarchic collaboration with SNTs. Anderson and Östlund (2019) demonstrate that SNTs express that paraprofessionals' contribution to the learning process of students with ID is seen as valuable, even though there is limited time for co-planning and co-assessing. Paraprofessionals' responsibility for providing educational support to students with ID is pervasive.

In summary, research on paraprofessionals shows that they work in teams with SNTs. They take responsibility for similar tasks in teaching as SNTs and make decisions on pedagogical instruction. Moreover, their education is often regarded as insufficient. Since research on paraprofessionals' work and assignments in Sweden is rare, it is our ambition to critically discuss in this area of research. Based on a paraprofessional perspective, we raise questions concerning their occupational role and collaboration with SNTs, in self-contained classrooms for students with ID. Therefore, our research addresses three research questions:

(1) What are the conditions for paraprofessionals' cooperation with SNTs?
(2) What are paraprofessionals' specific assignments?
(3) What support do paraprofessionals receive for their occupational development?

Our research is relevant as it exemplifies basic questions about conditions for paraprofessionals in self-contained settings. From a larger perspective, this chapter sets the foundations for an open discussion on the tensions and dilemmas that arise in collaboration between special needs teachers (e.g. Broer, Doyle and Giangreco 2005). Thus, our study supports a discussion about the current situation of the paraprofessional occupation in relation to students with ID in self-contained settings and, at the same time, contributes knowledge to an area that is seldom explored in a Scandinavian context.

Theoretical framework

The theory taken for this study is from Michael Lipsky (2010), which describes how street-level bureaucrats, who are in direct contact with their clients, carry out or implement measures that are legislated by the legislature and through decisions made in the public sector. There are core components of the description of what constitutes a street-level bureaucrat working within an organisation. These individuals work with clients and have great freedom of action in relation to the client. However, there are unclear goals that street-level bureaucrats are working towards. Freedom of action is necessary for them to be able to do the work because it is considered so complex that it is not possible to formulate ready-made manuals. To shed light on the paraprofessional role and to interpret their views when dealing with assignments, professional development and cooperation with SNTs in self-contained classrooms, street-level bureaucracy (Lipsky 2010) has been a theoretical inspiration. In their daily work, paraprofessionals are guided by overall education policies; however, there are no specific guidelines or instructions to guide them. Street-level bureaucrats generally have limited control over the outcome of their work and cannot choose individual clients (Lipsky 2010). This means that they are bound to the overall structures in education for students with ID, including the curriculum and their working conditions. However, there is no clear policy governing their work and paraprofessionals have great discretion in relation to these students. In previous research (Brock and Carter 2013; Broer, Doyle and Giangreco 2005), the role and assignments of paraprofessionals appear to be complex, with low demands on education and high demands on performance of work because these professionals often work closely with students who have the most complex needs. This theoretical view aims to clarify how paraprofessionals experience cooperation with SNTs, their assignments in self-contained classrooms and what support paraprofessionals receive for their occupational development.

Method

To investigate paraprofessional experiences, a mixed methods approach (Creswell 2014) based on a questionnaire and qualitative interviews has been chosen. We collected both descriptive quantitative data and qualitative data, which have helped to provide a deeper understanding of paraprofessional cooperation, assignments and support. The use of mixed methods is taken to capture paraprofessional statements in a nuanced way. All participants were informed about the research study's ethics policy applied in this project (Swedish Research Council 2002), which was based on confidentiality and participants taking part voluntarily.

First, we conducted a digital questionnaire with open and closed responses in two municipalities. 60 paraprofessionals ($N = 60$) working in four schools for students with ID participated with a response rate at ~67%. All four schools were located in two municipalities with 50,000–100.00 One of the inhabitants. The municipalities were selected by a convenience sample method. All schools were sharing campus with general education students and the teaching for students with ID were organised in self-contained classrooms. Due to the sample size and the sample method, we only used descriptive statistics when presenting the numerical data and qualitative data of the questionnaire. The paraprofessionals have experience from 0 to 2 years ($N = 13$), 3 to 10 years ($N = 32$), 11 to 20 years ($N = 12$) and 21 years and more ($N = 3$). Quotes from the questionnaire are identified as para 1 to para 60.

Second, we received permission from one municipality, based on convenience selection method to conduct interviews with paraprofessionals ($N = 5$; identified as PARA a to PARA e) and SNTs ($N = 4$; identified with the abbreviation SNT a to SNT d). We used a purposive sampling strategy to find participants, and searched for SNTs and paraprofessionals working in teams with experience of working with education students with ID. In the final sample, we prioritised participants working in joint teams rather than having extensive experience, which resulted in one of the interviewed paraprofessionals having only three months' experience being included in the sample. Within the group of interviewees, four female paraprofessionals, one male paraprofessional and all four SNTs were females. Working with qualitative data is a common procedure for researchers to identify, analyse and interpret themes (Bryman 2016). The analysis of the interviews can be divided into four stages. (1) All interviews were transcribed verbatim; (2) the transcript was initially read in order to identify an overview; (3) a thematisation was carried out in light of the study's research questions; and (4) the final analysis was carried out and quotes were selected that related to the research questions, theory and previous research studies. Due to the study design, limitations exist in generalising the results.

Results

The analysis of the survey and the interviews was guided by the research questions and yielded three themes. We summarise them as *Conditions for cooperation between paraprofessionals and SNTs; Being an educator and a care-giver; Lack of support for professional development*.

Conditions for cooperation between paraprofessionals and SNTs

Paraprofessionals working with students with ID are included in working teams alongside SNTs. From both interview and questionnaire data there are different responsibilities in the work team and the prerequisites for working together vary. All informants share the view that lack of time places limits on how cooperation works and state this is an organisational issue. The interviewed SNTs and paraprofessionals describe that they set aside 15–30 minutes a week for meetings. This time is the only scheduled time for meetings every week.

> We have a short meeting every Monday morning, but that time is very much spent on what is going to happen and not so much on assessment.
> (PARA b)

Time allocated for educational discussions focused on learning and assessment is often consumed by other more urgent practical tasks. The lack of joint planning time is confirmed in the survey responses, but with the difference that they have more time at their disposal: up to one hour (73%) and in some cases up to two or three hours (27%). The survey also states that the time for co-planning and co-assessment disappears because of practical problems that need to be solved. Despite the shortage of time, paraprofessionals often receive information about what the teaching should contain at the same time as the students. Time is also a prerequisite to keeping informed about SNTs' written plans and students' IEP and is something that does not fit within the working hours. The interviewed paraprofessionals also keep themselves updated on student documentation outside their working hours. Even though there is a lack of time for joint planning, the survey shows that many paraprofessionals report they are familiar with the content in the weekly education plan (Figure 2.1).

The interviewed SNTs and paraprofessionals describe a constant exchange of information during the school day. Often these are ad hoc, unplanned reconciliations in connection with the beginning or end of a lesson. It is primarily an oral exchange of information, but there are examples of paraprofessionals mentioning that they write down reflections on students' learning and provide these to the SNT after a lesson. Some participants describe the importance of these brief reconciliations about students' learning process directly when the lesson ends; otherwise, the information will be forgotten.

It is also expressed that the staff share their thoughts with each other while the students are having a lesson, as some situations occur when the students have independent work and have the opportunity to catch these moments.

> You complement each other in good cooperation. I can contribute what I see and then my colleague comes up with their opinions. You have to listen and trust each other and together you can create a clearer picture of the student.
> (SNT b)

I am well acquainted with the SNTs educational planning for a school week.

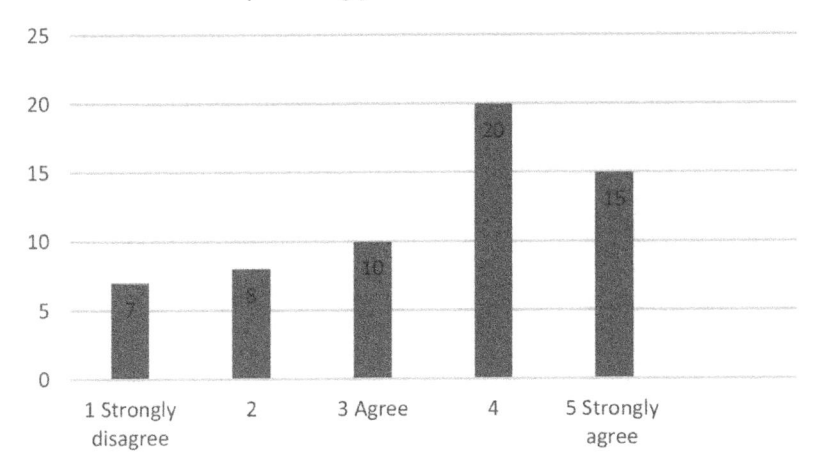

(Bar chart showing responses: 1 Strongly disagree = 7; 2 = 8; 3 Agree = 10; 4 = 20; 5 Strongly agree = 15)

Figure 2.1 Paraprofessionals' self-reported knowledge about special needs teachers' educational planning for a school week (N = 60).

The interviewees point towards the importance of giving opportunity for dialogues within the team to utilise all knowledge about the students' learning and they believe that their knowledge is well used if they strive to do a good job together. They suppose that responsibility rests on the SNT to lead the cooperation, but also invite the paraprofessional to participate in the educational work and in the formative assessment.

> It is what interests you have as paraprofessional, but also how the SNT invites me and what I want with my work. It's a bit of both I think.
> (PARA c)

In the interviews the importance of the SNT's overall role in the work team is identified together with the formal mandate to assess, and do not indicate that the conversations held in the work team affect teaching to any significant degree. Another participant argues that there is a clear difference in the roles, but that the role of paraprofessional is underestimated. The SNTs do not see everything the paraprofessional does. The interviewees also point out that the role of a paraprofessional is to follow the student throughout the school day, but that they may also take over a SNT's assignments, such as being a substitute due to SNTs' absence.

> Yes, but I have the role of being everywhere. Then we will be substitutes when the SNT is absent. Then you have both your own role and the SNT's role.
> (PARA b)

It also appears that some participants experience a large difference between the two occupational categories in terms of status. Some paraprofessionals describe a hierarchy within this cooperation:

> Many of us in the team where everyone is equally worthy of whatever title they have. In the class I am now, it is *not* like that.
>
> (PARA e)

Furthermore, some paraprofessionals claim to be divided into a 'first' and a 'second' team and that it is the SNT who has the main responsibility – being the 'first' team – and sets the agenda. The paraprofessionals feel as though they are not valued in the same way because they lack a title and education.

> I can sometimes feel that when you have an education that I have, you look at things sometimes in a different way. Paraprofessionals may not always have the overall picture.
>
> (SNT b)

In the survey responses, on being familiar with the content in the curriculum shows variation among paraprofessionals. It is stated in the interviews that the SNT has the main responsibility for planning, making the teaching work and completing assessments. The paraprofessional has a supportive and important role, working closely with the student all day. It seems contradictory that a lack of time for planning is highlighted as an issue at the same time as many paraprofessionals believe they are familiar with their SNT's weekly planning schedule. Information about students' learning objectives and what kind of learning activity to perform is given ad hoc to the paraprofessional, often whilst the students are informed. Even though there are difficulties in organising joint time for SNTs and paraprofessionals, it is stated as a strength that the work team representatives have different roles, can focus on different parts and can then take advantage of this. In the interviews some participants explained that the different occupational roles complement each other with their different knowledge, which contributes to a holistic view of the student.

Being an educator and a caregiver

Both the interviews and the survey data point to the complexity of the paraprofessionals' occupation, role and assignments. In relation to students, they have a responsibility for educational activities and pedagogical decision making. They also have the main responsibility for a student's well-being, peer-to-peer relations and being accountable for more care-orientated work tasks. The paraprofessional's work consists mainly of working closely with a student throughout the day: in the classroom, in recess and in the cafeteria – thus supporting the student in a variation of situations. Being a significant adult for the student and working with them each day means the paraprofessional's pedagogical decision making becomes important. Some of the paraprofessionals express that besides their direct work with students they also have other specific responsibilities to procure subs, make the schedules for the staff, order materials and teach single subjects (such as music or arts). Although they always work closely with the students, they are expected to support them in their learning, and many have direct responsibility for teaching a subject. The survey results show that paraprofessionals' self-reported knowledge of content in the curricula varies (Figure 2.2).

Most participants see the team's joint work as a resource that benefits all of the students. The collegial work is seen as a strength in relation to the student and that paraprofessionals and SNTs see different aspects of the students' learning and development. Participants also mention that students work and behave in different ways depending on which member of staff is closest to the learning situation. One benefit highlighted by the interviews is that the paraprofessionals follow the students throughout the school day. The paraprofessionals describe that they have responsibilities for their students in other situations than in the classroom. That circumstance gives them a holistic picture of a student's learning during all activities in the school, not just the formalised ones.

> Yes, but it is very important that you see the whole of the student, that is, their entire development everywhere and you listen to each other because we have different knowledge and we look at the student in different ways and in different situations.
>
> (PARA c)

I feel well acquainted with content in the curricula.

Response	Count
1 Strongly disagree	6
2	11
3 agree	14
4	21
5 Strongly agree	8

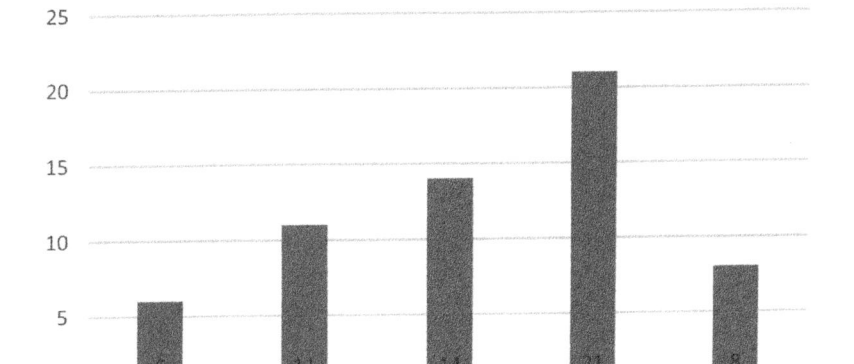

Figure 2.2 Paraprofessionals' self-reported knowledge about content in the curriculum (N = 60).

There are statements that differ from the others, and these indicate that the time for learning is not always seen throughout the school day. Content learned in a formalised lesson is sometimes seen as more important than learned in other situations and some paraprofessionals state that they contribute with a holistic understanding of the students' learning:

> There are different SNTs [...] some just see the learning in the classroom and do not think that this time between leisure time is also a learning to be assessed. We can see that the knowledge is in other places than in the classroom. For example, the math: you can see traces of it when the student works in the wood craft lesson.
>
> (PARA b)

This statement points to the importance of recognising a student's knowledge in a subject in different contexts. Paraprofessionals follow students in all subjects with different teachers and have the potential to observe them learning and how knowledge is used in different situations. Both SNTs and paraprofessionals are needed in the team to ensure a student is guaranteed a valid and reliable formative assessment.

> If you think about the formative assessment, this an ongoing assessment in everyday life all the time. When you are several staff members you see different things, you see different pieces, you contribute with different parts. If I was the one who assessed everything myself, [...] then it is just my eyes and my thoughts. If there are more people, you see more angles, I think.
>
> (SNT d)

This quotation highlights the importance of members in the team around the students' contributions in the formative assessment. In addition to tasks that are directly related to teaching, paraprofessionals have a variety of other tasks directly related to students' disabilities and their need for care. In the survey, the paraprofessionals provide examples of tasks they perform every day:

> Nasogastric intubation, toilet/diaper change, providing medication, transfers between different aids/wheelchairs, assisting students to get dressed.
>
> (para 1)

> Supports social interaction in recess, supports students' dressing, for example, in PE; ensures that students wash properly and dress in clean clothes, reminds students to wash hands after a visit to the toilet, support in school lunch cafeteria.
>
> (para 39)

The quotations pin down the variety and complexity of the paraprofessionals' work and where they are expected to be able to support students academically, but also support them in issues such as their social interactions in recess, hygiene and medical conditions. The results show that the paraprofessionals' role is an important contribution to a holistic view of the students' learning. On the other hand, there is a large variation in their knowledge on what content the students are supposed to learn. As a group, paraprofessionals also take on the main responsibility for activities outside of formal teaching. They are in recess with the students, provide medicine, help with toilet activities (such as changing diapers), mediate conflicts between students and help with nasogastric intubation. The assignment may also include coordinating student journeys with the school bus and arranging subs when someone is absent, and in some cases making schedules for the paraprofessionals. Both the interviews and the survey provide instructions on the complexity and the various tasks that are part of paraprofessionals' work.

Lack of supervision for professional development

The data indicate a lack of support for paraprofessionals' professional development and few opportunities for them to be supervised by SNTs. Only 10% (N = 6) of survey respondents report they have access to supervision continuously.

One of the paraprofessionals clarified:

> Our SENCO meets with me and another paraprofessional once every 14 days to help us design our support around our students. We discuss different arrangements and give each other feedback. The SENCO makes observations during lessons to see how we work.
>
> (Para 42)

Since SNTs are the ones expected to lead the work and have overall responsibility for planning, conducting teaching, assessment and documentation, they need to guide and supervise the paraprofessionals. The lack of common time is an obstacle to being able to supervise and the supervision often becomes superficial when SNTs only provide feedback in connection with the teaching when the student is present. The lack of time is a dilemma for the SNTs who are unable to practice their skills in supervising; this requires supervision to be a continuous element in the team's preparation and evaluation. The interviewees believe it is important to have a respectful attitude in all forms of supervision, describing examples of both external and internal supervision. Engaging an external supervisor was mainly related to dealing with students' behavioural problems, while internal supervision was in the form of guidance from SNTs to paraprofessionals within the same team. One of the SNTs emphasised that external supervision at the start of the semester could be helpful because they were then completely new colleagues who formed a new team and needed support. In the interviews, paraprofessionals expressed what skills a supervisor should have:

> A supervisor must be responsive and have both education and experience. It is good to have experience in mentoring someone, but you do not become a good supervisor overnight. Almost everyone needs guidance to be able to develop the work.
>
> (PARA e)

Participants believe that a good supervisor should have experience and a respectful attitude. SNTs do not consider themselves qualified interlocutors, nor are they considered qualified interlocutors by the paraprofessionals. SNTs must guide paraprofessionals on issues related to content in the curriculum and learning objectives, questions on assessment and student development. It became clear that newly hired paraprofessionals need guidance, and this is seen as a shared responsibility between the SNTs and more experienced paraprofessionals.

> The paraprofessionals need an adjustment period to get into the way they work. They are thrown in and have no idea what they should be able to work with. It is everyone's responsibility when any new colleague starts with us.
>
> (PARA d)

Discussion

Our results revealed a large variety in paraprofessionals' experiences. It is remarkable to note the time paraprofessionals report they spend with students and the responsibilities they have. Our results confirm the results in international research (Brock and Carter 2013; Broer, Doyle and Giangreco 2005; Martin and Alborz 2014; Saufley Brown and Stanton Chapman 2017; Symes and Humphrey 2011), as both the interviews and the survey report a variation between no time at all up to three hours for cooperation around planning, assessments and supervision. Due to the complexity of teaching and assessing students' progress, the variation in time for cooperation in the team is problematic. The assessment of students' progress is something that affects the entire team, not only the SNTs. The results demonstrate two stakes. First, there is not enough time for SNTs and paraprofessionals to prepare and evaluate their joint efforts for students' learning. Second, paraprofessionals have limited access to and limited time for supervision from SNTs or external supervision. Therefore, students with ID are expected to receive instruction and formative assessment from a varied and diverse group of paraprofessionals.

Anderson and Östlund (2017) reached a similar conclusion where ambiguity exists in the roles of different occupations. The results lead to similar conclusions where boundaries between the various occupational categories have faded, as paraprofessionals have an increasingly informal responsibility for pedagogical decisions, including direct instruction and formative assessment. For cooperation to work, good guidance is required for paraprofessionals, but also commitment and motivation in the group of paraprofessionals. It also turns out that there are partial opportunities for dialogue and educational conversations among the staff. However, time limitations for teachers and paraprofessionals become a barrier for cooperation and for student learning outcomes.

From the theoretical perspective of street-level bureaucracy, Lipsky (2010) has developed four main parts of the description over what constitutes a street-level bureaucrat in an organisation: (1) they work with people; (2) have great freedom of action; (3) unclear goals that the street-level bureaucrats are working towards; and (4) they often have too few resources at their disposal. In our results, it becomes clear that paraprofessionals are trapped between organisational conditions, unclear expectations and expanding discretion in meeting students. Lipsky (2010) believes that street-level bureaucrats are expected to be able to make balances and assessments based on each unique situation they encounter. Based on participants' accounts, our research suggests that they also feel a great influence over direct meetings with students. When there are no predetermined courses of action, formal rules or supervision guiding them, teaching is conducted on the basis of street-level bureaucratic subjective interpretation of a situation. This may explain that reviews of education for students with ID by the Swedish Schools Inspectorate (2010) indicate that the teaching places low demands on students and becomes more caring oriented than knowledge oriented (Swedish National Audit Office 2019). Another explanation is the paraprofessionals' lack of formalised pedagogical education and the lack of professional development for this occupational group.

Both SNTs and paraprofessionals point towards tensions in overall cooperation; from the paraprofessionals' point of view, they are sometimes feeling like being seen as the 'second team' compared to SNTs. On the other hand, they are also valued as competent enough to be a sub for the SNT. The SNTs point to the problem of paraprofessionals often lacking a formal education, but in contrast they also highlight the importance of good cooperation and that paraprofessionals contribute with knowledge and student experiences. In a working cooperation, balance in the relationship is important as well as the staff working together to enable students to make use of transferability in knowledge acquisition. For students to succeed in school, persistent work teams are required, with the students' learning objectives in focus and that they strive for a holistic approach. For the cooperation to be favourable, common goals, functioning communication and planning time are central. Our results demonstrate this, and it emerges that respect is an important building block in relationship building among staff. This confirms Saufley Brown and Stanton Chapman (2017) study, which shows that hierarchical structures can damage teamwork unless paraprofessionals' participation and influence are encouraged. However, this is a matter of the paraprofessionals showing an interest in increasing the opportunity to participate. There is a risk that hierarchical structures will build up in the work team and damage the teamwork unless paraprofessionals' participation and influence are encouraged. The paraprofessionals have a multifaceted assignment where they work with knowledge-oriented tasks, but also social, medical and nursing tasks. This places great demand on them. All of these areas are important for a student's well-being and growth as a future citizen. The work with medical, social and nursing tasks is a prerequisite for the teaching environment to function properly.

It will need further research to replicate our results. However, some tendencies become visible Due to the sampling strategy used, the results can only be applied to other groups with great caution. The samples are very limited in size, but the results from the questionnaire and the interviews are compatible and complement each other. The observed tendencies are valuable and could inspire future research.

Conclusion

Paraprofessionals are the occupational group who spend the most time with students during the school day and therefore become especially important for students' social and academic development. In the light of the street-level bureaucracy approach (Lipsky 2010), paraprofessionals' work is between the organisation, SNT and student with the task of accommodating all parties. Paraprofessionals have the discretion to make their own pedagogical decisions in relation to the student, but with very limited support and resources. Paraprofessionals' time for co-planning with SNTs varies, leaving the paraprofessional to make decisions about teaching and assessment on their own with few possibilities for supervision. The paraprofessionals' perceived ambivalence can be a reaction to the fact that there are several contradictory values that they are expected to support. Due to conflicting values, Lipsky (2010) argues that the role of street-level bureaucracy is complex and difficult. The results lead to similar a conclusion, as Broer, Doyle and Giangreco (2005) point to paraprofessionals being responsible for direct instructions and pedagogical decisions. The conflicting values place high demands on street-level bureaucrats' level of competence and responsibility. We conclude that paraprofessionals' role is complex due to leeway and the demands on pedagogical decision making with a lack of policy and regulations steer their work. The importance of joint time for supervision, co-planning and co-assessment (to reduce barriers developing) cannot be stressed enough. In view of the requirement since 2011 that teachers of students with ID must have a special needs teacher's degree and supplementary education at an advanced level, questions are raised about paraprofessional education. As paraprofessionals have a comprehensive responsibility for both teaching and social development, the issue of their education needs to be addressed by policymakers as well as government and local officials. It is also the case that students with ID should be entitled to an education with highly skilled SNTs and paraprofessionals. Our results indicate that there are organisational barriers preventing paraprofessionals from developing within their profession. The lack of time for co-planning and co-assessment and non-supervision also becomes an obstacle to further development. Although the dilemmas described are related to the school's organisation, the issue is larger and needs to be addressed by both school authorities and policymakers. There is reason to believe that it is students with ID who will not make progress from a qualitatively worse teaching environment unless paraprofessionals are paid attention and receive support. Requirements for statutory planning time and supervision are two initiatives that would raise awareness of pedagogical decisions within the professional group. An increased focus on the group through training requirements, professional development programs and formalised education would probably contribute to the professionalisation and help that the group requires for joint time with SNTs for co-planning and co-assessment.

Acknowledgements

Originally published as Daniel Östlund, Thomas Barow, Kajsa Dahlberg & Anette Johansson (2021) In between special needs teachers and students: paraprofessionals work in self-contained classrooms for students with intellectual disabilities in Sweden, European Journal of Special Needs Education, 36:2, 168-182, DOI: 10.1080/08856257.2021.1901370.

© Taylor & Francis Ltd (2021), reprinted by permission of the publisher.

References

Anderson, L., and D. Östlund. 2017. "Assessments for Learning in Grades 1–9 in a Special School for Students with Intellectual Disability in Sweden." *Problems of Education in the 21st Century* 75 (6): 508–524. doi:10.33225/pec/17.75.508.

Anderson, L., and D. Östlund. 2019. "Swedish Special Needs Teachers' Views on Their Work and Collaborations in Education for Students with Intellectual Disabilities." *The New Educational Review* 57 (3): 225–235.

Balshaw, M. 2010. "Looking for Some Different Answers about Teaching Assistants." *European Journal of Special Needs Education* 25 (4): 337–338. doi:10.1080/08856257.2010.513534.

Biggs, E., C. Gilson, and E. Carter. 2016. "Accomplishing More Together: Influences to the Quality of Professional Relationship between Special Educators and Paraprofessionals." *Research and Practice for Persons with Severe Disabilities* 41 (4): 256–272. doi:10.1177/1540796916665604.

Brock, M. E., and E. W. Carter. 2013. "A Systematic Review of Paraprofessional-delivered Educational Practices to Improve Outcomes for Students with Intellectual and Developmental Disabilities." *Research and Practice for Persons with Severe Disabilities* 38 (4): 211–221. doi:10.1177/154079691303800401.

Broer, S. M., M. B. Doyle, and M. F. Giangreco. 2005. "Perspectives of Students with Intellectual Disabilities about Their Experiences with Paraprofessional Support." *Exceptional Children* 71 (4): 415–430.

Bryman, A. 2016. *Social Research Methods*. 5th ed. Oxford: Oxford University Press.
Cipriano, C., T. N. Barnes, M. C. Bertoli., L. M. Flynn., and S. E. Rivers. 2016. "There Is No I in Team: Building a Framework for Teacher-paraeducator Interactions in Self-contained Special Education Classrooms." *Journal of Classroom Interaction* 51 (2): 4–19.
Creswell, J. W. 2014. *A Concise Introduction to Mixed Methods Research*. London: Sage Publications.
Egilson, S. T., and R. Traustadottir. 2009. "Participation of Students with Physical Disabilities in the School Environment." *American Journal of Occupational Therapy* 63 (3): 264–272. doi:10.5014/ajot.63.3.264.
Giangreco, M. 2021. "Maslow's Hammer: Teacher Assistant Research and Inclusive Practices at a Crossroads." *European Journal of Special Needs Education*.
Haycock, D., and A. Smith. 2011. "To Assist or Not to Assist? A Study of Teachers' Views of the Roles of Learning Support Assistants in the Provision of Inclusive Physical Education in England." *International Journal of Inclusive Education* 15 (8): 835–849. doi:10.1080/13603110903452325.
Hedegaard-Sørensen, L., and S. Langager. 2012. *Samarbetskunst, Arbejdsfælleska-ber Og Samarbejdsrelationer På Specialsko-ler*. Aarhus: Institut for Uddannelse og Pædagogik (DPU), Aarhus Universitet.
Hemmingsson, H., L. Borell, and A. Gustavsson. 2003. "Participation in school- School Assistants Creating Opportunities and Obstacles for Pupils with Disabilities." *OTJR: Occupation, Participation, and Health* 23 (3): 88–98.
Klang, N., K. Göransson, G. Lindqvist, C. Nilholm, S. Hansson, and K. Bengtsson. 2019. "Instructional Practices for Pupils with an Intellectual Disability in Mainstream and Special Educational Settings." *International Journal of Disability, Development and Education* 67 (2):151–166.
Lindqvist, G., C. Nilholm, L. Almqvist, and G.-M. Wetso. 2011. "Different Agendas? the Views of Different Occupational Groups on Special Needs Education." *European Journal of Special Needs Education* 26 (2): 143–157. doi:10.1080/08856257.2011.563604.
Lipsky, M. 2010. *Street-level Bureaucracy: Dilemmas of the Individual in Public Services*. New York: Russell Sage Foundation.
Martin, T., and A. Alborz. 2014. "Supporting the Education of Pupils with Profound Intellectual and Multiple Disabilities: The Views of Teaching Assistants regarding Their Own Learning and Development Needs." *British Journal of Special Education* 41 (3): 309–327. doi:10.1111/1467-8578.12070.
Mason, P., K. Timms, T. Hayburn, and C. Watters. 2013. "How Do People Described as Having a Learning Disability Make Sense of Friendship?" *Journal of Applied Research in Intellectual Disabilities* 26 (2): 108–118. doi:10.1111/jar.12001.
Mitchell D. 2008. *What Really Works in Special and Inclusive Education. Using Evidence-based Teaching Strategies*. London. Routledge.
National Agency for Education. 2001. Kvalitet i särskolan - en fråga om värderingar [Quality in schools for students with intellectual disability - a question about values]. Dnr 2000:2037, National Agency for Education.
Östlund, D. 2015. "Students with Profound and Multiple Disabilities in Education in Sweden: Teaching Organisation and Modes of Student Participation." *Research and Practice in Intellectual and Developmental Disabilities* 2 (2): 148–164. doi:10.1080/23297018.2015.1085327.

Saufley Brown, T., and T. L. Stanton Chapman. 2017. "Experiences of Paraprofessionals in US Preschool Special Education and General Education Classrooms." *Journal of Research in Special Educational Needs* 17 (1): 18–30. doi:10.1111/1471-3802.12095.

Sharma, U., and S. J. Salend. 2016. "Teaching Assistants in Inclusive Classrooms: A Systematic Analysis of the International Research." *Australian Journal of Teacher Education* 41 (8): 118–134. doi:10.14221/ajte.2016v41n8.7.

Swedish National Agency for Education. 2011. *Curriculum for the Compulsory School for Students with Intellectual Disability.* Stockholm: Skolverket.

Swedish National Agency for Education. 2018. "Statistics on Compulsory School for Students with an Intellectual Disability." Accessed 22 January 2020 https://www.skolverket.se/skolutveckling/statistik/sok-statistik-om-forskola-skola-och-vuxenutbildning

Swedish National Audit Office. 2019. "The Task of Promoting Knowledge in Compulsory Schools for Students with Learning Disabilities – Control, Support and Follow-up." RIR:13 Stockholm, Sweden: Swedish National Audit Office.

Swedish Research Council. 2002. "*Forskningsetiska Principer Inom Humanistisk-samhällsvetenskaplig Forskning*" [Research Ethical Principles in Humanities and Social Science Research]. Accessed 16 January 2020 http://codex.vr.se/texts/HSFR.pdf

Swedish Schools Inspectorate. 2010. "*Undervisningen I Svenska I Grundsärskolan* [Teaching in the Swedish Compulsory School for Students with Intellectual Disability]." Quality Review. Report:9. Stockholm: Skolinspektionen.

Symes, W., and N. Humphrey. 2011. "The Deployment, Training and Teacher Relationships of Teaching Assistants Supporting Pupils with Autistic Spectrum Disorders (ASD) in Mainstream Secondary Schools." *British Journal of Special Education* 38 (2): 57–64. doi:10.1111/j.1467-8578.2011.00499.x.

Takala, M. 2007. "The Work of Classroom Assistants in Special and Mainstream Education in Finland." *British Journal of Special Education* 34 (1): 50–57. doi:10.1111/j.1467-8578.2007.00453.x.

Thompson, J., V. Walker, K. Shogren, and M. L. Wehmeyer. 2018. "Expanding Inclusive Educational Opportunities for Students with the Most Significant Cognitive Disabilities through Personalized Supports." *Intellectual and Developmental Disabilities* 56 (6): 396–411. doi:10.1352/1934-9556-56.6.396.

3 The ambiguous role of paraprofessionals in inclusive education in Germany

Anika Lübeck and Christine Demmer

Introduction

Paraprofessionals have been working in the German school system for many years, supporting pupils with special needs. In this respect, paraprofessionals are not an entirely new occupational group in Germany, especially not in special schools. However, since the ratification of the UN Convention on the Rights of Persons with Disabilities (UN-CRPD) and the associated expansion of inclusive schools, this occupational group has acquired a new significance. While there has been a very differentiated special school system in Germany, more and more special schools are now being closed and pupils with special needs are increasingly attending mainstream schools. Yet often, these mainstream schools are insufficiently adapted to the needs of these pupils. As a result, schools increasingly try to rely on paraprofessionals to fill this gap.

In this chapter, we argue that paraprofessionals have an ambiguous role in inclusive schooling. On the one hand, they are supposed to promote inclusion, yet on the other hand, they cannot fulfil many aspects of a high-quality and non-stigmatising inclusive education. In order to substantiate this diagnosis, we will first describe the conditions of employment and deployment of paraprofessionals in Germany, in which we see this ambivalence laid out, as the application process represents a high hurdle and stigmatises children. We will then localise the ambiguous roles of paraprofessionals within a school system that has so far not been sufficiently oriented towards systemic inclusion, and within a job description that explicitly prohibits paraprofessionals from taking responsibility for pedagogical and teaching activities.

In order to theoretically underpin these diffuse roles and responsibilities, we will draw on the concept of the 'Grammar of Schooling' (Tyack and Tobin 1994). It describes unconscious concepts of a 'real school', which, according to our own work, also includes beliefs about the complementary roles of teachers and pupils (Lübeck 2019). We argue that this implicit Grammar of Schooling does not yet define a specific role for paraprofessionals. This results in different and problematic forms of practice that add to the structural deficiencies mentioned above. Based on these findings, we conclude this chapter by outlining possible scenarios for future developments in

DOI: 10.4324/9781003265580-5

the field of paraprofessionals, and for an inclusive school development that does not rely as much on the concept of paraprofessionals in its current form.

Background: Employment and deployment of paraprofessionals in Germany

The situation of paraprofessional deployment and employment in Germany is a complex matter. One reason for this is the educational sovereignty of the 16 federal states, which results in 16 different sets of school laws, and represents 16 different stages in the development of an inclusive school system. Another reason is that in most federal states, paraprofessionals do not belong to the school system, but to the welfare system. From a legal point of view, paraprofessionals represent a kind of 'integration assistance', and depending on the nature of the special needs of the child, they are financed by the youth welfare office, by the social welfare office or even by the child's health insurance. Accordingly, paraprofessionals are not centrally organised; there are no national standards for their application, approval, qualification or deployment.

Due to the diffuse circumstances, we lack reliable data on this, but in most cases, it is the parents who have to apply for a paraprofessional for their child with special needs. The social welfare office is responsible for pupils with a physical or learning disability; while those with a mental disability or a suspected mental disability or emotional disorder fall into the responsibility of the youth welfare office (Thiel 2017). This distinction is not always clear – especially for pupils with combined impairments, neither office may consider themselves responsible. As a result, applications are pushed back and forth, ending up in 'switchyards' or 'black holes' (Federal Ministry for Family Affairs, Senior Citizens, Women and Youth 2009, 13, translation by authors). As a reaction to this problem, the so-called inclusive solution has been discussed for years now. It is an intended reform of the social law aimed at bundling all future services for children and young people under the umbrella of the youth welfare office, regardless of the type of disability (Federal Ministry of Labour and Social Affairs 2015, 28). So far, however, several draft laws have failed, and implementation of the reform is not in sight for the time being (Lüders 2019).

Applications for a paraprofessional submitted to the office in charge need to be assessed, as the school system and the social system are different and do not have a common definition of disability. Even if a child has been diagnosed with a special educational need in school, for example, a physical disability, this is not yet a sufficient criterion for the approval of a paraprofessional (Thiel 2017). For this purpose, a separate assessment procedure must first be carried out, which can differ from office to office. In any case, it implies a medical assessment that the child has to go through.

Once the application process has been successfully completed, the approval statement determines both the extent and the duration of the service.

Usually, paraprofessional assistance is only being granted for one school year, sometimes for even a shorter period of time, after which either the whole procedure needs to be repeated or the child is assessed to no longer needing individual assistance. With the approval of the financing of a paraprofessional, it is then up to the parents to choose a service provider, as this is not the responsibility of the authorities. Service providers are often providers of youth welfare or handicapped aid, but also private providers, who take care of the selection and recruitment of paraprofessionals and who, due to the increasing demand in recent years, have in many cases already specialised in this service. It is also possible, however, that the parents themselves act as the employer of a paraprofessional.

There are no standards to determine who is ultimately hired to work as a paraprofessional. As a result, there is a wide range of people who carry out this activity, and they differ in age, qualifications, job experience and motivation. Looking at the working conditions (e.g. the temporary employment, low wages, at times even predictable unemployment during the summer holidays), it is no surprise that there is high employee turnover (Dworschak 2012a; Henn et al. 2014).

The ambiguous role of paraprofessionals in inclusive school development processes

In the German context, assessing for and obtaining paraprofessional support is a highly complex undertaking. For practitioners, this situation leads to great confusion and uncertainty, while for researchers, there are problems connected to field access and systematic data collection. It is a young field of enquiry. For example, a representative survey of the whole of Germany does not yet exist, and under these circumstances would also be a major undertaking. The existing studies are limited to individual federal states, or more often regions, and are only comparable to a limited extent. For an overview of empirical studies on paraprofessionals in Germany, see Lübeck and Demmer (2017).

Paraprofessionals vs. inclusive school development

The reliance on paraprofessionals is seen as highly controversial with regard to inclusive school development. In addition to many critical aspects which are inherent of a one-to-one support model, and which have been already and repeatedly pointed out in international literature on paraprofessionals (Blatchford et al. 2009; Giangreco et al. 1997; Sharma and Salend 2016), the location of paraprofessionals in the welfare system exacerbates these aspects. The UN-CRPD (2007) calls for an education system in which 'Persons with disabilities can access an inclusive, quality and free primary education and secondary education on an equal basis with others in the communities in which they live' (Article 24, Paragraph 2b), and in which 'Persons with disabilities receive the support required, *within the general education system*, to facilitate their effective education' (Article 24, Paragraph 2d, emphasis added). Against this background, the complex application procedure for paraprofessionals in Germany seems quiet grotesque, as:

> ...while all the other pupils simply need to sign up at the school of their district, pupils who are entitled to a paraprofessional first need to undergo this stigmatizing and by no means barrier-free application procedure in order to get adequate support at the regular school.
> (Demmer, Heinrich, and Lübeck 2017, 17, translation by authors)

An education system that meets the requirements of the UN-CRPD, on the other hand, would have to be an education system that, in regard to its 'structural and communicative accessibility, material and personal equipment as well as methodical-didactic diversity, is in a position to provide *all children and young people* with high-quality shared educational offers' (Blömer-Hausmanns 2014, 226, translation by authors; emphasis added).

Schools which are not (yet) able to do this themselves currently rely on paraprofessionals, who ensure that the child and school 'fit together.' In this sense, the paraprofessional acts as an 'adapter' between the pupil's needs and what the school can provide in terms of support. As Dworschak, emphasises, this is particularly the case for pupils with intellectual disabilities:

> To put it bluntly, one could say that pupils with intellectual disabilities can attend mainstream schools in the model of individual integration if they bring along a paraprofessional that compensates for their deficits to such an extent that they can be integrated into the existing concept of the general school without major effort.
> (Dworschak 2017, 48, translation by authors)

In this way of thinking, however, the reliance on paraprofessionals implies that only pupils whose 'deficits' can be more or less compensated for by paraprofessionals can attend mainstream schools, whereas it is concluded that whenever such compensation cannot be provided, a pupil cannot be integrated and must continue to attend a special school (where available). Given that inclusion does not only aim at the common education of all children but also at access to education that is as free as possible from labelling and discrimination (see above), the realisation of inclusion in the school system can be considered insufficient. In addition, there is a danger that the strong reliance of paraprofessionals may draw attention away from the development of an inclusive school system, that major efforts are avoided and individual support is made permanent. This danger is particularly relevant since in this constellation, the school system relies on the financing by the welfare office. Thus, the reliance on paraprofessionals can be interpreted as a 'reward' for school authorities who 'make no effort to transform their schools into inclusive schools' (Lindmeier and Polleschner 2014, 204, translation by authors).

Consequently, paraprofessionals resemble a double-edged sword. On the one hand, they enable many pupils with disabilities to attend mainstream schools in the first place, and are therefore seen as 'a contribution to inclusion' (Fegert et al. 2016). But on the other hand, the reliance on paraprofessionals may also delay important inclusive school development measures (see also Giangreco 2021) and may furthermore stigmatise the pupils they are allocated to based on a deficit-oriented perspective. The role of paraprofessionals at the level of inclusive school development processes is therefore highly ambiguous.

Role confusion in everyday interaction

This ambivalence also applies to their role at the level of everyday interaction. Paraprofessionals are in constant contact with a large number of different stakeholders. Besides the child they are assigned to, they are also in touch with the child's parents, the teachers, other pupils in class, their employer, authorities and sometimes even therapists and doctors relevant to the child. All these different stakeholders have their own expectations of the paraprofessional, and these may contradict one another. For example, due to their location in the welfare system and the absence of standards for qualification, paraprofessionals in Germany are usually neither explicitly allowed to do pedagogical work, nor to teach – which is why the internationally common nomenclature of 'teaching assistants' is not suitable for the German form of individual assistance. Paraprofessional in the German context are:

> …not second teachers, tutor assistants, homework supervisors or assistants to the teachers in teaching the contents of the lessons. The pedagogical and didactic responsibility for the teaching of the curriculum to young people with disabilities lies exclusively with the teachers.
> (Bayerisches Staatsministerium für Unterricht und Kultus and Verein der Bayerischen Bezirke 2012, 5, translation by authors)

Although this requirement is understandable from a legal perspective, it can be difficult to comply with in practice. Not only because pedagogical and non-educational tasks cannot always be clearly distinguished from one another, but also because paraprofessionals are inevitably confronted with pedagogical requirements. This is due to their proximity to the child, the necessities in the classroom and the expectations of classmates who may not always differentiate between teachers and paraprofessionals (Böttcher et al. 2019, 54). Many studies conclude that paraprofessionals act pedagogically and even instructionally (e.g. Blasse et al. 2020; Dworschak 2012b). It is up to the paraprofessional to respond to and deal with these partially contradictory expectations, even though they are in an extremely weak negotiating position and run the risk of quickly falling victim to the whims of different interests (ebd., 4; Demmer, Heinrich and Lübeck 2017).

The result is a considerable intra-role conflict for the paraprofessional (Lübeck 2019), while at the same time there is no authority that takes responsibility for the bigger picture and for paraprofessionals specifically. These observations can theoretically be placed within the concept of the 'Grammar of Schooling' by Tyack and Tobin (1994). In this chapter, we use this concept to discuss the question of what development opportunities exist for the role of paraprofessionals.

'Grammar of Schooling'

Grammar of Schooling refers to the historically grown 'regular structures and rules that organize the work of instruction' (Tyack and Tobin 1994, 454), such as 'standardized organizational practices in dividing time and space, classifying students and allocating them to classrooms, and splintering knowledge into "subjects"' (Tyack and Tobin 1994, 454). On a theoretical level, it may provide a valuable insight regarding this question, and explain why, in our view, school development often fails. Similar to the grammar of speech, the Grammar of Schooling does not need to be:

> ...consciously understood to operate smoothly. Indeed, much of the grammar of schooling has become so well established that it is typically taken for granted as just the way schools are. It is the departure from customary practice in schooling or speaking that attracts attention.
> (Tyack and Tobin 1994, 454)

It is partly as a result of the 'taken for granted' nature of this form of organisation that '[d]espite many assaults on the standard grammar of schooling, it seems remarkably durable' (Tyack and Tobin 1994, 455). From this perspective, paraprofessionals seem to be more of an adjustment and indirect stabilisation of the known grammar of schooling, since they do not change existing structures (see below), but represent a resource to enable individual children to participate in those structures.

In contrast, the development of an inclusive education system can be viewed as a major departure from customary practice, as it involves changes to a significant number of aspects of our familiar Grammar of Schooling. Among other things, these changes include a complete reorganisation of the secondary school system (which in Germany still divides pupils into different types of schools according to their academic performance); a reorganisation of teacher training which specialises future teachers for a specific type of school; and a stronger emphasis on multi-professional cooperation. While over the past few years new professions such as special educators, social workers and sometimes even therapists have established themselves in the regular school system, bringing along different ideas of education and participation, none of them are as directly involved in the classroom as paraprofessionals are, and none of them spend as much time with the pupils and the teachers as paraprofessionals do.

The presence of paraprofessionals draws attention to yet another element of our familiar Grammar of Schooling that is challenged by inclusive developments: the specific role structure of teachers and pupils. A closer look at this established role structure reveals that the role patterns of teachers and pupils are, in many respects, complementary: teachers teach, pupils learn; teachers are trained or professionalised, pupils are not; teachers give instructions and sanctions received by pupils; teachers are part of the staff, pupils belong to the pupil body (Lübeck 2019).

Paraprofessionals, however, cannot be classified into any of these established complementary roles. They are neither allowed to teach, nor is it their task to learn in school. In many cases they are not trained for their task, and they certainly lack the status of a profession, but neither is it their aim to acquire a qualification at school. They belong neither to the pupils nor to the teaching staff. Lastly, there are ambiguities regarding questions of authority. The role of paraprofessionals is not provided for in the school system. In the already established, interrelated role structure of teachers and pupils – to stay with the analogy of grammar – no syntax yet exists for the deployment of paraprofessionals.

So, paraprofessionals challenge the current Grammar of Schooling, which raises the question of what will happen to this oversight. In principle, we see three possible development options:

1   Paraprofessionals adapt to the prevailing grammar and fit into one of the two complementary roles already established
2   Paraprofessionals fail to establish themselves permanently and remain merely a transitional phenomenon
3   A specific role for paraprofessionals is established, which goes along with a transformation of the Grammar of Schooling.

Integrating paraprofessionals into the existing role structure

On the one hand, we know from research that paraprofessionals often assume teacher-like roles in the classroom, as they teach, supervise pupils and stay in touch with the individual pupil's parents (Giangreco, Suter and Doyle 2010; Lindmeier and Ehrenberg 2017, 141; Sommer et al. 2017). In this way, they can decrease the workload of the teacher, even though it is widely known that due to lacking standards in the qualification of paraprofessionals, this poses a risk to educational quality and pupil achievement (Blatchford et al. 2009; Lübeck and Heinrich 2016). On the other hand, studies sometimes find paraprofessionals to be closer to role, position or status of the pupil. Depending on the paraprofessionals' (lack of) qualification, pedagogical skills, age and life experience, teachers interviewed about this can perceive paraprofessionals as 'just another pupil' in the class who needs supervision and support (Lübeck 2019). Although paraprofessionals and pupils are formally not equivalent learners, we find evidence of paraprofessionals' role/status being nearer to that of the pupil when, for example, they raise their hand to speak during class, when they queue up with the pupils in front of the teacher (Blasse 2017, 114), when they are admonished for using their smartphones during class, or when they describe themselves as the pupils' friends (Lübeck 2019). Either mode can be interpreted as an attempt to integrate the paraprofessional into the existing role structure, which is understandable insofar as systems are generally prone to self-preservation. Successfully integrating paraprofessionals into the existing role structure would consequently leave the system intact and unmodified.

Although it is obvious that an orientation towards the pupil role is not an adequate form of practice, an orientation towards the teacher role also seems difficult under the structural conditions described. It is doubtful whether it is possible to integrate paraprofessionals into the existing role structure. Adapting paraprofessionals to the existing Grammar of Schooling without a specific role is therefore not simple, and could cause lasting confusion. Firstly, for the teachers who do not know what to expect from the paraprofessional and how to evaluate their performance. Secondly, for the pupils, to whom it is not obvious to what extent the paraprofessional is a 'peer' they can confide in or a person of authority. And, thirdly, for the paraprofessionals themselves, who will most likely experience difficulties when trying to do justice to the contradictory expectations others have of them.

Paraprofessionals as a transitional phenomenon

Another possible scenario is a reduced deployment of paraprofessionals. Considering the unsatisfactory current situation mentioned above, this might even be a desirable development, provided that it is accompanied by a sound inclusive school development that itself would reduce the necessity of one-to-one assistance for individual pupils.

So far, however, there has been a steady increase in the number of paraprofessionals, and in the recent past, an association for paraprofessionals has been founded. This hints at an increase of visibility and significance, and it can be assumed that the 'phenomenon of paraprofessionals' is here to stay. It is also possible, however, that inclusive school reform will not be able to assert itself against the established Grammar of Schooling. At the time of writing, several German federal governments are already backpedalling in their efforts to expand an inclusive school system (Johannsen 2018, 90). Against this background, it is important to ensure that paraprofessionals are not taken out of the school system without alternative inclusive structures being put in, and that there is little or no resistance to the joint teaching of pupils with and without disabilities.

Changing the established role structure and the Grammar of Schooling

The third possible scenario would involve changing the established role structure and augmenting it with an independent role of paraprofessionals. This would significantly challenge the 'cultural construction of school' itself

(Tyack and Tobin 1994, 456) and public concepts of what makes a school a 'real' school. The greater the discrepancy with the usual concept of school, the lower the social acceptance, and thus the probability of a sustainable implementation of these changes. A change in the established role structure, therefore, could only go along with a durable change of those beliefs in a 'real' school. However, various challenges confront this form of development. Firstly, there currently seems to be no basis for establishing an independent, solid role for paraprofessionals considering the contradictory expectations they face, the ambiguous contribution they make to inclusive school development and the current lack of qualification standards. Without this starting point, it is difficult to imagine a corresponding change in the overall structure.

Secondly, it is difficult to imagine that such fundamental changes in the system can be initiated from the weakest position in the structure, in the sense of an effective grassroots movement. Due to the large number of positions involved, there is no central authority that is responsible for the development of paraprofessional deployment and the integration of paraprofessionals into school development processes (both at the level of the individual school and at the level of the school system as such). Despite first initiatives to train paraprofessionals and to implement multi-professional cooperation, this does by no means represent the reality of everyday school life.

Thirdly, in order to initiate the rewriting of the Grammar of Schooling, we believe that the establishment of a pool model in connection with incentives for inclusive school development would be necessary (Demmer, Heinrich and Lübeck 2017). This also includes bundling responsibilities and structurally linking paraprofessionals to schools in order to enable continuous and robust high-quality teamwork.

Implications

What implications do our reflections have for practice? First of all, it might help to explain some phenomena that cause friction in their everyday cooperation, and to sensitise and prepare us to address the challenges related to paraprofessionals, teachers and pupils working together. Furthermore, we have seen how the ambiguities in the work paraprofessionals do and the role they occupy, after all, affect all other stakeholders who work with or alongside them. The stakeholders have to negotiate how they work together, which suggests that the professional roles of others are to some extent up for discussion and readjustment. Accordingly, it is necessary to discuss questions of roles and responsibilities in inclusive schools with the other actors; for example, in ways that are currently being pursued via the state-funded research project 'ProFiS' (Professionalization through case work for inclusive schools) (Heinrich et al. 2019). This qualitative research project investigates the ways in which stakeholders in multi-professional and inclusive teaching settings negotiate their roles with one another, and which role models, expectations and attributions are empirically evident. The results of these analyses are then condensed into authentic case narratives, which are in turn used as the foundation for further training courses aimed at the multi-professional pedagogical staff of the school and students of teacher training (Demmer, Lübeck and Heinrich 2021). In further trainings, the participants can use these case narratives as an opportunity to reflect on their own roles and their professional identities in light of the multi-professional cooperation, but also the structural ambiguities that shape their work environments. We believe this approach will have a more lasting effect than asking the participants to adapt to a normative model of 'good cooperation' (Lau, Heinrich and Lübeck 2019).

Rewriting the Grammar of Schooling and the traditional complementary roles of pupils and teachers in this perspective would imply understanding multi-professional teamwork as fundamental for inclusive schooling, and at the same time as a process of negotiation. Structural changes we consider indispensable include anchoring support systems in schools as part of an inclusive school development. Assigning paraprofessionals to teachers instead of pupils (Giangreco 2021), and thus strengthening multi-professional cooperation and team structures, seem to be a step into the right direction. Furthermore, time is a critical factor that studies on liaison and cooperation between teachers and paraprofessionals have repeatedly point out (Lindmeier and Polleschner 2014; Blatchford et al. 2009, 72–82; Giangreco and Broer 2005). Teachers and paraprofessionals need time to talk about and reflect on their work; not only to plan and discuss for the current day's lessons and events, but also to reflect on their cooperation in its entirety, and to be able to discuss fundamental questions about their respective roles.

Studies show how the power of a Grammar of Schooling unfolds in established structures that comprise, for instance, hierarchies among school staff, notions of normalcy, and the primacy of teaching (Buchna et al. 2016). To change the current Grammar of Schooling, a broader concept of education that encompasses extracurricular and life-world learning could be established. In addition to classroom learning, this would include other forms of 'engagement with the world' as part of the school's core business and thus significantly strengthen the systematic involvement of other specialists.

References

Bayerisches Staatsministerium für Unterricht und Kultus and Verein der Bayerischen Bezirke. 2012. 'Einsatz von Schulbegleitern an allgemeinen Schulen (Regelschulen) bei der Beschulung von Schüler/innen mit Behinderung i.S.d § 54 Abs. 1, Satz 1 Nr.1 SGB XII.' (1): 1–6.

Blasse, Nina. 2017. 'Vielfältige Positionen von Schulbegleitung im Unterricht.' In Laubner, Lindmeier, and Lübeck 2017, 107–117.

Blasse, Nina, Jürgen Budde, Christine Demmer, Julia Gasterstädt, Martin Heinrich, Anika Lübeck, Georg Rißler, Albrecht Rohrmann,, Alicia Strecker,, Michael

Urban, and Hanna Weinbach. 2020. 'Multiprofessionelle Teams in der "inklusiven" Schule—Zwischen Transformation und Stabilisierung.' In K. Kunze, D. Petersen, G. Bellenberg, J.-H. Hinzke, A. Moldenhauer, L. Peukert, C. Reintjes and K. te Poel (Hrsg.), *Kooperation—Koordination—Kollegialität. Befunde und Diskurse zum (multi-)professionellen Zusammenwirken pädagogischer Akteur*innen an Schulen*. Bad Heilbrunn: Klinkhardt (in press).

Blatchford, Peter, Paul Bassett, Penelope Brown, Maria Koutsoubou, Clare Martin, Anthony Russell, and Rob Webster. 2009. 'The Impact of Support Staff in Schools. Results from the Deployment and Impact of Support Staff (DISS) Project. The Impact of Support Staff in Schools (Results from Strand 2, Wave 2).' (Department for Children, Schools and Families). http://maximisingtas.co.uk/assets/content/disss2w2r.pdf. Accessed June 8, 2018.

Blömer-Hausmanns, Sibylle. 2014. 'Integrationshilfe—eine Baustellenbesichtigung.' *Gemeinsam Leben* 4: 226–229.

Böttcher, Wolfgang, Gesa Klemp, Dirk Nüsken, Pierre Overesch, Sofia H. Peters, and Ariane Schmidt. 2019. 'Zwischenbericht der Evaluation des Projektes "Ein guter Ort für alle—wir gestalten Inklusion!" für den Zeitraum 2017/2018.'

Buchna, Jennifer, Thomas Coelen, Bernd Dollinger, and Pia Rother. 2016. 'Normalisierte Hierarchie in Ganztagsgrundschulen. Empirische Befunde zur innerorganisationalen Zusammenarbeit von Lehrkräften und weiterem pädagogisch tätigem Personal.' *Zeitschrift für Soziologie der Erziehung und Sozialisation (ZSE)*, 36 (3), 281–297.

Demmer, Christine, Martin Heinrich, and Anika Lübeck. 2017. *Funktion und Funktionalität von Schulbegleitung im inklusiven Schulsystem!? Expertise im Auftrag des AFET*. Hannover: Carl Küster.

Demmer, Christine, Anika Lübeck and Martin Heinrich. 2021. 'Wer hilft wem, wie, wann, warum,es selbst zu tun? Zur Reflexion der Antinomie von Autonomie und Heteronomie in der Tätigkeit von Schulbegleitungen und Lehrkräften.' *DiMawe—Die Materialwerkstatt*, 3(3), 28–36. https://doi.org/10.11576/dimawe-4138.

Dworschak, Wolfgang. 2012a. 'Schulbegleitung im Förderschwerpunkt geistige Entwicklung an der allgemeinen Schule.' *Gemeinsam Leben* 2: 80–94.

Dworschak, Wolfgang. 2012b. 'Assistenz in der Schule. Pädagogische Reflexionen zur Schulbegleitung im Spannungsfeld von Schulrecht und Eingliederungshilfe.' *Lernen konkret* 4: 2–7.

Dworschak, Wolfgang. 2017. 'Zur Gewährung von Schulbegleitung—Wer erhält in welchem Umfang eine Schulbegleitung?' In Laubner, Lindmeier, and Lübeck 2017, 37–49.

Federal Ministry for Family Affairs, Senior Citizens, Women and Youth. 2009. '13. Kinder- und Jugendbericht.' Accessed May 29, 2018. https://www.bmfsfj.de/blob/93144/f5f2144cfc504efbc6574af8a1f30455/13-kinder-jugendbericht-data.pdf.

Federal Ministry of Labour and Social Affairs. 2015. *Abschlussbericht des Bundesministeriums für Arbeit und Soziales über die Tätigkeit der Arbeitsgruppe Bundesteilhabegesetz, Teil A*. Bonn. Accessed June 8, 2018. http://www.bmas.de/SharedDocs/Downloads/DE/PDF-Publikationen/a764-abschlussbericht-bthg-A.pdf?__blob=publicationFileand v=4.

Fegert, Jörg M., Ute Ziegenhain, Lydia Schönecker, and Thomas Meysen. 2016. Schulbegleitung als Beitrag zur Inklusion. Bestandsaufnahme und Rechtsexpertise. Schriftenreihe der Baden-Württemberg Stiftung; Nr. 81.

Giangreco, M. F., Jesse C. Suter, and Mary B. Doyle. 2010. 'Paraprofessionals in Inclusive Schools: A Review of Recent Research.' *Journal of Educational and Psychological Consultation* 20 (1), 41–57. doi:10.1080/10474410903535356.

Giangreco, Michael F. 2021. 'Maslow's Hammer: Teacher Assistant Research and Inclusive Practices at a Crossroads.' *European Journal of Special Needs Education* 36(2).

Giangreco, Michael F., and Stephen M. Broer. 2005. 'Questionable Utilization of Paraprofessionals in Inclusive Schools: Are We Addressing Symptoms or Causes?' *Focus on Autism and other Developmental Disabilities* 20 (1): 10–26.

Giangreco, Michael F., Susan W. Edelman, Tracy Evans Luiselli, and Stephanie Z. C. MacFarland. 1997. 'Helping or Hovering? Effects of Instructional Assistant Proximity on Students with Disabilities.' *Exceptional Children* 64 (1): 7–16.

Heinrich, Martin, Nina Blasse, Jürgen Budde, Christine Demmer, Julia Gasterstädt, Anika Lübeck, Georg Rißler et al. 2019. 'Professionalisierung durch Fallarbeit für die inklusive Schule.' In *Vernetzung, Kooperation, Sozialer Raum—Inklusion als Querschnittaufgabe*, edited by Gabi Ricken and Sven Degenhardt. Bad Heilbrunn: Julius Klinkhardt.

Henn, Katharina, Leonore Thurn, Tanja Besier, Anne K. Künster, Jörg M. Fegert, and Ute Ziegenhain. 2014. 'Schulbegleiter als Unterstützung von Inklusion im Schulwesen.' *Zeitschrift für Kinder- und Jugendpsychiatrie und Psychotherapie* 42 (6): 397–403.

Johannsen, Hans-Werner. 2018. '"Nur unsere Leuchttürme strahlen noch!" Der schwierige Weg in die Inklusion.' *DDS—Die Deutsche Schule* 110 (1): 87–98.

Lau, Ramona, Martin Heinrich, and Anika Lübeck. 2019. 'Professionalisierung in Spannungsfeldern von Inklusion durch Fortbildung. Transferaktivitäten zu einem Forschungsdesiderat.' *Jahrbuch der Wissenschaftlichen Einrichtung Oberstufen-Kolleg an der Universität Bielefeld* 2: 82–99. https://doi.org/10.4119/we_os-3188. Accessed January 02, 2020.

Lindmeier, Bettina, and Katrin Ehrenberg. 2017. '"In manchen Momenten wünsch ich mir auch, dass sie gar nicht da sind."—Schulassistenz aus der Perspektive von Mitschülerinnen und Mitschülern.' In Laubner, Lindmeier, and Lübeck 2017, 137–149.

Lindmeier, Bettina, and Sandra Polleschner. 2014. 'Schulassistenz—ein Beitrag zu einer inklusiven Schule oder zur Verfestigung nicht inklusiver Schulstrukturen?' *Gemeinsam Leben* 4: 195–205.

Lübeck, Anika. 2019. *Schulbegleitung im Rollenprekariat: Zur Unmöglichkeit der "Rolle Schulbegleitung" in der inklusiven Schule*. Wiesbaden: Springer VS.

Lübeck, Anika, and Christine Demmer. 2017. 'Unüberblickbares überblicken—Ausgewählte Forschungsergebnisse zu Schulbegleitung.' In Laubner, Lindmeier, and Lübeck 2017, 11–27.

Lübeck, Anika and Martin Heinrich. 2016. *Schulbegleitung im Professionalisierungsdilemma. Rekonstruktionen zur inklusiven Beschulung*. Münster: MV-Wissenschaft.

Lüders, Christian. 2019. 'Inklusion und "große Lösung" in der Kinder- und Jugendhilfe. Eine Zwischenbilanz aus aktuellem Anlass.' In *Migration, Flucht und Behinderung*, edited by Manuela Westphal and Gudrun Wansing, 167–184. Wiesbaden: Springer Fachmedien Wiesbaden.

Sharma, Umesh, and Spencer Salend. 2016. 'Teaching Assistants in Inclusive Classrooms: A Systematic Analysis of the International Research.' *AJTE* 41 (8): 118–134. doi:10.14221/ajte.2016v41n8.7.

Sommer, Sabine, Stefanie Czempiel, Bärbel Kracke, and Ada Sasse. 2017. 'Zwischen Einzelfallhelfer/in und Zweitlehrer/in: Wie handeln Integrationshelfer/innen im Unterricht? Zum Zusammenhang zwischen der Zuständigkeit im Unterricht und dem Stand der inklusiven Schulentwicklung.' *Diskurs Kindheits- und Jugendforschung* 12 (1), 35–47.

Thiel, Sylvia. 2017. 'Die Beantragung und Bewilligung von Schulassistenz.' In Laubner, Lindmeier, and Lübeck 2017, 28–36.

Tyack, D., and W. Tobin. 1994. 'The "Grammar" of Schooling: Why Has it Been so Hard to Change?' *American Educational Research Journal* 31 (3): 453–479.

UN General Assembly. 2007. 'Convention on the Rights of Persons with Disabilities: A/RES/61/106.' https://www.refworld.org/docid/45f973632.html. Accessed December 04, 2019.

Part II
Teaching assistants and pupils

4 Inclusion moments for students with profound intellectual and multiple disabilities in mainstream schools

The teacher assistant's role in supporting peer interactions

Ineke Haakma, Anke A. de Boer, Sanne van Esch, Alexander E. M. G. Minnaert and Annette A. J. Van Der Putten

Introduction

Students with profound intellectual and multiple disabilities (PIMD) are not yet included in mainstream classrooms as a matter of course. However, this particular student population has the right to be included in mainstream schools (United Nations 2006), and their inclusion could lead to increased opportunities for social interaction with typically developing peers (hereafter called 'peers'). High-quality interactions are crucial for the quality of life of persons with PIMD (Hostyn and Maes 2009; Petry, Maes and Vlaskamp 2005). Therefore, it is important to explore the possibilities for including students with PIMD in mainstream schools, to assess whether inclusion has a positive effect on their social interactions with peers and to identify the role of a teaching assistant in supporting these interactions.

A 'To School Together' project was recently initiated in the Netherlands to promote the integration of students with PIMD into mainstream schools. In this project, a classroom in a regular primary school is specially designed and adapted for students with severe disabilities. In a 'To School Together' class, students with severe disabilities, such as PIMD, receive tailored care and education from trained direct support professionals during the school day. Direct support professionals are involved in the support of persons with PIMD on a daily basis. In the Dutch context, these are professionals with either a medical or educational background (Jansen, Van Der Putten and Vlaskamp 2016). Students in a 'To School Together' class undertake activities with other students with disabilities and occasionally join their typically developing peers during activities in regular classrooms. Since the 'To School Together' classroom is located within a regular primary school, it is a short distance from one classroom to another. Conversely, children in regular classes sometimes join in activities with students with disabilities in the 'To School Together' classroom. In addition to these inclusion moments,

DOI: 10.4324/9781003265580-7

a student with PIMD may be matched to a typically developing peer and take part in activities in either the mainstream classroom or the 'To School Together' classroom.

These inclusion moments provide opportunities for peer interaction. However, engaging in peer interaction is not self-evident for students with PIMD. Individuals with PIMD can experience difficulties during peer interactions due to their profound and multiple disabilities (Nijs et al. 2016). Their profound intellectual disabilities, profound or severe neuromotor dysfunctions, possible health problems, sensory impairments and limited understanding of verbal language (Nakken and Vlaskamp 2007; Van Timmeren et al. 2017) seriously hinder their ability to interact with others. Such interaction is also difficult because communication is mostly pre- or proto-symbolic and consists of movements, sounds, body postures, facial expressions or muscle tensions (Maes et al. 2007). Nonetheless, research shows that individuals with PIMD can show peer-directed behaviours (Nijs et al. 2016; Nijs, Vlaskamp and Maes 2015). These studies were conducted in day care facilities accommodating only children with PIMD. There is a lack of research on the interactions of students with PIMD with peers in mainstream primary schools.

We know from research on students with special educational needs (SEN) that including students with SEN in inclusive classrooms does not automatically lead to an increase in interaction (Koster et al. 2010). Koster et al. (2010) studied the social participation of students with special needs (behavioural disorders, autistic spectrum disorders, motor disabilities, intellectual disabilities or speech/language disabilities) in regular primary education. Their results show that, in general, students with SEN have fewer friends and fewer interactions with classmates than their typically developing peers. For some students, inclusion can even result in negative outcomes, such as loneliness and rejection, rather than the assumed positive outcomes. Teachers have the vital task of monitoring the social participation of students and, in doing so, they can prevent the harmful long-term effect of negative social experiences at school (Koster et al. 2009). As well as teachers, teaching assistants (TAs) also have an important role in facilitating the social participation of students with SEN.

Internationally, the movement towards including students with disabilities in general education classrooms has led to an increase in the number of TAs (Sharma and Salend 2016). TAs have been employed in the primary classroom, especially to support the needs of students with SEN (MacKenzie 2011). The TA's work includes tasks to make education accessible and available for a variety of students. TAs supplement teacher input, provide opportunities for one-to-one and small group work, and work with students outside the classroom (Webster et al. 2010). The main goal of their work is to assist and support students during the learning process (Takala 2007).

Earlier research has not always shown positive results regarding the impact of a TA's presence on peer interactions. TAs frequently teach students with SEN separately individually or in small groups, which means that students are rarely included in whole class instructions and spend less time in the classroom (Sharma and Salend 2016; Webster and Blatchford 2013). This leads to an experience of separation from the classroom, teacher and peers, which may have a negative effect on the interactions that students with SEN have with their peers (Blatchford and Webster 2018; Giangreco et al. 1997; Sharma and Salend 2016). The presence of the TA can therefore create a physical or symbolic barrier that interferes with interactions between a student with disabilities and their classmates (Giangreco et al. 2005).

Similarly, research suggests that the presence of a direct support professional in day care centres for children with PIMD does not positively influence peer interactions among children with PIMD. Research by Nijs, Vlaskamp and Maes (2015) revealed that children displayed significantly less peer-directed behaviour in the presence of a direct support professional than in situations where a direct support professional was absent. Rather than facilitating peer interactions, direct support professionals spent most of their time focusing on other things, such as organising the activity or one-on-one interaction with one child. They also displayed distracting behaviours that interrupted peer interaction, such as displacing an object used by playing peers, or calling a child's name. In addition, they paid little attention to the position of the children. Children were put in place at the start of an activity and were not moved during the activity. As a result, children who were placed where they could see and touch their peers displayed the greatest number of peer-directed behaviours. A study by Kamstra et al. (2019) also showed that interactions among peers with PIMD were nearly impossible due to their physical positioning by direct support professionals. These studies indicate that TAs and direct support professionals do not always have a facilitating role in promoting peer interactions and may in fact hamper such interactions.

In the context of the present study, direct support professionals provide care and/or education to students with PIMD throughout the school day. They do so during activities with other students with disabilities in the 'To School Together' classroom, as well as during inclusion moments when students with PIMD engage in activities with students without disabilities. During these inclusion moments the direct support professional is present to assist the student. The direct support professional may offer one-to-one support to the student when needed, by helping them to express themselves or by helping peers understand these expressions. Direct support professionals may also offer suggestions to peers on how to interact with the student with PIMD. In addition, they may offer medical support when needed. Since direct support professionals support the needs of students during inclusion moments and help to make education accessible and available for students, their task is similar to the role of a TA. However, we do not yet know how TAs (the direct support professionals in the context of the present study) actually support students, since research on this topic in this context has not yet been conducted.

We do not yet know what happens during these inclusion moments. There is no research on the kind of activities undertaken and whether students with

PIMD engage in interactions with peers during inclusion moments. More specifically, we do not know whether students with PIMD initiate contact with peers and whether peers respond. Nor do we know whether peers initiate contact with students with PIMD and whether students with PIMD respond. The role of TAs (i.e. the direct support professionals in the 'To School Together' classes) in supporting peer interactions is also unclear. Earlier research indicates that TAs and direct support professionals may have a negative influence on peer interactions. As mentioned, their presence seems to hamper, rather than facilitate, peer interactions. This study was set up to fill this knowledge gap by answering the following research questions:

1 How can we describe the inclusion moments for students with PIMD and the interactions between them and peers during these inclusion moments?
2 What is the TA's role in supporting interactions between students with PIMD and peers during these inclusion moments?

It is important to gain insights into what happens during inclusion moments, whether peer interactions take place and what the TA's role is during these moments. These insights will add new knowledge to the research base on inclusive education and social participation. They will also fill the research gap on the peer interactions of students with PIMD in mainstream schools and can be used to tailor and improve inclusive practices for students with PIMD.

Method

Participants

An approach was made to all Dutch primary schools with an inclusive classroom for students with severe disabilities (i.e. a 'To School Together' class). Eight students from three schools were selected to participate. These students met the following inclusion criteria: (a) they attended a 'To School Together' class in a mainstream primary school in the Netherlands; (b) they were aged between 3 and 12 years; (c) they had a profound intellectual disability not determinable by standardised instruments (Nakken and Vlaskamp 2007); and (d) they had a profound or severe motor disability (Nakken and Vlaskamp 2007) (Table 4.1) provides an overview of the students' characteristics.

Procedure

Written informed consent to participate in the current study was obtained from the parents of the students with PIMD. In accordance with the general policy and guidelines of the participating schools, passive consent was obtained from the peers' parents, the TAs and the teachers at the mainstream

Table 4.1 Students' characteristics

Student	Gender	Age (in years)	Sensory impairment	Specified motor impairment
1 (School A)	Boy	9	–	Spasticity
2 (School A)	Girl	9	Visual	Spasticity and malformations
3 (School A)	Boy	4	Visual	–
4 (School A)	Girl	3	Visual	Hypotension, malformation, scoliosis
5 (School B)	Boy	9	Auditory	Spasticity, hypotension, malformation, frontometaphyseal dysplasia, joint contractures
6 (School B)	Boy	7	Visual	Hypertension, spasticity
7 (School C)	Girl	9	Visual	Hypotension and hypermobility
8 (School C)	Boy	9	–	Hypertension

school. Approval was therefore assumed unless TAs or teachers indicated that they did not wish to participate, or parents indicated that they did not want their children to participate. Prior approval to carry out the current study was also obtained from the ethical committee of the Department of Pedagogical and Educational Sciences at the University of Groningen.

Data collection

Video recordings were made of inclusion moments in which the student with PIMD engaged in activities with peers. No criteria were formulated for inclusion moments: the TA and primary school teacher discussed and made decisions about the types of activities that were suitable for inclusion. Video observation is the method most frequently used to examine interactions of persons with PIMD (Hostyn and Maes 2009). Video recordings were made of three inclusion moments for each of the eight students. The video recording was carried out in 2016 (school A) and 2017 (schools B and C) in the second half of the school year, in March, April and May. The lengths of the inclusion moments differ, but most lasted about 45 minutes. A total of 24 video recordings were made. Each recording started at the beginning of the activity and ended when the activity ended (see Table 4.3 for an overview of the activities).

Coding scheme

To analyse the interaction between peers, the student with PIMD and the TA, we developed a coding scheme for the videos (see Table 4.2), based on previously developed coding schemes for peer interactions of students with severe disabilities (Baulminger, Shulman and Agam 2003; Hauck et al. 1995; Nijs et al. 2016; Nijs, Vlaskamp and Maes 2015). We coded all contact

Table 4.2 Coding scheme

Actor	Action		Example
– Student with PIMD – Peer – TA	Initiative		– Offering object – Physical contact (touching/grabbing) – Verbalisation (making sounds) – Asking questions – Giving information – Pointing
	Response	Positive response	– Physical contact – Eye contact – Accepting an object – Imitation – Verbal response
		No response Negative response	– No response of any kind – Turning away – Avoidance – Unrelated behaviour – Becoming irritated

initiations by students with PIMD, peers or TAs, as well as the response from the person addressed in this initiative. For example, if a student with PIMD touched the arm of a peer (an initiative by a student with PIMD) and the peer responded by touching the arm of the student (a response from the peer). We categorised the responses into three groups: a positive response (e.g. the peer responded by touching the student's arm), an absence of response (e.g. the peer did not respond) and a negative response (e.g. the peer pushed the student's hand away).

Data analysis

The video recordings varied in length, depending on the activity. To make the video recordings comparable, we selected 15 minutes from each of the 24 videos for data analysis. Since this study focuses on the TA's role in supporting peer interactions, we selected video fragments that showed (in this order): (1) interaction (at least one initiative followed by at least one response) between a student with PIMD and typically developing peer(s), facilitated by a TA; (2) interaction between a student with PIMD and typically developing peer(s) without the facilitation of the TA; (3) at least one initiative by a student with PIMD or a typically developing student, without a response of the addressed student; (4) no signs of interaction between the student with PIMD and typically developing peer(s). In other words, if the first occurred, we would select this fragment to code, followed by 2, 3 and 4.

To answer the first research question, the first author described the setting, location, activity and presence of other students with and without PIMD and teachers for each video. To answer the second research question, initiatives and responses were coded using the previously mentioned coding scheme. The first author coded all the selected video fragments. To ensure the reliability of the first author's coding, a research assistant coded 25% of the material. Cohen's Kappa statistic was 0.72, which is above the recommended cut-off value of 0.60.

We calculated the frequency of the initiations and responses (positive/negative/absent) by students with PIMD, peers and TAs. In addition to the frequencies, we added examples of initiative-response patterns to illustrate the nature of the initiatives and responses.

Results

Inclusion moments

The video recordings showed that inclusion moments occurred in various settings and locations (see Table 4.3). Students 1, 3 and 4 were included in a regular classroom, where they undertook an activity together with a class of typically developing peers. Student 2 joined a small group of peers during an activity in the corridor. Students 5 and 6 were each matched with a peer (buddy), with whom they engaged in various activities in the 'To School Together' classroom or the mainstream classroom. Students 7 and 8 were recorded during the same activities in the 'To School Together' classroom. Together with another student with PIMD and two peers, students 7 and 8 participated in activities guided by three TAs.

During all the inclusion moments for students 2, 4, 5, 6, 7 and 8, the TA was close to the student with PIMD (within a reachable distance) most of the time. One of the TAs for students 1 and 3 was close by, while the other two TAs were present at a distance (not within the student's reach). With regard to proximity to peers, students were closest to peers in freer and more open settings, such as physical education lessons and playtime (e.g. students 1 and 4), compared to more fixed settings, such as sitting at a desk or in a circle (e.g. students 2, 7, 8).

Some students engaged in the same activity in each of the three inclusion moments (students 1, 4, 7, 8), while the activities of others varied (students 2, 3, 5, 6). Due to their physical and intellectual disabilities, students had difficulty taking part in some activities, such as playing tennis, playing chess or learning about contradictions in a language lesson. Some TAs tried to adjust the activity to make it possible for the students to engage. For example, student 1 took part in a tennis lesson during physical education. Student 1 relied on his wheelchair and was not able to handle a racket and hit a ball independently. Student 1's TA explored various ways to engage him in the lesson. She took him out of his wheelchair and got him to stand up and lean against her as they held the tennis racket together and tried to hit the ball. After a few tries she sat down with the student, faced him and rolled the tennis ball towards him. Student 2 took part in a language lesson, in which typically developing students learned about contradictions.

Table 4.3 Description of inclusion moments

Student	Setting	Location	Activity	Presence of other people	
				Peers	Teachers
1.	Inclusion in the regular classroom	Physical education Classroom (1,2,3)	Physical education (1,2,3)	Full class of peers (1,2,3)	– Primary school teacher (1A,2A,3A) – TA, close by (1A) or at a distance (2B, 3C)
2.	Inclusion in a small group	Corridor (1,2,3)	Language class (1), playing board games (2), listening to a story (3)	Two peers (1,2) Group of peers (3)	– TA, close by (1A,2B,3C)
3.	Inclusion in the regular classroom	Mainstream classroom (1,2,3)	Music class (1,2), playtime (3)	Full class of peers (1,2,3)	– Primary school teacher (1A,2A) – TA, close by (2A) or at a distance (1B,3B)
4.	Inclusion in the regular classroom	Mainstream classroom (1,2,3)	Playtime (1,2,3)	Full class of peers (1,2,3)	– Primary school teacher, at a distance (1A) – TA, close by (1A,2B,3B) – TA, close by (1A,2B,3A)
5.	Inclusion in the 'To School Together' classroom	'To School Together' classroom (1,2,3)	Physical education (1), playtime (2), art class (3)	A buddy (peer) and other students with PIMD (1,2,3)	– TA, close by (1A,2B,3A)
6.	Inclusion in the 'To School Together' classroom Inclusion in the regular classroom	'To School Together' classroom (1,2) Mainstream Classroom (3)	Cooking class (1,3), cooking class and watching a movie (2)	A buddy (peer) and other students with PIMD (1,2). A buddy (peer) and other peers (3).	– Primary school teacher (3A,B) – TA, close by (1A,2B,3A)

| 7. | Inclusion in the 'To School Together' classroom | 'To School Together' classroom (1,2,3) | Art class (1,2,3) | Three students with PIMD and two peers (1,2,3) | – TA, close by (1A,B,C,2A,B,C,3A,B,C) |
| 8. | Inclusion in the 'To School Together' classroom | 'To School Together' classroom (1,2,3) | Art class (1,2,3) | Three students with PIMD and two peers (1,2,3) | – TA, close by (1A,B,C,2A,B,C,3A,B,C) |

Note: Numbers 1, 2 and 3 refer to inclusion moments 1, 2 and 3. Letters A, B, C refer to the primary school teacher or TA present. For example, the same teacher (A) was present during each inclusion moment for student 1. A different TA (A, B or C) was present during each inclusion moment.

The TA tried to include the student by writing down the words mentioned by the peers and showing them to the student. During the third inclusion moment for student 2, two peers played board games, including chess. The TA asked the peers how the student could join in their games. In addition, TAs often tried to find the best position for a student to join in an activity. For example, during playtime (students 3, 4 and 5), TAs would take the student out of their wheelchair and place them near a group of peers who were playing on the ground.

Interactions initiated by students with PIMD

Students 1, 3, 5 and 6 initiated contact towards peers 4, 4, 1 and 24 times respectively (see Figure 4.1). No initiations were observed for students 2, 4, 7 and 8. Peers responded positively to all four of student 1's initiations and either negatively (once), positively (once) or not at all (twice) to student 3. Student 5's single initiation was followed by a negative response from the peer. Peers responded negatively most often (23) to the 24 initiations by student 6, and positively only once. A total of 33 contact initiations by students with PIMD were observed. Most peer responses were negative (25 times), followed by positive responses (6 times) and the absence of a response (2 times). An example of interactions initiated by a student with PIMD is presented in the text box.

For an example of interactions initiated by a student with PIMD see Figure 4.2. In this 11 example, student 3 is included in a regular classroom setting with peers aged 4–5 years old. The teacher is giving a music lesson. All the peers are sitting on chairs in a circle. The student with PIMD is placed in his wheelchair in the middle of the circle. The TA is seated on the other side of the circle, next to the teacher. The teacher starts the lesson by telling the group that student 3 loves music and they are going to sing a song for him. The teacher hands out instruments to some students. The peer seated to the left of the student with PIMD is playing the maraca. The student tries to grab the maraca twice (11:06 and 11:13), without the peer noticing (see Figure 4.2). The peer seated to the right of the student is playing the tambourine, which the student also tries to grab. The peer notices this and pulls back the hand holding the instrument. The peer to the left with the maraca then makes physical contact with the student twice by stroking his head (11:45 and 13:33). The student does not respond to this.

Interactions initiated by peers

The peers present during student 1's inclusion moments made 11 contact initiations (see Figure 4.3). The student with PIMD responded negatively 6 times and did not respond the other 5 times. The peers of students 2 and 3 each made 28 initiations. Student 2 did not respond to any of these initiations, while student 3 showed a negative response 5 times, a positive response 7 times and no response 16 times. Student 4's peers made 30 contact

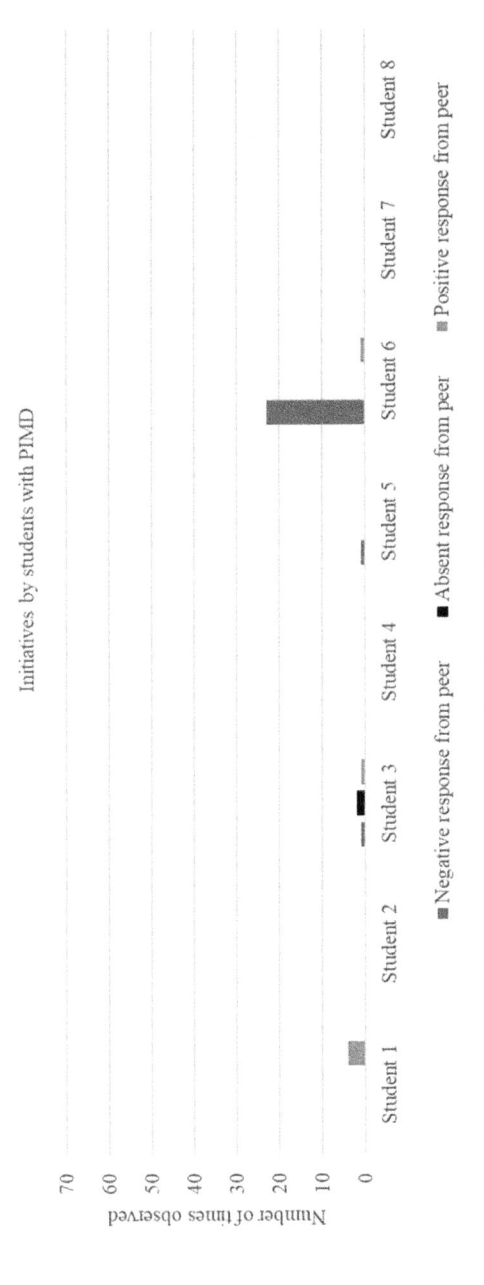

Figure 4.1 Initiatives by students with profound intellectual and multiple disabilities.

72 *Ineke Haakma et al.*

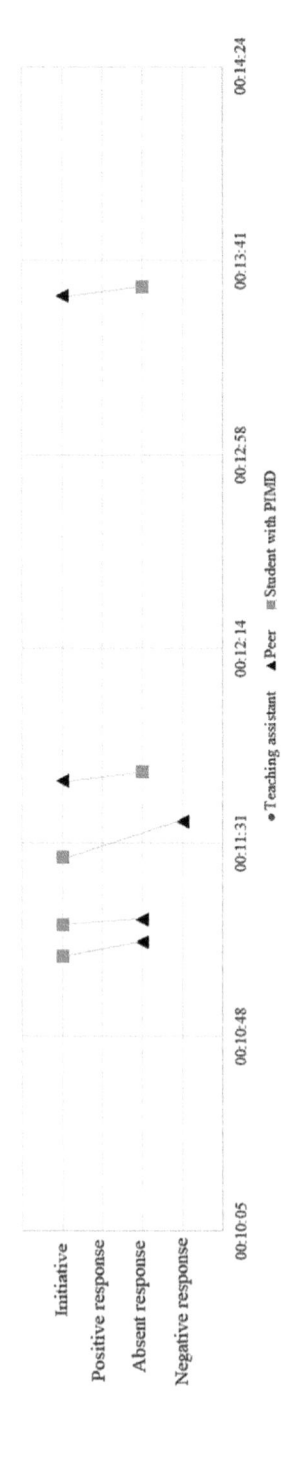

Figure 4.2 An example of student initiations (student 3).

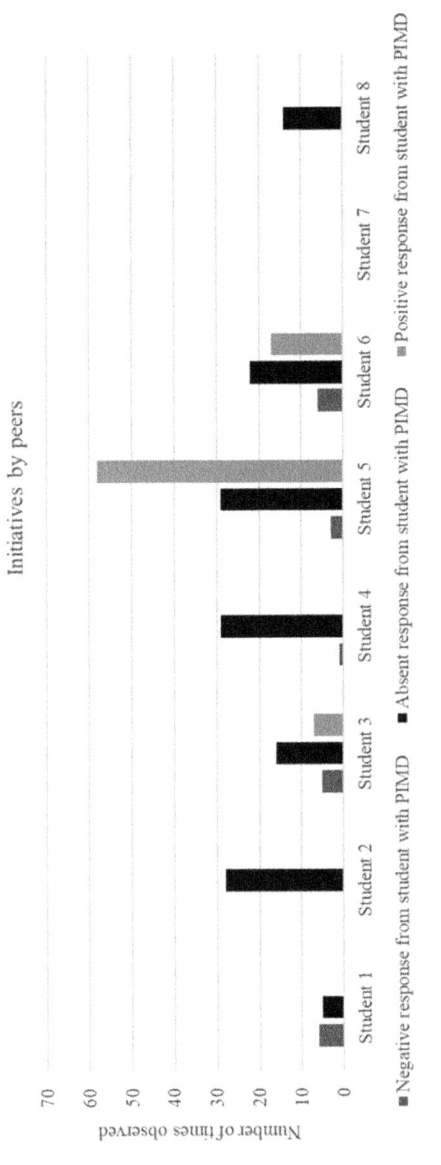

Figure 4.3 Initiatives by peers.

initiations, to which the student responded negatively once and did not respond the other 29 times. The peers present during student 5's inclusion moments made 90 initiations. The student reacted negatively 3 times, positively 58 times, and no response was observed 29 times. Student 6's peers made 45 initiations. The student reacted negatively 6 times, positively 17 times, and no response was observed 22 times. None of the peers present during student 7's inclusion moments made initiations. Student 8's peers made 14 initiations, none of which the student responded to. A total of 246 peer initiatives were observed. On most occasions, students with PIMD did not respond (143), followed by 82 positive responses and 21 negative responses.

For an example of interactions initiated by a peer see Figure 4.4. In this example, student 5 is sitting at a table in the 'To School Together' classroom, with a peer (buddy) sitting next to him. The TA is seated on the other side of the table with another student with PIMD. They are going to make a clay heart, a Mother's Day present. The peer gives a piece of clay to the student with PIMD (32:52) and the student starts pressing the clay. The peer starts rolling another piece of clay herself (34:29). The TA enthusiastically comments on the peer's work to the student, who does not respond. The student tries to take the peer's piece of clay, which the peer does not allow. The peer (35:39) places a heart shape on the clay and asks the student to press it. The student presses the form into the clay.

Interactions initiated by teaching assistants

The TAs present during student 1's inclusion moments did not initiate the facilitating of interaction between the students and peers (see Figure 4.5). The TAs present during student 2's inclusion moments made 25 attempts to create interactions between students with PIMD and peers. The student with PIMD did not respond to these initiations. One of student 3's TAs made an initiation that resulted in a negative response from the student. Student 4's TAs made four initiations that were not responded to by the student. The TAs present during student 5's inclusion moments made seven initiations, to which the student made seven positive responses. In the case of student 6, the TAs made four initiations. The student did not respond on one occasion and responded positively the other 3 times. Student 7's TAs made five initiations, to which the student responded positively once and made no response 4 times. The TAs present during student 8's inclusion moments made nine initiations, none of which provoked a response from the student. In sum, TAs tried to initiate interaction between the students with PIMD and peers 55 times. The students with PIMD mostly did not respond (43 times), followed by a positive response (11 times) and a negative response (once).

For an example of interactions initiated by a TA see Figure 4.6. In this example, student 6 and a peer (his buddy) are sitting at a table in the school

Figure 4.4 An example of peer initiations (student 5).

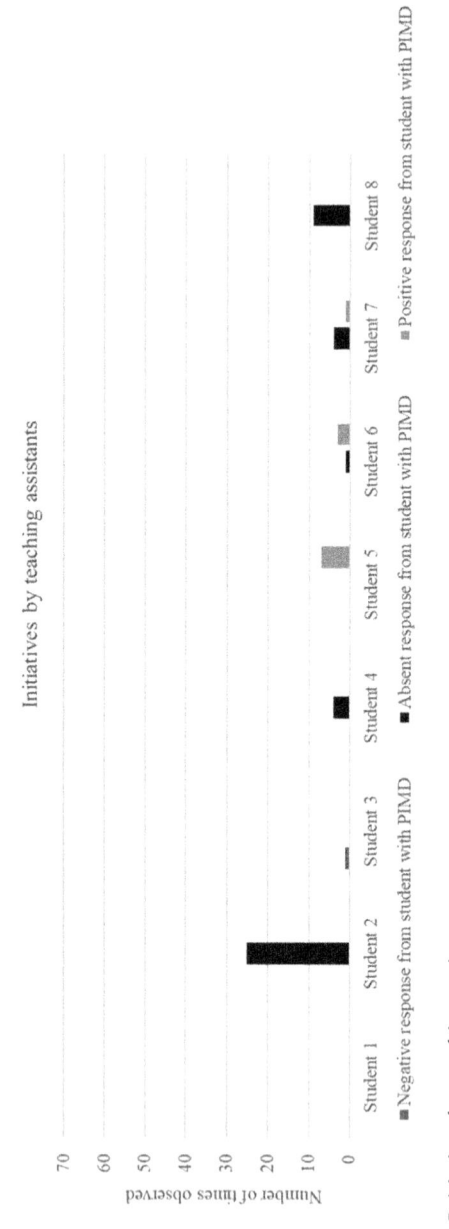

Figure 4.5 Initiatives by teaching assistants.

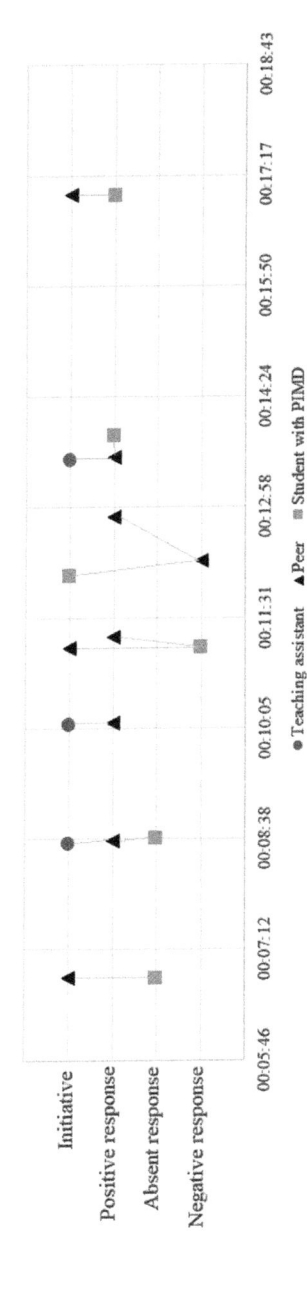

Figure 4.6 An example of TA initiations (student 6).

corridor near a kitchen. The TA and another student with PIMD are sitting at the same table. The peer sets out the ingredients to make a dessert. The student is watching the peer. The peer strokes the student's arm (6:50). The student does not respond. The TA suggests that the peer let the student smell the ingredients (8:36). The peer does so. The student does not seem to respond. The TA suggests that they go to the kitchen to use the mixer and let the student feel the mixer when it is switched on (10:09). The peer goes to the kitchen. He starts mixing (11:08) and lets the student feel the mixer. The student does not seem to like this. He pulls back his hands and covers his ears. The peer tries to calm him by stroking his arm. When the mixing is finished, the student puts his hand in the batter (12:05). The peer says the student's name and pulls his hand out of the batter. He then laughs and cleans the student's hand. The TA indicates that the peer can fill cups with the batter on the student's wheelchair tray. The peer does this so that the student can smell the dessert. The student looks at the peer filling the cups. The peer puts an apron on the student and lets him eat the batter left in the bowl.

Discussion

Our results indicated that inclusion moments occurred in various settings and locations. Overall, our findings show that peers initiated more contact with students with PIMD than vice versa. Students with PIMD did not respond to most of the initiations by peers. It is not possible to ask the students with PIMD to explain why they did not initiate contact or respond to initiations. However, there are possible explanations that could be explored in further research. The first is that some activities were difficult for students with PIMD to engage in because of their physical and intellectual disabilities. Examples are tennis lessons, language lessons and games of chess. Some TAs tried to make the activity accessible by adapting the content of the activity or adjusting the student's position, for example, by taking a student out of their wheelchair and placing them on the ground among a group of playing students. Research shows that the positioning of individuals with PIMD can be improved to encourage interactions with other people (Kamstra et al. 2019). Positioning can therefore influence the number of peer-directed behaviours. Given the perception behaviours of students with PIMD (looking, listening, tasting, touching and smelling), it is important to place the student near peers, which gives both the student and the peers opportunities to perceive each other and reach out to each other.

A second explanation could be a mismatch in the communication modes used by peers and students with PIMD. Peers, for instance, tend to opt for physical contact in contact initiations, such as stroking the student with PIMD, or laying an arm around their shoulder. Not all students with PIMD appreciate this physical approach. Peers may also fail to notice the expressions of students with PIMD, who usually communicate by subtle facial or bodily expressions and vocalisations that are difficult to interpret (Penne et al. 2012). In addition, they often do not show behaviours such as waving or pointing to attract the attention of others in order to initiate social interactions (Nijs and Maes 2014).

A third explanation is that the complex disabilities of students with PIMD can hamper interaction. For example, many students with PIMD have sensory impairments (Evenhuis et al. 2001), as was the case for six students in this study.

A fourth explanation is that students with PIMD do not necessarily need peer interactions in order to enjoy or benefit from inclusion moments. We gave an example of student 3 taking part in a music lesson. As mentioned in the text box, the teacher commented that the student loved music. The observations do indeed show that the student reacted positively when his peers sang a song. He was also very interested in the instruments that they played. In other words, this student seemed to enjoy listening to other students sing despite not being able to sing himself. Seeing and hearing peers playing instruments can also be very interesting in itself.

This raises the question of whether social interactions should be the main outcome of inclusion moments. Enjoying the presence of other students and being in a new, different environment that triggers a student's interest and alertness might also be very valuable outcomes. In addition, inclusion moments may have positive effects on peers who have an opportunity to meet students with PIMD.

With regard to the TA's role in supporting peer interactions, we found that TAs tried to facilitate interactions between students with PIMD and peers. However, they differed in the degree to which they tried to do so. A possible explanation is in our setting, TAs may have seen their main role as that of direct support professionals who offer medical and practical support to the students, while the teacher is responsible for the lesson content. These different views may lead to different approaches and could explain why one TA does not intervene in the situation, while another tries out a variety of ways to enhance peer interaction. However, even when TAs feel responsible for facilitating interaction, they still need the knowledge and skills to do so effectively. TAs may intend to foster interaction, while unintentionally hampering it. We know from previous research in other settings that the presence of TAs does not always have a positive influence on the peer interactions of students with disabilities. For example, a study by Blatchford and Webster (2018) showed that students with SEN have more interactions with TAs and fewer interactions with peers compared to students without SEN. For children with PIMD, research by Nijs et al. (2016) found that direct support professionals in day care centres for children with PIMD do not usually focus on facilitating peer interactions. Rather, they spend most of their time doing such things as organising the activity. Also, examples were found in which direct support professionals drew the attention of children with PIMD to themselves instead of to interaction with other students with PIMD. The results of our study did not indicate that

TAs drew attention away from peer interactions. Nor did TAs engage in interactions with the students that excluded peers.

The interplay between the TA, the peer and the student with PIMD seemed to be very effective in settings in which a peer (buddy) was matched to a student with PIMD. The text box examples of students 5 and 6 provide an illustration of how the three worked together. The TA was present, offering suggestions and answering the peer's questions when needed. However, the TA's focus was on supporting another student with PIMD. This left the peer to take the lead in executing the activity with their buddy. Since they had all known each other for some time, they were well attuned to one another, which is reflected in the interactions that took place. The peer tried various ways to activate the student's senses and include him in the process of making the dessert: he let him smell and taste the batter, which the student seemed to enjoy. When the student expressed his discomfort at the loud noise made by the mixer, the peer calmed him down, after which the student put his hand in the batter. This was not the peer's plan. The peer was startled and pulled the student's hand out of the batter, and then immediately started laughing at the student's action. They both seemed to find it very funny. Even though their contact initiations and responses were not always perfectly in tune (in the sense that every initiative was followed by a positive response), it is evident from the videos that they enjoyed each other's company. This particular setting – matching students to peers – allows an opportunity for friendships to develop. More interaction can occur as the student and peer get to know each other better.

Strengths and limitations

A strength of this study is that it adds to the knowledge on social interactions of students with PIMD. Most research so far has focused on interactions between children or adults with PIMD in residential or day care facilities (Kamstra et al. 2019; Nijs, Vlaskamp and Maes 2015). The current study offers a new perspective on the interactions of children with PIMD who are included in a mainstream school.

A limitation of this study is that we only used observations to answer our research questions. Although we cannot ask students with PIMD to describe their experiences, we could have asked TAs, teachers and peers about their views on and experiences of the inclusion of students with PIMD. We could also have used video-stimulated recall to invite them to reflect on their behaviours. Another limitation is that we did not consult knowledgeable others in the coding process. Students with PIMD often display very idiosyncratic behavioural expressions that are difficult to identify and interpret. This may have influenced our coding. Consulting the parents, for example, might have improved the coding process. Because they know their children best, they may have been able to identify idiosyncratic behavioural expressions that we perhaps missed.

Research implications

Our suggestion for future research is to investigate outcomes of inclusion moments for students with PIMD and their peers other than social interaction. We have already suggested aspects such as enjoyment, interest and alertness as potential positive outcomes of inclusion moments. A suggestion for practice would be to initiate meetings in which TAs, teachers, peers, parents and siblings of children with PIMD share their knowledge about the student. Integrating these various perspectives will provide insights into the student's abilities, disabilities, needs and preferences, which may help in the selection of activities that are adapted to the abilities and wishes of the student. Given the heterogeneity of students with PIMD and the severity of their disabilities, they are dependent on staff being sufficiently knowledgeable to provide them with appropriate activities. Therefore, teachers and TAs must have detailed and extensive knowledge about the preferences and abilities of each student in order to offer appropriate activities (Ten Brug, Van Der Putten and Vlaskamp 2013; Vlaskamp, Hiemstra and Wierdsma 2007).

Besides exploring what kind of activities can best be offered during inclusion moments, these meetings can also be used to discuss how students with PIMD can best be addressed by others. TAs, parents and siblings of students with PIMD could inform peers about how the student likes to be approached and how and when they might respond. Siblings grow up with the person with PIMD and adjust the way in which they make contact (Nijs et al. 2016). Siblings mainly use non-verbal attention-directing behaviours and often use physical support, such as helping the child with PIMD to grasp an object by manipulating their hand. Presenting a combination of verbal and non-verbal behaviours is more likely to attract the attention of the student with PIMD. Therefore, siblings might have valuable input for optimising inclusion moments. These meetings could be organised on a regular basis to evaluate how things are going and to make adjustments where necessary, in order to create inclusion moments that are most beneficial for students with PIMD and their peers.

Acknowledgements

We would like to thank all the schools, teaching assistants and parents, and children to participate in this study. Thanks to the student assistants who were involved in the data collection, with special thanks to Angela Jong.

Originally published as Ineke Haakma, Anke A. de Boer, Sanne van Esch, Alexander E. M. G. Minnaert & Annette A. J Van Der Putten (2021) Inclusion moments for students with profound intellectual and multiple disabilities in mainstream schools: The teacher assistant's role in supporting peer interactions, European Journal of Special Needs Education, 36:2, 231-247, DOI: 10.1080/08856257.2021.1901374.

© Taylor & Francis Ltd (2021), reprinted by permission of the publisher.

Funding

This study was funded by the Dutch foundation for the Handicapped Child (project nr. 20140333) and the unit Inclusive and Special Needs Education of the University of Groningen.

References

Baulminger, N., C. Shulman, and G. Agam. 2003. "Peer Interaction and Loneliness in High-functioning Children with Autism." *Journal of Autism and Developmental Disorders* 33 (5): 489–507. doi:10.1023/A:1025827427901.

Blatchford, P., and R. Webster. 2018. "Classroom Contexts for Learning at Primary and Secondary School: Class Size, Groupings, Interactions and Special Educational Needs." *British Educational Research Journal* 44 (4): 681–703. doi:10.1002/berj.3454.

Evenhuis, H. M., M. Theunissen, I. Denkers, H. Verschuure, and H. Kemme. 2001. "Prevalence of Visual and Hearing Impairment in a Dutch Institutionalized Population with Intellectual Disability." *Journal of Intellectual Disability Research* 45 (5): 457–464. doi:10.1046/j.1365-2788.2001.00350.x.

Giangreco, M. F., S. W. Edelman, T. E. Luiselli, and S. Z. C. Macfarland. 1997. "Helping or Hovering? Effects of Instructional Assistant Proximity on Students with Disabilities." *Exceptional Children* 64 (1): 7–18. doi:10.1177/001440299706400101.

Giangreco, M. F., S. Yuan, B. McKenzie, P. Cameron, and J. Fialka. 2005. "'Be Careful What You Wish for…': Five Reasons to Be Concerned about the Assignment of Individual Paraprofessionals." *Teaching Exceptional Children* 37 (5): 28–34. doi:10.1177/004005990503700504.

Hauck, M., D. Fein, L. Waterhouse, and C. Feinstein. 1995. "Social Initiations by Autistic Children to Adults and Other Children." *Journal of Autism and Developmental Disorders* 25 (6): 579–595. doi:10.1007/BF02178189.

Hostyn, I., and B. Maes. 2009. "Interaction between Persons with Profound Intellectual and Multiple Disabilities and Their Partners: A Literature Review." *Journal of Intellectual & Developmental Disability* 34 (4): 296–312. doi:10.3109/13668250903285648.

Jansen, S. L. G., A. A. J. Van Der Putten, and C. Vlaskamp. 2016. "Parents' Experiences of Collaborating with Professionals in the Support of Their Child with Profound Intellectual and Multiple Disabilities: A Multiple Case Study." *Journal of Intellectual Disabilities* 21 (1): 53–67. doi:10.1177/1744629516641843.

Kamstra, A., A. A. J. Van Der Putten, B. Maes, and C. Vlaskamp. 2019. "Exploring Spontaneous Interactions between People with Profound Intellectual and Multiple Disabilities and Their Peers." *Journal of Intellectual & Developmental Disability* 44 (3): 282–291. doi:10.3109/13668250.2017.1415428.

Koster, M., H. Nakken, S. J. Pijl, and E. Van Houten. 2009. "Being Part of the Peer Group: A Literature Study Focusing on the Social Dimension of Inclusion in Education." *International Journal of Inclusive Education* 13 (2): 117–140. doi:10.1080/13603110701284680.

Koster, M., S. J. Pijl, H. Nakken, and E. Van Houten. 2010. "Social Participation of Students with Special Needs in Regular Primary Education in the Netherlands." *International Journal of Disability, Development and Education* 57 (1): 59–75. doi:10.1080/10349120903537905.

MacKenzie, S. 2011. "Yet, But.: Rhetoric, Reality and Resistance in Teaching Assistants' Experiences of Inclusive Education." *Support for Learning* 26 (2): 64–71. doi:10.1111/j.1467-9604.2011.01479.x.

Maes, B., G. Lambrechts, I. Hostyn, and K. Petry. 2007. "Quality-enhancing Interventions for People with Profound Intellectual and Multiple Disabilities: A Review of the Empirical Research Literature." *Journal of Intellectual & Developmental Disability* 32 (3): 163–178. doi:10.1080/13668250701549427.

Nakken, H., and C. Vlaskamp. 2007. "A Need for A Taxonomy for Profound Intellectual and Multiple Disabilities." *Journal of Policy and Practice in Intellectual Disabilities* 4 (2): 83–87. doi:10.1111/j.1741-1130.2007.00104.x.

Nijs, S., and B. Maes. 2014. "Social Peer Interactions in Persons with Profound Intellectualand Multiple Disabilities: A Literature Review." *Education and Training in Autism and Developmental Disabilities* 49 (1): 153–165.

Nijs, S., A. Penne, C. Vlaskamp, and B. Maes. 2016. "Peer Interactions among Children with Profound Intellectual and Multiple Disabilities during Group Activities." *Journal of Applied Research in Intellectual Disabilities: JARID* 29 (4): 366–377. doi:10.1111/jar.12185.

Nijs, S., C. Vlaskamp, and B. Maes. 2015. "The Nature of Peer-directed Behaviours in Children with Profound Intellectual and Multiple Disabilities and Its Relationship with Social Scaffolding Behaviours of the Direct Support Worker." *Child: Care, Health and Development* 42 (1): 98–108. doi:10.1111/cch.12295.

Penne, A., A. Ten Brug, V. Munde, A. Van Der Putten, C. Vlaskamp, and B. Maes. 2012. "Staff Interactive Style during Multisensory Storytelling with Persons with Profound Intellectual and Multiple Disabilities." *Journal of Intellectual Disability Research* 56 (2): 167–178. doi:10.1111/j.1365-2788.2011.01448.x.

Petry, K., B. Maes, and C. Vlaskamp. 2005. "Domains of Quality of Life of People with Profound Multiple Disabilities: The Perspective of Parents and Direct Support Staff." *Journal of Applied Research in Intellectual Disabilities* 18 (1): 35–46. doi:10.1111/j.1468-3148.2004.00209.x.

Sharma, U., and S. J. Salend. 2016. "Teaching Assistants in Inclusive Classrooms: A Systematic Analysis of the International Research." *Australian Journal of Teacher Education* 41 (8): 118–134. doi:10.14221/ajte.2016v41n8.7.

Takala, M. 2007. "The Work of Classroom Assistants in Special and Mainstream Education in Finland." *British Journal of Special Education* 34 (1): 50–57. doi:10.1111/j.1467-8578.2007.00453.x.

Ten Brug, A., A. Van Der Putten, and C. Vlaskamp. 2013. "Learn and Apply: Using Multi-sensory Storytelling to Gather Knowledge about Preferences and Abilities of Children with Profound Intellectual and Multiple Disabilities – Three Case Studies." *Journal of Intellectual Disabilities* 17 (4): 339–360. doi:10.1177/1744629513508384.

United Nations. 2006. *Convention on the Rights of Persons with Disabilities*. New York: Author.

Van Timmeren, E. A., C. P. Van Der Schans, A. A. J. Van Der Putten, W. P. Krijnen, H. A. Steenbergen, H. M. J. Van Schrojenstein Lantman-de Valk, and A. Waninge. 2017. "Physical Health Issues in Adults with Severe or Profound Intellectual and Motor Disabilities: A Systematic Review of Cross-sectional Studies." *Journal of Intellectual Disability Research* 61 (1): 30–49. doi:10.1111/jir.12296.

Vlaskamp, C., S. J. Hiemstra, and L. A. Wierdsma. 2007. "Becoming Aware of What You Know or Need to Know: Gathering Client and Context Characteristics in Day Services for Persons with Profound Intellectual and Multiple Disabilities."

Journal of Policy and Practice in Intellectual Disabilities 42 (2): 97–103. doi:10.1111/j.1741-1130.2007.00106.x.

Webster, R., and P. Blatchford. 2013. "The Educational Experiences of Pupils with a Statement for Special Educational Needs in Mainstream Primary Schools: Results from a Systematic Observation Study." *European Journal of Special Needs Education* 28 (4): 463–479. doi:10.1080/08856257.2013.820459.

Webster, R., P. Blatchford, P. Bassett, P. Brown, C. Martin, and A. Russell. 2010. "Double Standards and First Principles: Framing Teaching Assistant Support for Pupils with Special Educational Needs." *European Journal of Special Needs Education* 25 (4): 319–336. doi:10.1080/08856257.2010.513533.

5 Give them wings to fly

Critiquing the Special Needs Assistant scheme through the lens of pupil independence

Claire Griffin and Peter Blatchford

Introduction

The educational landscape for persons with special educational needs (SEN) has changed significantly over recent decades. This has been fuelled by a rights-based movement, where a focus on inclusive education is recognised as a fundamental pillar in building inclusive societies (UNESCO 1994). Across many international education systems, an increase in paraprofessional support has been implemented as a means of facilitating inclusion. Examples include in the United States (Giangreco, Doyle and Suter 2014), the United Kingdom (Blatchford et al. 2007), Australia (Sharma and Salend 2016), Iceland (Egilson and Traustadottir 2009) and Ireland (Department of Education and Skills [DES] 2014).

Irish policy context

Within Ireland, the paraprofessional workforce is realised through the Special Needs Assistant (SNA) scheme. The SNA role is defined in terms of a *non-teaching care* remit to 'provide schools with additional adult support staff who can assist children with SEN who also have additional and significant care needs' (DES 2014, 1). Moreover, a key goal of SNA support is to help children develop independent living skills (DES 2014). The SNA scheme differs from many international paraprofessional roles. Although the Irish SNA may *assist* with the delivery of teaching or therapeutic interventions, the role is prescribed as nonteaching in nature (DES 2011, 2014). Accordingly, SNA access is not sanctioned for pupils presenting with learning difficulties or specific learning disorders. Rather, SNAs are only sanctioned where professional reports outline that the pupil presents with *significant care needs* arising from (i) a significant medical need, (ii) a significant impairment of physical or sensory function or (iii) a disability categorisation including emotional behaviour disorder (EBD), severe EBD (SEBD), behavioural disturbance or behaviour-related care needs (DES 2014).

DOI: 10.4324/9781003265580-8

Research rationale and focus

Over the past two decades, the SNA scheme has grown exponentially, from 293 posts in 1998 (DES 2011) to almost 17,000 posts in 2020 (DES 2019). Most research has focused on the unintended expansion of the role into non-care duties including behaviour, therapeutic support, teaching and administration (DES 2011; National Council for Special Education [NCSE] 2018). In contrast, the relationship between SNA support and pupils' development of independence remains significantly under-researched both nationally and internationally, as identified from an in-depth literature review (Griffin 2018). Accordingly, the current authors sought to explore this gap, given the importance of independence as a lifelong skill.

Previous research in the field

Focusing on the link between paraprofessional support and pupils' development of independence, a review of national and international literature identified several overarching themes (Griffin 2018). Within Ireland, early, small-scale studies highlighted issues of pupil over-dependency, learned helplessness and over-reliance on the SNA, as deduced through interviews with SNAs, teachers, parents and pupils (Elliott 2004; Keating and O'Connor 2012; Logan 2006). Some opposing findings emerged from Shevlin, Kenny and Loxley (2008), where selected SNAs sought to maintain a caring yet supportive distance from pupils, including supporting pupils at the group level. More recently, findings revealed mixed school-based practices linking SNA support and pupil independence. Positive practices included SNA rotation, flexible provision of SNA support and individualised planning comprising independence-focused targets. In contrast, negative practices included over-proximity of SNAs to pupils and a lack of reduction in SNA support over time, with many pupils identified as inadequately equipped for life post-schooling (National Disability Authority [NDA] and NCSE 2017; Rose et al. 2015). Although these findings shed some light on the link between SNA support and independence development, the scarcity of Irish studies, the small sample sizes and the over-reliance on interviews reduce the generalisability of findings.

Internationally, large-scale UK studies, including the *Deployment and Impact of Support Staff* (DISS) project (Blatchford et al. 2008), the *Making a Statement* (MaSt) project (Webster and Blatchford 2013) and the *Special Educational Needs in Secondary Education* (SENSE) study (Webster and Blatchford 2017), have highlighted the high levels of proximity between Teaching Assistants (TAs) and pupils with SEN in comparison to TAs' proximity to non-SEN pupils. Although close TA–pupil proximity reduced negative behaviour and supported on-task behaviour (Blatchford et al. 2009; Webster and Blatchford 2013), unintended consequences included less contact time with teachers and peers than that experienced by non-SEN pupils (e.g. Blatchford and Webster 2018). Such research extends findings from earlier studies, where inappropriate levels of pupil assistance were shown to limit children's skills and perception of control, creating unhealthy dependencies on paraprofessionals (Egilson and Traustadottir 2009; Harris 2011).

In spite of the growing international studies on paraprofessional support and pupil independence, in-depth Irish research was deemed essential to inform policy and practice. The researchers also sought to integrate systematic observations and case studies to capture classroom events and behaviours connected to SNAs and pupil independence, presenting as the first time this methodology would be used for SNA research in the Irish context. Independence was defined as *being able to do things for oneself, to be self-supporting and self-reliant* (Reindal 1999). This construct was viewed along a continuum from *fully dependent*, i.e. requiring full-time assistance, to *fully independent*, i.e. operating autonomously, without help or assistance, in line with the child's stage of development. This definition mirrored that of the DES (2011, 2014), linking independence with adaptive behaviour and self-care skills. In addition, positive and negative SNA practices for supporting independence were defined in terms of *pupil proximity and intensity of SNA support*, as informed by the DES (2011) and NCSE (2018). Negative patterns included the SNA acting as a constant assistant/teacher to the child, acting as a barrier between the pupil and his/her teacher or peers, over-shadowing or constantly monitoring the child, and/or limiting the development of pupils' capabilities. In contrast, positive practices included SNAs' usage of various support patterns including close proximity and distance, as appropriate, with SNA provision at the minimum level required to meet the pupil's care needs (DES 2011; NCSE 2018). Nonetheless, neither list was deemed exhaustive, presenting scope for future research.

The first author undertook research from September 2016 to September 2017. The project aimed to obtain a detailed and integrated account of the preparedness and deployment of SNAs when supporting pupils with behavioural care needs and developing such pupils' independence. This chapter focuses on one research question, namely: *To what extent do SNAs support/hinder the development of independence of pupils presenting with behavioural care needs in mainstream primary schools in Ireland?*[1]

The research sought to investigate

(a) The level and nature of target pupils' independence/dependence on SNAs
(b) SNA practices which served to support/hinder target pupils' independence, with reference to
- SNA–pupil assignment
- SNA–pupil proximity
- Other SNA–pupil support strategies

Methodology

Research design and participants

The research was modelled on Strand 2 Wave 1 of the DISS project (Blatchford et al. 2008). A convergent parallel mixed methods design was adopted comprising systematic observations and case studies. Using a stratified sampling approach, 20 'target pupils' were recruited across 20 urban and rural DEIS[2] and non-DEIS mainstream primary schools in the Munster region of Ireland. All target pupils presented with behaviour-related care needs, as per DES (2014), and received SNA support for more than 50% of the schoolday. The final sample comprised 19 boys and 1 girl, ranging from 5 to 12 years (M = 9.1 years, SD = 1.91).

Systematic observations and case studies were built around each target pupil. The observations were conducted in each target pupil's classroom and provided systematic and quantitative data on the class context, SNA deployment and behaviours of the class teacher, target pupil and peers. Three comparison children were also selected within each target pupil's class. Following the procedure outlined in the MaSt project (Webster and Blatchford 2013), comparison children were identified by teachers as academically and behaviourally 'average' and gender-matched to target pupils. Thereafter, case studies adopted a multi-method, pupil-centred approach comprising:

(a) Semi-structured interviews with the target pupil, class teacher and SNA
(b) Documentary review of target pupil planning
(c) Field notes.

In total, 120 participants partook in the research including 20 target pupils, 20 class teachers, 20 SNAs and 60 comparison pupils.

Research tools

(a) *Systematic observation schedule*
An original observation schedule was designed, informed by the SENSE schedule (Webster and Blatchford 2017), MaSt schedule (Webster and Blatchford 2013) and the Observing Pupils and Teachers in Classrooms (OPTIC) schedule (Merrett and Wheldall 1986). Observation categories included: *ID and logging information* (pupil ID, school ID, date); *contextual information* (target pupil context, adult context, lesson type, target task, number of people in classroom); *interaction data* (social mode of pupils' interactions, interaction level, interaction context) and *OPTIC schedule data* (the nature of the focused interactions between the target pupil and adults). The schedule was divided into two halves to

facilitate concurrent data-logging on the target pupil and comparison pupil on a minute-by-minute basis. A copy of the schedule is available in Griffin (2018, 353–356).
(b) *Case studies*
To support case studies, original semi-structured interview schedules and templates for documentary analysis and field notes were created. These were informed by the research questions and international literature (see Griffin 2018, 373–380).

Procedure

Prior to data collection, ethical approval was obtained from the Institute of Education Research Ethics Committee. At all times, the researcher abided by the Psychological Society of Ireland's (PSI) Code of Professional Ethics (PSI 2010). Following a pilot study, the researcher spent two days in each of the 20 schools. Systematic observations were conducted in each target pupils' classroom for an average of four hours. Observations and coding took place on a minute-by-minute basis, moving between the target pupil (first 30 seconds) and the comparison child (second 30 seconds). Across the 20 cases, a total of 74 hours 55 minutes of observations took place across 77 lessons, yielding 4,495 data points. Two rounds of interrater reliability checks were undertaken near the start and mid-point of observational data collection. All semi-structured interviews occurred in a private room within the schools and were audio-recorded with prior consent/assent. Documentary analysis and field note-taking also took place over the two days.

Data analysis

(a) *Quantitative data: systematic observations*
Using SPSS Statistics 25 Programme, systematic observational data were analysed using descriptive and inferential statistics. Reliability coefficients were calculated for the observational data for the main sets of mutually exclusive categories. Based on the Landis and Koch (1977) benchmarks for agreement, all scores lay between 0.61 and 1, denoting 'substantial' to 'almost perfect' agreement.
(b) *Qualitative data: case studies*
NVivo 11 software was used to support qualitative case study analysis, based on the principles of 'Interpretative Phenomenological Analysis' (IPA). Although IPA is typically applied to studies with a small sample size, researchers support the application of IPA to larger sample sizes, facilitating detailed insight into particular phenomena (Smith, Flowers and Larkin 2009). This involved examination of each case in isolation, followed by cross-case comparisons. Data analysis was iterative in nature, ensuring depth of analysis and the relationship between 'part' and 'whole'.

Findings

Systematic observations

Total SNA context

Table 5.1 presents the total classroom context of all SNAs across all observations. SNAs' most frequent context was with target pupils on a one-to-one basis (41%). This was followed by 'not working with pupils' (23%), where the SNA mainly undertook secondary care-associated tasks.[3] In contrast, SNAs spent considerably less time with groups (5%) or other individual pupils (13%).

Total interaction data

Table 5.2 presents the total frequency of interaction data across all cases. This was calculated by totalling the number of observed interactions across each interaction category for target and comparison pupils. Findings show the disparate daily classroom interactions of target pupils when compared with comparison pupils.

Firstly, target pupils' most frequent interactions were at an individual, 'focused'[4] level with the SNA (38%). Comparable one-to-one interactions between SNAs and comparison pupils were not observed in any case. In contrast, comparison pupils' most frequent interactions were at a whole-class level with the teacher, as part of the class 'audience'[5] while the teacher led the class (62%). Comparable teacher interactions for target pupils were substantially lower (36%), superseded by individual interactions with the SNA.

Secondly, comparison pupils engaged in peer interactions almost double the frequency of target pupils (14% and 9%, respectively), albeit at a low level.

Thirdly, the frequency with which pupils had no interaction differed across target and comparison pupils; typically logged when pupils engaged in independent, uninterrupted work. Data show that comparison pupils had 'no interaction' over twice the frequency of target pupils (22% and 10%, respectively).

In summary, target pupils' classroom experiences consisted of very high levels of individual focused SNA support. This contrasted with comparison pupils, whose main interactions were at a whole-class level with the teacher

Table 5.1 Total special needs assistant classroom context across all cases

SNA context	Frequency (# observations)	%
With group <10	240	5.4
With individual non-target	590	13.2
With target (1–1)	1836	41.1
Part of audience	–	–
Roving/monitoring	787	17.0
Not working with pupils	1042	23.3
Total	4495	100.0

Give them wings to fly 91

Table 5.2 Total frequency of interaction data across all cases, comparing target pupil interactions with comparison pupil interactions

			Target pupils		Comparison pupils	
			Frequency	%	Frequency	%
Teacher	Audience	Part of class	1618	36.00	2806	62.42
		Part of group	1	.02	–	–
	Focused	Part of class	86	1.91	55	1.22
		Part of group	–	–	–	–
		Individual	147	3.27	10	.22
	Total teacher interactions		1852	41.20	2871	63.86
SNA	Audience	Part of class	2	.04	–	–
		Part of group	–	–	–	–
	Focused	Part of class	1	.02	–	–
		Part of group	88	1.96	3	.07
		Individual	1700	37.82	–	–
	Total SNA interactions		1791	39.84	3	.07
Peer	Total peer interactions		389	8.66	645	14.35
No	Total no interaction		463	10.30	976	21.72
	Total interactions		4495	100	4495	100

in audience mode. Such high levels of one-to-one support for target pupils were observed to result in reduced levels of interactions with the class teacher (in 'audience' mode), with peers, as well as opportunities for 'no interaction', when contrasted with that experienced by peers.

OPTIC schedule data

Table 5.3 presents OPTIC schedule data for target pupils across all cases. This details the nature of the focused interactions between the target pupil and teacher/SNA, spanning categories of positive/negative academic and positive/negative social or conduct interactions. The most frequent focused interactions between SNAs and target pupils were *academic and positive* in nature (54% of all focused interactions), followed by *positive social/conduct* interactions (30%). Comparable data for teacher–pupil interactions was lower; with 39% *positive academic* interactions and 28% *positive social/conduct* interactions. Interestingly, teachers' engagement in *negative social/conduct* interactions with target pupils was over double that of SNA–pupil interactions (15% versus 7% of all focused interactions). This suggests that teachers took the lead in providing corrective social/conduct feedback to target pupils, albeit at a low level. Overall, OPTIC data highlight that SNAs engaged in the majority of focused interactions with target pupils, with interactions primarily positive and related more to academic than social/conduct matters.

Total target task

Finally, Table 5.4 shows the nature of academic tasks undertaken by target pupils across all observed lessons ($n = 77$). Findings show the dominant form

Table 5.3 OPTIC schedule observation data for target pupils across all cases, as sourced from Griffin (2018, 198)

Type of focused interaction with target pupil	Teacher Frequency	% of focused interactions	% of total observations	SNA Frequency	% of focused interactions	% of total observations
Positive Academic	91	39.06	2.02	970	54.22	21.58
Negative Academic	1	.43	.02	13	.73	.29
Positive Social/Conduct	65	27.90	1.45	537	30.02	11.95
Negative Social/Conduct	34	14.59	.76	125	6.98	2.78
Bin	42	18.02	.93	144	8.05	3.20
Total	233	100	5.18	1789	100	39.80

Table 5.4 Type of academic task undertaken by target pupils across all observed lessons (n = 77)

Target task	Frequency (# lessons)	%
Same/not differentiated	67	87.0
Differentiated classwork	2	2.6
Different topic/subject	8	10.4
Total	77	100.0

of academic work was not differentiated (87%), despite 17 of the 20 target pupils presenting with learning difficulties.

Case study data

Case study data from interviews and field notes shed light on the level and nature of target pupils' independence/dependence on SNAs. Overall, target pupils' level of independence lay below their typically developing peers. Needs spanned numerous domains including self-care, social, emotional, physical, organisation, behaviour and learning. Pupils' dependence on SNAs varied across cases and typically correlated with their level of needs. On one hand, 12 target pupils (60%) displayed high SNA dependence. A sample comment included, 'He's not self-sufficient in any way'. Field notes verified that many of these pupils displayed poor self-management skills and sought SNA support before attempting tasks independently. Some teachers and SNAs referred negatively to related pupil dispositions with reports of 'learned helplessness'. Eight pupils (44%) communicated high psychological dependence on their SNA. Sample comments included, 'She's my SNA and she's the only one that can help me' and 'She always helps me and without her, I don't know what I would be able to do'. Although all cases highlighted positive SNA–pupil relationships, various teachers and two SNAs (10%) outlined concerns of target pupils becoming socially and emotionally dependent on SNAs. For example, one SNA stated, 'He would tell you things you know he just wouldn't tell others'. This was reported to regularly occur during pupils' one-to-one movement breaks. Additionally, some pupils outlined over-reliance on SNAs during paired-work, including pupils partnered with SNAs in lieu of classmates. Such social/emotional issues highlight the need for clear SNA role boundaries to ensure positive implications for pupils' holistic development.

In contrast, eight pupils (40%) were described as rejecting SNA support, a scenario more prevalent amongst older pupils. A sample comment included, 'He doesn't want to be dependent, he wants to be like the boys'. This was echoed by some pupils, with one boy stating, 'I want to be like everyone else in the class ... I don't want anyone sitting next to me'. Such data point to the importance of listening to pupils' voices in relation to the nature and level of SNA–pupil assignment.

Secondly, case studies provided insight into SNA practices which serve to support/hinder target pupils' independence. These spanned categories of SNA–pupil assignment, SNA–pupil proximity and additional forms of support.

SNA–pupil assignment

The time-frame for SNA–pupil assignment varied across cases. In over half of cases (n = 11, 55%), SNAs were rotated annually to reduce pupil dependency. In contrast, SNA–pupil assignment in the remaining cases ranged from 1 to 7 years, perceived to provide consistency for vulnerable pupils. In almost all cases, SNA support extended to other pupils either within (n = 7, 35%) or outside the target pupil's class (n = 8, 40%). Four cases (20%) also rotated SNA–pupil assignment on a daily or weekly basis. This shared-SNA model was recognised positively, with one SNA stating, 'When you are there for others, it does give them that little bit of independence'. In contrast, five target pupils (25%) had full-time one-to-one SNA support.

Considering the developmental nature of independence, almost half the cases described how SNA–pupil assignment had reduced over time, in light of pupil progress. One teacher explained, 'He's in sixth class so he's been weaned off it [SNA support]'. This was not common practice in all schools, due to enduring pupils' needs and/or, a lack of progress review.

SNA–pupil proximity

Pupil proximity was employed by all SNAs as a support mechanism. Half the SNAs (n = 10, 50%) expressed awareness of how proximity could impact on pupils' independence. Field notes verified some positive practices, where 12 SNAs positioned themselves away from pupils and employed intermittent support. For example, one SNA stated, 'Sitting away from him is probably better because if you are sitting right next to him he could sit back ... he'd hand you the book nearly'. Five pupils (25%) expressed positive feedback on intermittent support, with one pupil stating, 'I have my own space now'. In contrast, eight SNAs (40%) were seated directly beside the target pupil for the majority of the schoolday. Of concern, some SNAs justified this in terms of 'pupil control'. Nonetheless, the main justification related to curriculum access and academic support, despite the latter falling outside of SNAs' prescribed remit. SNAs referred to pupils' learning needs, their struggle to keep classroom pace and SNAs' role in preventing learning-based frustrations. Case studies identified a strong correlation between pupils' level of SNA dependence, their academic difficulties and the degree of task differentiation. For example, one SNA stated, 'He'd be very dependent on me because is he illiterate ... so I've to read for him'. In general, observations highlighted that during academic tasks, SNA support mainly related to task completion rather than pupil understanding, skill development or work quality.

Other SNA–pupil support strategies

Pupil prompting was also identified as a strategy used by SNAs to support on-task behaviour, positive behaviour and academic work. A significant over-reliance on verbal prompts was generally observed, with minimal employment of visual or gestural prompts. During interviews, only two SNAs noted the negative implications of 'intervening too soon'. This was verified by one pupil who stated, 'Like we do a circle time and I'm just trying to think of the answers ... and [the SNA] tells me it'. Overall, the incessant levels of pupil prompting were deemed a significant inhibitory factor in supporting pupils' development of independence.

In contrast, nine cases (45%) used reward strategies to effectively support target pupils' independence, including use of tick charts, token systems and the 'first-then' strategy. SNAs primarily assumed a monitoring role, with some SNAs supporting reward implementation. The remaining 11 cases (55%) did not use any motivational strategies to encourage independence.

Finally, some SNAs were observed to effectively reinforce pupils' skill development, as previously taught by the Special Education Teacher (SET). Examples included prompting pupils to use de-escalation techniques or encouraging oral communication over aggression. Conversely, this was not common practice, where skills taught by the SET were generally not reinforced by SNAs. In lieu, many SNAs hindered skill development through over-support of pupils, particularly related to self-management skills. This was attributed to a lack of teacher-SNA communication and minimal SNA training.

Discussion

This chapter sought to explore the extent to which SNAs support/hinder independence development of pupils presenting with behavioural care needs in mainstream primary schools. Overall, the data provides insight into the varied needs and independence levels of pupils accessing SNA support, serving to extend the construct of pupil 'independence' beyond that originally presented. In addition, findings build on previous research regarding SNA practices that support/hinder pupils' independence. In light of findings, key themes are discussed, with reference to national and international research.

Level and nature of target pupils' independence/dependence

Firstly, data show a general trend towards heightened target pupil dependence on SNAs, as compared to comparison pupils. Akin to previous research, SNA dependence varied across pupils, ranging from elevated levels of SNA over-reliance to more autonomous pupil self-management (Egilson and Traustadottir 2009; NDA and NCSE 2017). Although pupils' needs spanned numerous domains, the main focus of SNA support was academic in nature. This echoes a myriad of previous Irish research, highlighting the expansion of SNAs' role beyond their prescribed remit (DES 2011; NCSE 2018). Observation data revealed that 87% of tasks were undifferentiated for target pupils, despite 17 of the 20 pupils presenting with learning difficulties. Accordingly, SNAs frequently served as agents of differentiation, enabling curriculum access and preventing academic-related frustrations. This mirrors findings by Ware et al. (2011), which showed SNA support as the most frequent form of differentiation for children with SEN, despite the prescribed SNA role being non-teaching in nature. These findings align with the UK's MaSt study (Webster and Blatchford 2013), which identified that 81% of statemented pupils' tasks were the same as comparison pupils.

SNAs' academic support of target pupils is concerning, given that UK research revealed the negative relationship between the level of TA support and pupils' academic progress (Blatchford et al. 2011). Akin to the UK findings (Rubie-Davies et al. 2010), the main focus of SNA support related to task completion rather than task quality or pupil understanding. Although SNAs may *assist* in the delivery of class teaching, curriculum differentiation should fundamentally be the role of qualified teachers (DES 2014). Moving forward, priority must be given to enhancing curriculum differentiation to enable more autonomous pupil behaviour. In line with DES (2017b), higher levels of in-class support, group-based learning and Universal Design for Learning approaches are recommended (CAST 2018). In this way, reliance on SNAs as agents of differentiation could be replaced by greater pupil access to teacher expertise and increased pupil opportunities for autonomous functioning.

In addition to academic support, findings extended the construct of pupil independence to issues of social-emotional dependence. Although SNAs often serve as that 'one caring adult' in a child's life (National Educational

Psychological Service 2015), the lack of SNA training in working with emotionally vulnerable pupils cannot be overlooked. As one-to-one movement breaks emerged as a typical period for emotionally sensitive conversations, it is recommended that breaks are conducted at the group level and focused on socialisation and emotional regulation. Thereafter, pupils' needs must be addressed therapeutically by trained teachers and therapists. The role of regional support teams, as recommended by the NCSE (2018), may be a positive means of providing appropriate supports to pupils with EBD/SEBD, in lieu of over-reliance on SNAs.

Finally, the construct of pupil independence extended to include pupils' right to a voice. During semi-structured interviews, some pupils appealed for greater opportunities for autonomous functioning, referencing issues of SNA over-support. This underscores the long-standing issue of lack of pupil voice within education, particularly for pupils with SEN (Rabiee, Sloper and Beresford 2005; Shevlin and Rose 2008). Moving forward, the views of pupils with SEN must be given due weight during individualised planning, particularly when deploying SNA support. This is heralded as best practice both nationally and internationally (NCSE 2006).

Reflecting on findings, it is clear that 'independence' expands beyond initial definitions of adaptive behaviour or pupil self-reliance. Rather, pupil independence extends to all domains of functioning, including cognitive, social, emotional, behavioural and physical. Moreover, independence surpasses autonomous functioning alone and rather, encompasses an individual's ability to be in control and make decisions about his/her life (Reindal 1999). Accordingly, the definition of independence no longer pertains solely to one's physical or intellectual capacity to act autonomously. Rather, it extends to include matters of pupil voice and psychological empowerment, where one can access supports on one's own terms, without external control. Therefore, it is argued that one's need for care support should not automatically equate with dependence, where both constructs should remain dichotomised when pupil voice taking precedence. This definition builds on arguments forwarded by Morris (1997), Palm (2014) and Oliver (1989), and draws on theories of self-determination (Ryan and Deci 2000) and empowerment (Rappaport 1987, as quoted in Zimmerman 1990).

SNAs' support/hindrance of pupils' independence

School leadership

Beyond the definition of independence, findings provided insight into means by which SNAs support/hinder target pupils' development of independence. At a whole-school level, findings echo previous research which shows varied practices in SNA deployment including SNA rotation, shared SNA models and a phased reduction in support over time (Daly et al. 2016; NDA and NCSE 2017). In accordance with national policies (DES 2014), school leaders must aim to monitor and adjust the quantum of support allocated to pupils, taking cognisance of pupils' changing needs over time. Moreover, schools must strive to consider alternate strategies to support target pupils' daily functioning. The work of Giangreco (2013) could serve to stimulate alternative thinking within schools, to ensure pupil independence is considered at a systems level.

Pupil proximity and prompting

Focusing specifically on SNAs' behaviour, findings extended previous research regarding SNAs' use of pupil proximity and prompting. Data revealed the high level of SNA–pupil proximity, characterised predominantly by positive one-to-one academic interactions. Akin to international findings (Blatchford et al. 2009), intensive support aided pupils' on-task behaviour, organisation and curriculum access. In contrast, negative implications included a significant reduction for target pupils in whole-class teacher and peer interactions when contrasted with comparison peers. These findings echo the MaSt project (Webster and Blatchford 2013), where statemented pupils were in excess of three times more likely to interact with TAs than teachers and experienced roughly half as many peer interactions compared to control pupils. Nonetheless, disparate findings emerged across UK and Irish data regarding pupils' frequency of not interacting. Specifically, 'no interactions' were observed for Irish target pupils only 10% of the time, typically during periods of independent work, with comparison Irish pupils and counterparts in the UK over double that figure (22% and 24%, respectively). Such data highlight the negative impact of incessant SNA support on pupils' independent functioning; stemming from the nonalignment of academic tasks with pupils' abilities, alongside excessive SNA support. This is concerning and highlights the importance of providing all pupils with opportunities for independent skill development within their zone of proximal development (Vygotsky 1978).

Although many SNA–pupil interactions were supportive in nature, the negative implications of incessant verbal prompting cannot be overlooked, including promotion of prompt dependence, pupil passivity and learned helplessness (Goodson et al. 2007). Moving forward, SNAs need higher awareness of the broad prompting hierarchy, including visual and gestural prompts (Causton-Theoharis 2009). SNAs also need to implement more 'wait time' with pupils, i.e. time before the pupil receives instructional help, and use more planned ignoring of inappropriate behaviours. Finally, SNAs need to reflect on the potential opportunity costs for pupils during SNA–pupil interactions to ensure that SNA–pupil interactions always outweigh alternate, concurrent classroom experiences.

SNA training in evidence-based practice and frameworks

In addition to SNA proximity and prompting, findings showed SNAs' limited support of pupils' skill development for independent functioning.

Such findings highlight the need for SNA training in effectively balancing the support-independence dichotomy, with particular focus on evidence-based frameworks for independence development. Previous research has highlighted the direct application of scaffolding theory to paraprofessional practice (Bowles, Radford and Bakopoulou 2017; Radford et al. 2015). This theory outlines the temporary nature of contingent pupil support, with the focus on gradually fading support and transferring responsibility to the child (Bosanquet, Radford and Webster 2016). Various frameworks deconstruct the skillset required in this process including the *Scaffolding Framework* (Radford et al. 2015) and the *Planning and Assessing for Independence model* (The Education Endowment Foundation, 2018, as adapted from Bosanquet, Radford and Webster 2016). Although framework adaptations may be required for application to the Irish context, they offer strong direction for informing future training and practice.

Renewed thinking

Overall, this study shows that the non-teaching care role of the Irish SNA continues to extend beyond its prescribed remit into domains of academic, behavioural, social and emotional support. For many SNAs, their role has moved beyond the care remit alone; now occupying a *third space* along a continuum between care and education. This concept of the 'third space' is forwarded by Whitchurch (2008, 384), with reference to less bounded forms of professions. Considering the holistic nature of children's development, it is argued that constructs of care and education should not be separated but, rather, viewed as complementary and inextricably linked.

Accordingly, it is proposed that for SNAs to effectively execute their dual role of care support and independence development, a re-envisaged *edu-carer* role is required. This is pictured as neither a teaching nor care role but rather, a scaffolding role, operating between the pupil's receipt of direct teaching input from a trained teacher and the pupil's independent functioning. From a theoretical viewpoint, this would involve gradually supporting the pupils' movement along a continuum from adult-support to pupil control through a scaffolded approach, with the ultimate goal of pupil independence.

To realise this goal, a collaborative approach to pupil planning would be essential, including elicitation of the voice of the child and a clear focus on targets for independence. Skill development would be prioritised through direct teaching input by appropriately trained teachers/professionals. Thereafter, SNAs would provide contingent support to pupils as pupils enact the newly acquired skills, with SNAs guided by scaffolding frameworks and evidence-based strategies. By focusing on pupils' skill development, the SNA/edu-carer role would therefore constitute one that *bridges the gap* for pupils between tailored skill-based learning and autonomous pupil functioning by fading supports and transferring responsibility to the child over time (Van De Pol, Volman and Beishuizen 2010).

Nonetheless, for positive changes to occur, national policy reform is required. In this regard, the *New School Inclusion Model* cannot be overlooked, as proposed by the NCSE (2018). This advocates for a continuum of support to address pupils' needs, including increased school-based expertise, the frontloading of SNA posts and a national SNA training programme with particular focus on independence. This model offers potential for the Irish education system to pave the way internationally in relation to inclusive education and the paraprofessional role. Nonetheless, careful consideration must be given to the applied practice of this SNA/edu-carer scaffolding role to ensure that movement from theory to practice would serve to best support pupils' development, rather than constituting a continued blurring of role boundaries.

Conclusion

This study presents as a highly significant piece of research, with reference to the research design, the rigour of data collection and analysis, and the inclusion of multiple stakeholders, including the voice of the child. The research also presents as the first Irish study to examine the SNA role using systematic observations. It is anticipated that findings will inform national and international research and practices, with specific focus on paraprofessionals' role in fostering pupil independence. Nonetheless, limitations of this study must be acknowledged. Firstly, longer time duration for each case study would have been preferential rather than the two days spent in each school. Secondly, more age-appropriate methodologies could have been utilised with target pupils beyond the semi-structured interview. Examples include draw-write-tell, use of photographs and/or dolls and puppets. Finally, future research might consider audio-recording SNA–pupil interactions, akin to the work of Radford et al. (2015). This would serve to increase the reliability of the OPTIC schedule data and allow greater depth of analysis.

This study serves to extend national and international research related to paraprofessional support and independence. Importantly, this research develops the construct of 'independence' beyond adaptive behaviour. Moreover, it highlights the importance of situating tasks within pupils' zone of proximal development and ensuring that the voice of the child is given due weight when deciding the level and nature of SNA access. Finally, the research offers potential for the future direction of the SNA role through focusing explicitly on a scaffolding role between the teachers' skill-based input and the child's independent functioning. In this way, it is anticipated that adherence to clear, evidence-based frameworks may reduce the long-standing issues that exist within the SNA role, thereby supporting inclusive education for all.

Acknowledgements

The authors wish to thank all of the schools, teachers, SNAs, parents and pupils who generously partook in this research.

Originally published as Claire Griffin & Peter Blatchford (2021) Give them wings to fly: critiquing the Special Needs Assistant scheme through the lens of pupil independence, European Journal of Special Needs Education, 36:2, 198-214, DOI: 10.1080/08856257.2021.1901372.

© Taylor & Francis Ltd (2021), reprinted by permission of the publisher.

Notes

1 Primary schools in Ireland cater for children aged 4–12 years (TechLifeIreland 2020).
2 DEIS schools are under the 'Delivering Equality of Opportunity in Schools' scheme, aimed at providing better opportunities for those in communities at risk of disadvantage and social exclusion (DES 2017a).
3 Secondary care associated tasks involve SNA tasks that do not have direct pupil involvement (see DES 2014, 6–7). Examples included tidying classrooms, organisation of pupils' materials and SNA–teacher discussions.
4 A focused interaction was defined as the pupil being the focus of the adult's attention at an individual, group, or whole-class level through a verbal or physical interaction (Brown and Blatchford 2015).
5 An 'audience' interaction was defined as the adult addressing a group or class, of which the child is a member (Brown and Blatchford 2015).

References

Blatchford, P., P. Bassett, P. Brown, C. Martin, A. Russel, R. Webster, S. Babayigit, and N. Haywood. 2008. "Deployment and Impact of Support Staff in Schools and the Impact of the National Agreement: Results from Strand 2 Wave 1-2005/06." Institute of Education: University of London.

Blatchford, P., P. Bassett, P. Brown, C. Martin, A. Russell, and R. Webster. 2007. "Deployment and Impact of Support Staff in Schools: Report on Findings from the Second National Questionnaire Survey of Schools, Support Staff and Teachers (Strand 1, Wave 2–2006)." Institute of Education, University of London: Department for Children, Schools and Families.

Blatchford, P., P. Bassett, P. Brown, C. Martin, A. Russell, and R. Webster. 2011. "The Impact of Support Staff on Pupils' 'Positive Approaches to Learning' and Their Academic Progress." *British Educational Research Journal* 37 (3): 443–464. doi:10.1080/01411921003734645.

Blatchford, P., P. Bassett, P. Brown, and R. Webster. 2009. "The Effect of Support Staff on Pupil Engagement and Individual Attention." *British Educational Research Journal* 35 (5): 661–686. doi:10.1080/01411920902878917.

Blatchford, P., and R. Webster. 2018. "Classroom Contexts for Learning at Primary and Secondary School: Class Size, Groupings, Interactions and Special Educational Needs." *British Educational Research Journal* 44 (4): 681–703. doi:10.1002/berj.3454.

Bosanquet, P., J. Radford, and R. Webster. 2016. *The Teaching Assistant's Guide to Effective Interaction: How to Maximise Your Practice*. Abingdon, Oxon; New York: Routledge.

Bowles, D., J. Radford, and I. Bakopoulou. 2017. "Scaffolding as a Key Role for Teaching Assistants: Perceptions of Their Pedagogical Strategies." *British Journal of Educational Psychology* 88 (3): 1–14.

Brown, P., and P. Blatchford. 2015. "Deployment and Impact of Support Staff in Schools Research Project: Systematic Observations." Unpublished work, Institute of Education, University College London.

CAST. 2018. "About Universal Design for Learning." Accessed 10 May 2020. http://www.cast.org/our-work/about-udl.html#.WyY9OlVKjIU

Causton-Theoharis, J. N. 2009. "The Golden Rule of Providing Support in Inclusive Classrooms: Support Others as You Would Wish to Be Supported." *Teaching Exceptional Children* 42 (2): 36–43. doi:10.1177/004005990904200204.

Daly, P., E. Ring, M. Egan, J. Fitzgerald, C. Griffin, S. Long, E. McCarthy, et al. 2016. *An Evaluation of Education Provision for Students with Autism Spectrum Disorder in Ireland*, National Council for Special Education Research Report. Meath: National Council for Special Education.

Department of Education and Skills. 2011. *The Special Needs Assistant Scheme: A Value for Money Review of Expenditure on the Special Needs Assistant Scheme 2007/8-2010*. Dublin: Government of Ireland.

Department of Education and Skills. 2014. *Circular to the Management Authorities of Primary Schools, Special Schools, Secondary, Community and Comprehensive Schools and the Chief Executive Officers of the Educational Training Boards*. Westmeath: Department of Education and Skills.

Department of Education and Skills. 2017a. *DEIS Plan 2017: Delivering Equality of Opportunity in Schools*. Dublin: Department of Education and Skills.

Department of Education and Skills. 2017b. *Guidelines for Primary Schools: Supporting Pupils with Special Educational Needs in Mainstream Schools*. Dublin: Department of Education and Skills.

Department of Education and Skills. 2019. "09 October, 2019 – Record Investment in Education and Skills with Hundreds of New Teachers and More than 1,000 Additional Special Needs Assistants." Accessed 21 September 2020. https://www.education.ie/en/Press-Events/Press-Releases/2019-press-releases/PR19-10-09-1.html

Egilson, S. T., and R. Traustadottir. 2009. "Assistance to Pupils with Physical Disabilities in Regular Schools: Promoting Inclusion or Creating Dependency?" *European Journal of Special Needs Education* 24 (1): 21–36. doi:10.1080/08856250802596766.

Elliott, S. 2004. "The Role and Training of Special Needs Assistants for Students with Autistic Spectrum Disorders in Ireland." *Good Autism Practice* 5 (2): 22–34.

Giangreco, M. F. 2013. "Teacher Assistant Supports in Inclusive Schools: Research, Practices and Alternatives." *Australasian Journal of Special Education* 37 (2): 93–106. doi:10.1017/jse.2013.1.

Giangreco, M. F., M. B. Doyle, and J. C. Suter. 2014. "Italian and American Progress toward Inclusive Education: Common Concerns and Future Directions." *Life Span and Disability* 17 (1): 119–136.

Goodson, J., J. Sigafoos, M. O'Reilly, H. Cannella, and G. E. Lancioni. 2007. "Evaluation of a Video-Based Error Correction Procedure for Teaching a Domestic Skill to Individuals with Developmental Disabilities." *Research in Developmental Disabilities* 28 (5): 458–467. doi:10.1016/j.ridd.2006.06.002.

Griffin, C. 2018. "Fostering Independence through Care? A Study of the Preparedness and Deployment of Special Needs Assistants When Supporting Pupils' Behavioural Care Needs and Independence Development in Mainstream Primary Schools in Ireland." PhD diss., Institute of Education, University College London.

Harris, B. A. 2011. "Effects of the Proximity of Paraeducators on the Interactions of Braille Readers in Inclusive Settings." *Journal of Visual Impairment & Blindness* 105 (8): 467–478. doi:10.1177/0145482X1110500803.

Keating, S., and U. O'Connor. 2012. "The Shifting Role of the Special Needs Assistant in Irish Classrooms: A Time for Change?" *European Journal of Special Needs Education* 27 (4): 533–544. doi:10.1080/08856257.2012.711960.

Landis, J. R., and G. G. Koch. 1977. "The Measurement of Observer Agreement for Categorical Data." *Biometrics* 33 (1): 159–174. doi:10.2307/2529310.

Logan, A. 2006. "The Role of the Special Needs Assistant Supporting Pupils with Special Educational Needs in Irish Mainstream Primary Schools." *Support for Learning* 21 (2): 92–99. doi:10.1111/j.1467-9604.2006.00410.x.

Merrett, F., and K. Wheldall. 1986. "Observing Pupils and Teachers in Classrooms (OPTIC): A Behavioural Observation Schedule for Use in Schools." *Educational Psychology* 6 (1): 57–70. doi:10.1080/0144341860060107.

Morris, J. 1997. "Care or Empowerment? A Disability Rights Perspective." *Social Policy and Administration* 31 (1): 54–60. doi:10.1111/1467-9515.00037.

National Council for Special Education. 2006. *Guidelines on the Individual Education Plan Process*. Dublin: National Council for Special Education.

National Council for Special Education. 2018. *Comprehensive Review of the Special Needs Assistant Scheme: A New School Inclusion Model to Deliver the Right Supports at the Right Time to Students with Additional Care Needs: NCSE Policy Advice Paper No. 6*. Meath: National Council for Special Education.

National Disability Authority and National Council for Special Education. 2017. *A Qualitative Study of How Well Young People with Disabilities are Prepared for Life after School*. Dublin: RSM PACEC.

National Educational Psychological Service. 2015. *Well-Being in Primary Schools: Guidelines for Mental Health Promotion*. Dublin: Department of Education and Skills.

Oliver, M. 1989. "Disability and Dependency: A Creation of Industrial Societies." In *Disability and Dependency*, edited by L. Barton, 6–22. London: Falmer Press.

Palm, E. 2014. "A Declaration of Healthy Dependence: The Case of Home Care." *Health Care Analysis* 22 (4): 385–404. doi:10.1007/s10728-012-0228-x.

Psychological Society of Ireland. 2010. *Code of Professional Ethics*. Dublin: Psychological Society of Ireland.

Rabiee, P., P. Sloper, and B. Beresford. 2005. "Doing Research with Children and Young People Who Do Not Use Speech for Communication." *Children & Society* 19 (5): 385–396. doi:10.1002/chi.841.

Radford, J., P. Bosanquet, R. Webster, and P. Blatchford. 2015. "Scaffolding Learning for Independence: Clarifying Teacher and Teaching Assistant Roles for Children with Special Educational Needs." *Learning and Instruction* 36: 1–10. doi:10.1016/j.learninstruc.2014.10.005.

Reindal, S. M. 1999. "Independence, Dependence, Interdependence: Some Reflections on the Subject and Personal Autonomy." *Disability & Society* 14 (3): 353–367. doi:10.1080/09687599926190.

Rose, R., M. Shevlin, E. Winter, and P. O'Raw. 2015. *Project IRIS – Inclusive Research in Irish Schools, National Council for Special Education Research Report*. Meath: National Council for Special Education.

Rubie-Davies, C. M., P. Blatchford, R. Webster, M. Koutsoubou, and P. Bassett. 2010. "Enhancing Learning? A Comparison of Teacher and Teaching Assistant Interactions with Pupils." *School Effectiveness and School Improvement* 21 (4): 429–449. doi:10.1080/09243453.2010.512800.

Ryan, R. M., and E. L. Deci. 2000. "Self-determination Theory and the Facilitation of Intrinsic Motivation, Social Development, and Well-being." *American Psychologist* 55 (1): 68–78. doi:10.1037/0003-066X.55.1.68.

Sharma, U., and S. Salend. 2016. "Teaching Assistants in Inclusive Classrooms: A Systematic Analysis of the International Research." *Australian Journal of Teacher Education* 41 (8): 118–134. doi:10.14221/ajte.2016v41n8.7.

Shevlin, M., M. Kenny, and A. Loxley. 2008. "A Time of Transition: Exploring Special Educational Provision in the Republic of Ireland." *Journal of Research in Special Educational Needs* 8 (3): 141–152. doi:10.1111/j.1471-3802.2008.00116.x.

Shevlin, M., and R. Rose. 2008. "Pupils as Partners in Education Decision-Making: Responding to the Legislation in England and Ireland." *European Journal of Special Needs Education* 23 (4): 423–430. doi:10.1080/08856250802387430.

Smith, J. A., P. Flowers, and M. Larkin. 2009. *Interpretative Phenomenological Analysis*. London: SAGE.

TechLifeIreland. 2020. "Guide to Ireland's School System." Accessed 13 April 2020. https://techlifeireland.com/moving-to-ireland/find-schools-ireland/

UNESCO. 1994. *The Salamanca Statement and Framework for Action on Special Needs Education*. Spain: UNES.

Van De Pol, J., M. Volman, and J. Beishuizen. 2010. "Scaffolding in Teacher–Student Interaction: A Decade of Research." *Educational Psychology Review* 22 (3): 271–296. doi:10.1007/s10648-010-9127-6.

Vygotsky, L. S. 1978. *Mind in Society: The Development of Higher Psychological Processes*. Cambridge, MA: Harvard University Press.

Ware, J., C. Butler, C. Robertson, M. O'Donnell, and M. Gould. 2011. *Access to the Curriculum for Pupils with a Variety of Special Educational Needs in Mainstream Classes: An Exploration of the Experiences of Young Pupils in Primary School, National Council for Special Education Research Report*. Meath: National Council for Special Education.

Webster, R., and P. Blatchford. 2013. *The Making A Statement Project Final Report: A Study of the Teaching and Support Experienced by Pupils with A Statement of Special Educational Needs in Mainstream Primary Schools*. University of London, London, UK: Dept. of Psychology and Human Development, Institute of Education.

Webster, R., and P. Blatchford. 2017. *The Special Educational Needs in Secondary Education (SENSE) Study Final Report*. London: UCL Institute of Education.

Whitchurch, C. 2008. "Shifting Identities and Blurring Boundaries: The Emergence of *Third Space* Professional in UK Higher Education." *Higher Education Quarterly* 62 (4): 377–396. doi:10.1111/j.1468-2273.2008.00387.x.

Zimmerman, M. A. 1990. "Toward a Theory of Learned Hopefulness: A Structural Model Analysis of Participation and Empowerment." *Journal of Research in Personality* 24 (1): 71–86. doi:10.1016/0092-6566(90)90007-S.

6 The perspectives and experiences of children with special educational needs in mainstream primary schools regarding their individual teaching assistant support

Hayley Pinkard

Introduction

TAs: Developments

The significant increase in the number of TAs employed within schools in England, over the past two decades, has been influenced by various factors, including the move to educate more children with SEN within mainstream (rather than special) schools, the introduction of the National Literacy and Numeracy Strategies in 1998 to boost pupils' progress relative to international levels, and the National Agreement (DfES 2003) which promoted delegation of tasks from teachers to TAs. Between the years 2000 and 2018 the number of full-time equivalent TAs increased from 79,000 to 263,900 (DfE 2019).

The TA role has also undergone significant change. Whilst TAs once assisted the teacher in administrative tasks as an 'extra pair of hands' in the classroom (Groom and Rose 2005, 20) they have increasingly taken on 'greater responsibility for instructional decision-making' (Tews and Lupart 2008, 40). Lamb (2009, 29) reports that the teaching and support for pupils with SEN has largely 'been handed over to TAs', and Webster and Blatchford (2013) found that pupils with SEN are almost constantly accompanied by a TA. Researchers debate the appropriateness of this pedagogical role (e.g. Warhurst et al. 2014; Webster 2014) and highlight ethical issues around assigning TAs 'to students whose learning support requirements (through no fault of their own) often challenge teachers' (Rutherford 2011, 95).

The focus of Education Health and Care Plans (EHCPs: statutory records of an individual pupil's SEN and required provision) on the weekly hours of TA support required continues to reinforce one-to-one assignment of TAs to pupils with SEN. Webster and Blatchford (2019, 110) suggest that TAs should instead be 'part of a wider, more balanced and coherent set of responses to meeting the needs of pupils' with SEN. Whilst the Special Educational Needs and Disabilities (SEND) Code of Practice clarifies that 'teachers are responsible and accountable for the progress and development of the pupils in their class, including where pupils access support from TAs'

DOI: 10.4324/9781003265580-9

(DfE 2014, 99), a review of the deployment of TAs found that head-teachers were still 'aware and concerned that the responsibility for appropriately supporting and progressing their most vulnerable learners was often being given' to TAs (Skipp and Hopwood 2019, 8).

Impacts of TA support

It was previously assumed that TA support must promote pupil progress. The Deployment and Impact of Support Staff (DISS) study (Blatchford, Russell and Webster 2012) contradicted this assumption, finding a negative relationship between the amount of TA support received and levels of pupil progress (across seven Year groups, three curriculum subjects and controlling for prior attainment and SEN status). Klassen (2001) found that pupils with specific learning difficulties who were assigned individual TA support during literacy lessons made less progress than those receiving no TA support. Muijs and Reynolds (2003) found that pupils receiving TA support during numeracy lessons made slightly less progress than those receiving no TA support.

When explaining the DISS project findings, Rubie-Davies et al. (2010) concluded that compared to teachers, TAs are more likely to focus on task completion (rather than advancing understanding), to ask closed questions, to give incorrect explanations and to provide prompts which give the answer. Researchers highlight that the impact of TA support is due to the 'decisions made about rather than by TAs' (Webster et al. 2010, 139) and can be linked to the five factors of the Wider Pedagogical Role model (Webster et al. 2011): 'practice' (e.g. TAs' explanations, demonstrations, questioning techniques), 'preparedness' (e.g. professional development opportunities, planning-sessions with teachers before lessons), 'deployment' (e.g. one-to-one working, small-group work, targeted interventions), 'TA characteristics' and 'conditions of employment'.

In a review of the TA literature, Alborz et al. (2009) highlighted a number of studies with more positive outcomes, usually where TAs delivered structured, targeted academic interventions (with adequate preparation and resources) rather than working one-to-one in the classroom. Qualitative studies have often found that 'key stakeholders perceive the presence of TAs in classrooms as contributing to improved outcomes' (Alborz et al. 2009, 30). Groom and Rose (2005) interviewed teachers, TAs, parents and pupils, finding an overwhelming view that TAs help pupils with SEN to manage lesson tasks and play a critical role in supporting their social, emotional and behavioural needs.

Pupil voice

'One of the simplest and most powerful steps we can all do more frequently is to listen to our students' voices in an effort to better understand their perspectives' (Giangreco 2021, 287). Even though children 'can reveal new issues about a setting that could go undetected' (Fitzgerald, Jobling and Kirk 2003, 124) and can offer 'intelligible and realistic ideas about TAs and their work' (Fraser and Meadows 2008, 359), there 'appears to be little research on whether pupils value working with TAs' (Bland and Sleightholme 2012, 173). In perspective-seeking studies, TAs (not pupils) are the most common participants (Alborz et al. 2009) and the voices of children with SEN are 'markedly absent from the literature' (Tews and Lupart 2008, 40).

When they are asked, pupils often report that TA support improves their approach to learning and access to tasks. Rose and Doveston's (2008) pupil interviewees expressed that they completed more work and were more engaged with education when supported by a TA. Fraser and Meadows (2008) found that pupils generally felt positive about being withdrawn from lessons to work with TAs.

Studies of pupil perspectives have also, however, confirmed the blurring of teacher–TA roles and the degree of separation between pupils and teachers. Pupils with SEN suggest that they spend more time with a TA than their teacher, learn more from them (Tews and Lupart 2008) and struggle to explain the difference between the two professionals (Eyres et al. 2004). Broer, Doyle and Giangreco (2005) interviewed young adults about the TA support that they had received in school, finding that many viewed the TA as their primary educator.

In relation to social outcomes, Broer, Doyle and Giangreco's (2005) participants' discussions also reflected views of the TA as a mother and friend, suggesting a level of closeness and admiration but also interference with peer socialisation. Seeing the TA as a 'friend' was a positive factor for Fraser and Meadows' (2008, 354) participants; 'she feels like a friend ... we don't feel embarrassed to go up to her', and Tews and Lupart (2008) found that pupils with SEN reported that TAs increased their opportunities to socialise with peers, supported friendships, boosted the peer group's empathy/understanding of their SEN and helped pupils to follow rules during play.

Within pupil voice research, there is greatest consensus about the impact of TA support on pupils' emotional experiences (compared to other pupil outcomes); findings are overwhelmingly positive. Rose and Doveston (2008, 151) suggested that TAs can act as a 'safe haven' or a 'temporary container for the excessive anxiety' experienced by pupils. Pupils value nurturing qualities in TAs, including being calm, patient, caring (Fraser and Meadows 2008), kind, respectful and helpful (Bland and Sleightholme 2012). They suggest that TAs are 'there for you ... they back you up ... you feel like if you've got a problem they will help you get through it' (Groom and Rose 2005, 27).

Purpose of current study

'The prerogative of pupils, regardless of their need or ability, to be involved in decisions which affect their lives has been established' (Shevlin and Rose 2008, 425), and research has shown that pupils can provide important insights about their support (Fraser and Meadows 2008). The present study recognises the abilities and rights of children (United Nations Convention on the Rights of the Child 1989) to express their views and to be heard, and was designed to enable and empower them to do so. The research was designed to explore the question: what are the perspectives and experiences of pupils with SEN in mainstream primary schools regarding their individual TA support?

Methods

Design

This chapter reports a small-scale qualitative research project, which used child-friendly interviews, designed to gather rich examples of the lived experiences of children with SEN, in relation to their individual TA support.

Sample

A purposive sample of ten children (aged 10–11) was recruited by the Educational Psychology Team within one Local Education Authority in the South of England (see Table 6.1 for participant details). Requests were sent to Special Educational Needs Coordinators (SENCOs) in local schools, to identify pupils who: were in the final year of primary school, had an EHCP (or Statement: the previous equivalent of an EHCP), and received at least 25 hours of TA support weekly. Participants' SEN included: Autism Spectrum Disorder, physical needs, social emotional and mental health needs, speech, language and communication needs, attention deficit hyperactivity disorder (ADHD) and learning difficulties. Participants were recruited from eight primary schools spread across one city; in five of these schools, over 20% of pupils were eligible for free school meals (a measure of lower household income).

Table 6.1 Participant information

Participant (names have been changed)	Primary SEN
Scott	Autism spectrum disorder
Paul	Physical disabilities
Toby	Social emotional & mental health needs
Amy	Hearing impairment
Mariusz	Speech language & communication needs
Ben	Autism spectrum disorder
Thomas	Learning difficulties
Joseph	Physical disabilities
Lauren	Attention deficit hyperactivity disorder
Becky	Hearing impairment & autism spectrum disorder

Instrument

Individual semi-structured interviews lasted between 11 and 52 minutes (on average 32 minutes), with the duration depending on participants' level of detail given in their responses, and levels of comfort within the interview situation. Interviews were recorded electronically. The interview schedule covered questions about many aspects of TA support, including: role, impacts, characteristics, examples of working together, comparisons with teachers. A participatory communication tool was included within the interviews, referred to as the Ideal TA activity. This was a modified version of the Ideal Self technique (Moran 2001). Participants were asked if they would like to draw or model (with modelling clay) their current and later their imagined ideal TA. Accompanying discussions prompted participants to think about what an ideal TA might be like, might do, and might say, and to make comparisons between their own TA and imagined ideal TA.

Inspiration was taken from the Mosaic Approach (Clarke and Moss 2001) which combines verbal interviewing with visual methods of gathering children's views, and suggests children are 'experts in their own lives' (Clarke and Moss 2005, 5). Eyres et al. (2004, 150) report that drawing the adults in the classroom gives children a 'concrete starting point from which to elaborate' and Thomas and O'Kane (1998, 343) report that in their research, the 'use of these participatory techniques greatly assisted in breaking down imbalances of power' between adult (interviewer) and child (interviewee).

Toy props supported expectation-setting and rapport-building. Participants were invited to place a Lego Judge figurine facing away from them, to aid explanations that there were no right or wrong answers in the interview. A stop sign (from a Lego set) could be presented to the interviewer if participants wanted to stop the interview or skip a question. The use of props was guided by the person-centred planning work of Newton and Wilson (2011, 14) who claim that 'when we playfully talk about the serious subjects of judgement ... we can create a safer climate'.

Procedures

Approval was granted by the University of Southampton Ethics Committee. Data were collected in schools during the academic year 2015–2016. Interviews started with informal discussions to build rapport, and then the props were jovially explained. Participants were assured of anonymity and confidentiality (with the exception of safeguarding issues).

The interviewer followed the interview schedule, adapting in-the-moment for individual pupils' needs, interests and engagement, and prompting for more information. Participants were given the choice of engaging with the drawing and modelling resources during the Ideal TA segment of the interviews.

Data analysis

Interviews were transcribed verbatim. Data were analysed using inductive thematic analysis, following the six phases described by Braun and Clarke (2006) and using the computer software QSR N-Vivo 10. Thematic analysis provided a structured and transparent process of analysis and was suitable for the combination of visual and verbal data. During the coding phase, participants' spoken words/phrases, as well as key elements within their drawings/models were highlighted, and allocated a code, based on their interpreted meaning.

Results

The thematic analysis process established five overarching themes based on the data, each comprising a number of sub-themes (see Figure 6.1).

Logistics of my TA support

All participants highlighted the close proximity of the TA and the frequency of their support; Scott suggested that 'Miss X would already be by me so I'd ask her', and when asked how much time they spent with their TA, Mariusz replied, 'always' and Thomas said, 'lots'. Becky talked about feeling frustrated that she was unable to work more independently: 'yeah I like to work by myself ... I'm okay with that (working with TA) but sometimes I find it frustrating'. However, seven participants (with a wide range of SEN) described examples of their TA encouraging independent work; Ben explained: 'she broke down the steps and showed me how to do it on the whiteboard. Then I could do it by myself,' Scott said that 'sometimes I can do it on my own and she lets me get on', and Lauren described how 'sometimes they help me for a while and then when they feel like I've got the idea they'll go and help other people'.

Suggestions of dependency on TA support arose in discussions about secondary school; Paul suggested that without a TA, secondary school 'would be so bad, I need that, I would rather get home-schooled' and Mariusz felt he would 'never learn nothing'. Eight participants identified that although the TA had a certain level of responsibility to prioritise their needs, they were also involved in other forms of support including small-group work, supporting other pupils in class, and helping the teacher. Participants suggested that working outside of the classroom helped them to learn things that they could then apply back in the classroom, but some comments seemed to suggest a feeling that being withdrawn was an automatic and inevitable response to their struggles; 'I was stuck and Miss had to take out me, Millie and Jake' (Lauren).

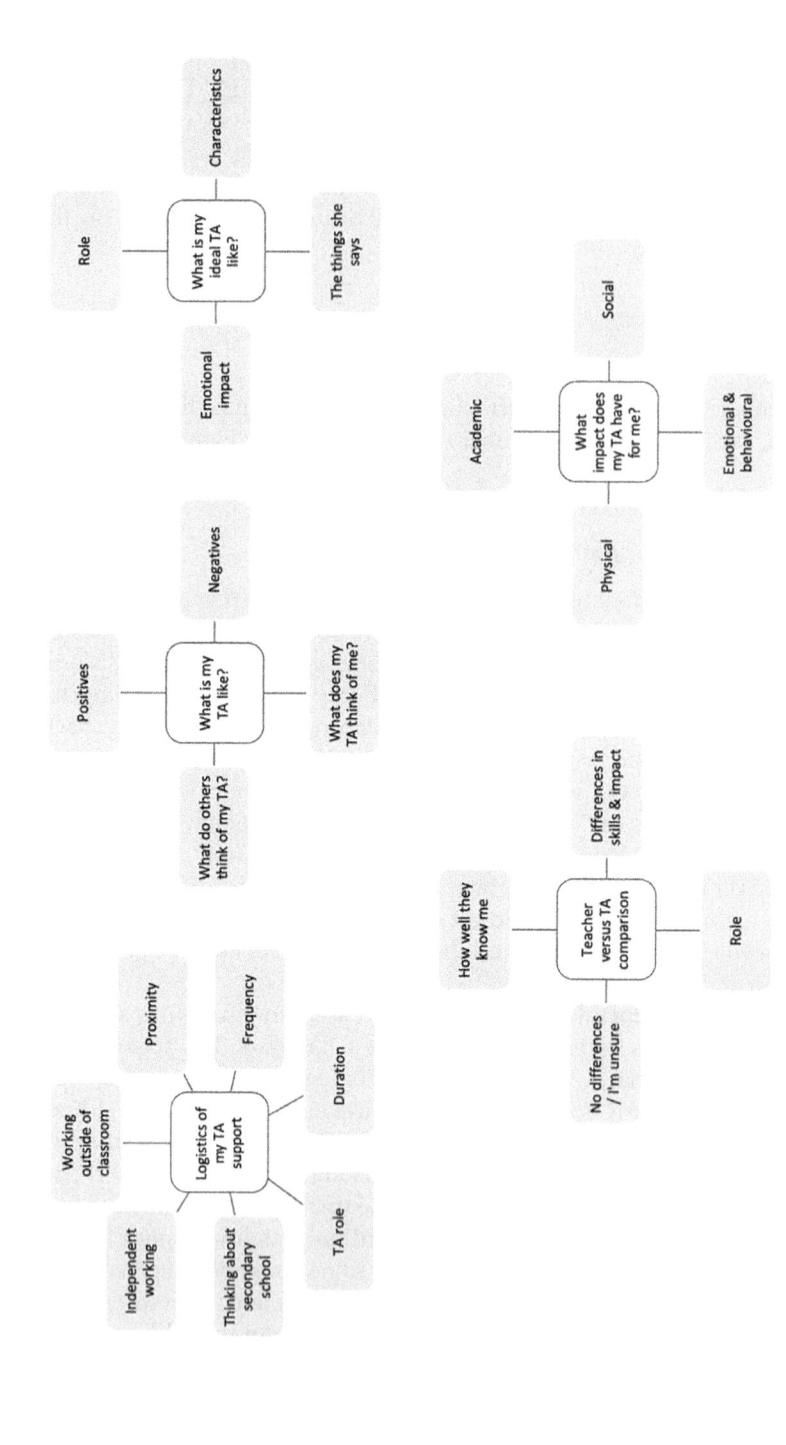

Figure 6.1 Thematic analysis themes and sub-themes.

What is my TA like?

Participants talked positively about their TAs' characteristics; seven considered them to already be ideal. When asked an open question about how they would describe their TAs, most responses related to the TA's nurturing nature, and their positive interactions. Amy reported that her TA was 'funny, chatty and kind' and Paul stated, 'they're funny ... yeah they've got character'. Participants' drawings and models of their TAs also depicted kind and cheerful characters (see Figure 6.2). Lauren's model was smiling and waving, Amy's model was smiling, Paul's drawing was smiling and asking if he was okay, and Scott's model was labelled 'happy' and 'kind'.

Joseph held a less positive view of his current TA, describing her as being 'pushy' and 'mean'; the examples he gave suggested a lack of patience and a failure to understand his needs, as well as an impact on his emotional well-being. He suggested that one way in which his TA could become closer to his ideal TA would be if she smiled more (see Figure 6.3). Other participants suggested that their TAs could sometimes be 'sad', 'bored', 'tired' and 'grumpy'.

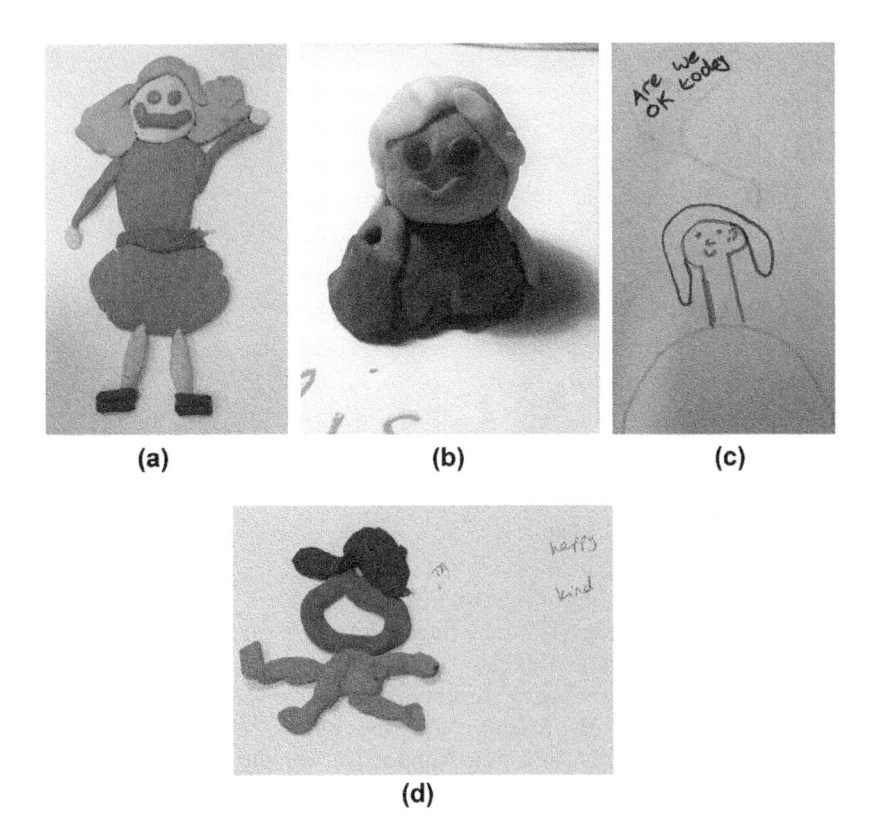

Figure 6.2. 'What is my TA like' 1.

112 *Hayley Pinkard*

(a)

(b)

Figure 6.3. 'What is my TA like' 2.

Eight participants thought that their peers liked their TAs. Paul explained that 'my best friends they like her, they think she's funny and that she's a good character to have in the class', and Lauren suggested that her peers thought that the TA was 'nice'. Teachers were perceived to think highly of TAs: Paul believed that the teachers 'like having their help and stuff', whilst Thomas described his TA as being 'supportive' for the teacher. Ben commented that (without the TA): 'maybe she (teacher) could cope but it would be hard'.

When asked to consider what their TA thought about them, participants said that the TA liked them, would use a variety of positive adjectives to describe them, felt proud when they had done well ('and that makes me feel happy' – Ben) and understood their difficulties. Their comments described positive, respectful relationships, apart from Joseph, who wondered if his TA preferred other pupils, and thought that he was 'rude', especially when he struggled to do something.

Teacher versus TA comparisons

When Toby was asked whether there were differences between his TA and his teacher, he replied 'no'. Paul explained, 'they (TA) know me much better … the teacher has to know everyone … but the TA, I'm the first person, so they know the most about me' and Mariusz stated, 'she (teacher) doesn't even know all of my names'. Amy explained: 'well, my teacher doesn't really come to me, like if I need help, but my TA comes to me whenever I need help' and Mariusz highlighted that 'teachers are like writing on the massive whiteboard … she doesn't help'. Teachers were viewed as having greater knowledge/awareness of lesson content, and as being more highly skilled; Lauren commented, 'I think they're different because … teacher knows what they're doing, feels confident about what we're learning … sometimes, they (TAs) don't know what they're doing'. Ben highlighted that his TA would not always know the answer: 'say if I was stuck on such a hard question that even Miss X didn't know the answer'.

What is my ideal TA like?

It was important for all participants (apart from Toby who was unable to respond on this topic) that the ideal TA was a nice person; they would be 'happy', 'smiling', 'kind', 'caring', 'sweet', 'friendly', 'funny' and 'encouraging'. Ben was the only participant to also refer to academic skills; his ideal TA would be 'knowledgeable'. Joseph explained that the ideal TA would 'help other people as well as me', a view echoed by other participants. He also suggested that his imagined ideal TA (compared to his actual TA) would 'understand me more'.

Participants' ideal TAs would say encouraging things and ask questions about the support they might need; 'keep going' (Paul) and 'are you okay with this?' (Joseph). For nine participants, the emotional support that their ideal TA would provide was emphasised. An ideal TA would help pupils to feel happy and to look forward to going to school. Lauren's ideal TA was described as being 'like a counsellor who helps … their job is to help people with their problems', and Paul felt that an ideal TA should be a good listener and could lift his mood (see Figure 6.4).

Figure 6.4 'My ideal TA'.

What impact does my TA have for me?

Eight participants thought that they would struggle in lessons without the TA providing academic support. Becky said 'sometimes she tells me to carry on, try to extend my sentences' and Thomas (the only participant to have 'learning difficulties' as his primary SEN) suggested that the TA helped to clarify his thoughts: 'by helping with my thinking … sometimes my head feels really clogged up with ideas'. For Ben, TA support appeared to be important for his access to tasks as well as his motivation, and he explained that without TA support he would be 'just thinking … about how I wouldn't even try at school since it would be too hard'. Joseph recognised that academic support from a TA tended to mean greater separation from the teacher, highlighting that 'sometimes I'm relieved, like when Miss X goes somewhere else, cuz I get to spend a bit more time with other teachers'.

Nine participants described the positive impact of TA support on their social inclusion and emotional well-being. Thomas' TA helped him to 'be kind' and to 'make friends', Paul's TA helped him to become involved in games with peers at break times, and when Lauren had experienced difficulties with friends, her TA had supported reconciliations. Lauren also described how the TA helped her to feel a sense of belonging in school: 'like I'm meant to be here', Amy suggested that school would be 'not fun … and less laughtery' without her TA, and Scott suggested that TA support helped him to feel 'happy! She's the only one that makes me happy'. For Paul, the TA helped to soothe his anxiety, Lauren suggested, 'she'll calm me down', and Ben explained that his TA helped him to use positive coping strategies (e.g. going to his safe space) when he was feeling distressed. Even Toby, who had remained very quiet throughout the interview highlighted that 'I talk to him about stuff'. Four participants (two with Autism, one with learning difficulties and one with ADHD) mentioned that the TA helped them to manage their behaviour, for example intervening to stop them swearing and shouting-out, and reflecting on challenging behaviour afterwards. For Joseph too, his TA and their interactions brought implications for his emotional well-being in school, only for him, these were negative: 'sometimes it's just a misery ... sometimes I wish I could just go somewhere else'. He had not spoken to anyone else in school about these experiences because he feared he would get into trouble.

TAs were described as providing physical support for those participants with such needs, including physiotherapy interventions, 'quiet times' where hearing aids could be taken out, and supporting movement and basic needs (e.g. eating).

Discussion

When provided with the opportunity to express their views, in a child-friendly interview scenario, participants generated insight and feedback about the support that they received from TAs. Participants discussed the logistics and nature of the TA role, the impacts of TA support (in particular for their academic, social and emotional development) and the ideal qualities and behaviours that a TA might demonstrate.

Participants' discussions often suggested they felt that TA support enabled them to access the curriculum, to persevere with tasks and to make academic progress, as had been found in previous qualitative studies (e.g. Groom and Rose 2005; Tews and Lupart 2008). Pupil voice in this study echoed the positive opinions of TAs, teachers and parents reported in previous qualitative research (e.g. Farrell, Balshaw and Polat 2000; Lacey 2001). Several participants appeared to describe the TA providing effective scaffolding for their learning, for example breaking tasks into smaller steps, encouraging them to extend what they had written, and modelling and coaching before encouraging pupils to apply learned skills independently. Some pupils also suggested that TAs would check-in with them to see if they needed help, before automatically stepping-in. Their experiences possibly suggest some progress having been made since previous observational studies in schools where the practice of TAs was criticised (e.g. for limiting independence, for providing the answer without progressing understanding). However, the feeling that TAs were needed to make the work more accessible for pupils raises questions about how effectively and by whom the work had been set and differentiated originally. Additionally, of the eight participants who talked about the support they received with their learning, only one had 'learning difficulties' as their primary SEN reported on their EHCP, raising a question about whether their TA support was specifically targeted to their individual needs or had sometimes spread into other areas of support.

It seems likely that whilst pupils could describe in-the-moment examples of the TA helping them to engage with the work, this support does not necessarily translate into longer-term academic progress, when taking into consideration the findings of quantitative studies such as the DISS project. The perspectives and experiences of participants tended to complement current understandings of why this might be the case, relating to the Wider Pedagogical Role model (Webster et al. 2011).

There was a feeling amongst participants that because they struggled with the work within the classroom, the natural response would be for them to work one-to-one with the TA, separately from peers, often outside of the classroom. Whilst participants generally felt okay about this arrangement, they may not have known any different. The extent to which this strategy of TA deployment (one-to-one working and withdrawing pupils from class) seemed to be the norm raises questions about whether these pupils were able to feel that they had as much right to be in the classroom as everyone else (as suggested by Broer, Doyle and Giangreco 2005) and about other strategies that could have been implemented to support pupils with SEN more inclusively within the classroom. It has been argued that a more appropriate deployment of TAs would be as part of a more balanced and more individualised set of responses to pupils' needs (Webster and Blatchford 2019); expressing the provision section of EHCPs without stating a number of weekly TA hours, and instead adding more detail about specific targeted, and evidence-based strategies would help to promote this. Evidence suggests that when TAs are trained and supported to deliver targeted, discrete academic interventions, (rather than working more frequently and ad hoc, one-to-one) they are more likely to promote pupils' academic progress (Alborz et al. 2009). TA support is not always the most appropriate strategy of support for particular pupils, and schools ought to consider alternative solutions, such as supporting teachers to become more engaged and confident in teaching children with SEN, clarifying the teacher's role and promoting natural support systems such as peers (Giangreco 2021).

Participants' discussions highlighted that they were frequently in close proximity to the TA, echoing previous research findings, both quantitative (Webster and Blatchford 2013) and qualitative (Tews and Lupart 2008). Whilst this was likely a helpful factor (for all but one participant) in fostering a positive and close relationship, the significant amount of time spent with a TA is perhaps why several participants believed that they wouldn't be able to manage without them. Participants' reflections in this area also highlighted a substantial degree of separation from the class teacher. Many participants felt that the TA knew them better than the teacher did, and several participants reported that the teacher didn't help them. TA support had become an alternative rather than an additional support, to teacher-led instruction/intervention.

Such findings relate to research which has suggested that TAs are taking on the main responsibility for pupils with SEN (Lamb 2009; Skipp and

The perspectives and experiences of children with SEN 117

Hopwood 2019) and playing a largely pedagogical role (Giangreco, Suter and Doyle 2010). It seems that these strategies of TA deployment have been internalised by pupils, who can come to see the TA as their 'teacher' ('she's my best teacher' – Amy). The idea that the teacher teaches the class whilst the TA teaches pupils with SEN links to the view of a participant without SEN from the study of Fraser and Meadows (2008, 355) who stated that 'I think those some people (children with SEN) would otherwise be dragging the rest of the class down so that the teacher can't give their full assistance to us'. Handing over the responsibility for those pupils with the greatest level of need within the classroom to TAs has consistently been highlighted as unethical (Giangreco, Suter and Doyle 2010; Rutherford 2011), and a TA-led educational package 'would be considered unacceptable if suggested for students without disabilities' (Giangreco 2021, 280), but it appears that pupils as well as staff (Skipp and Hopwood 2019) continue to see this as the norm. A number of pupils in the study suggested that an ideal TA would play a wider role, also supporting other pupils, and the teacher. A more effective and ethical TA deployment would be to include regular portions of time where individual or small-groups of children with SEN work with the teacher, whilst the TA looks after the rest of the class.

Further comparisons between the teacher and TA helped to illuminate pupils' experiences of their support, and provide helpful indications about the practice and preparedness of TAs. Whilst some participants struggled to explain the difference between the two adults (as was found by Eyres et al. 2004), others indicated that the teacher might be more knowledgeable, be more likely to give correct explanations and to know the answers. One participant explained that the teacher rather than the TA would 'know what was going on', possibly suggesting that TAs were 'thinking on their feet' with no previous information from the teacher. Despite participants often thinking that the teacher could be more likely to know the answers, they still suggested that the first and often only person that they would turn to for help was the TA. If TAs are to be able to bring positive academic impacts for pupils, then schools need to provide the appropriate training, support and information prior to lessons.

One participant's experiences of the TA coming across as mean and seeming to find him rude when he was struggling with the work, and other participants' reports that their TAs could be irritable or grumpy, highlight instances of ineffective practice and difficult interactions, and potentially speak of the strains quite naturally placed on a relationship when two people spend such a lot of time together, and/or of the difficult working conditions for some TAs. These findings also emphasise the importance of pupils with SEN being given regular opportunities to feedback about the TA support that they are receiving (without feeling that they are doing something wrong) and to be included in decisions made about them (SEND Code of Practice; Convention on the Rights of the Child).

When asked to consider what their TA was like, participants overwhelmingly showed great admiration towards them; most participants stated that their TA was already ideal. Their descriptions generally focused on positive and nurturing personality traits and characteristics, including being kind, humorous, chatty and cheerful. Such findings are in line with previous qualitative studies (Bland and Sleightholme 2012; Fraser and Meadows 2008) and suggest that an emphasis should be placed on these TA characteristics when recruiting and training TAs, and that a good level of consideration should be given to the likelihood of a positive, friendly relationship being formed when a particular TA is working with a particular pupil. A further implication is that TAs should feel supported within their workplace to be able to maintain such cheery and enthusiastic personas.

A particularly strong theme within the interviews was the social-emotional support that TAs provided (both current and ideal TAs). By facilitating positive interactions with peers, supporting group work, providing prompts about social-rules and supporting pupils to problem-solve in social scenarios, TAs helped participants to feel more included within their peer group. Participants' friends were perceived to think highly of TAs, admiring their sociable and fun qualities, suggesting that within the social environment of the school, TAs were providing good modelling of social skills for the pupils they supported. In discussions about their relationships with TAs, participants' comments indicated that TAs got to know pupils well, showed an understanding of their needs and advocated for them. A significant message in relation to social outcomes was that TA support fostered a sense of belonging for pupils within school ('she makes me feel like I'm meant to be here'). In this way, TAs appear to support greater inclusion of pupils with SEN within mainstream settings, in line with previous suggestions (Saddler 2013). The magnitude of this is clear; when pupils feel a greater connection with others in school, they are more engaged (Vollet, Kindermann and Skinner 2017) and demonstrate greater academic performance (Allen et al. 2016).

In a review of the literature in 2009, Alborz et al. concluded that more information was needed about the impacts of TA support on pupils' emotional outcomes. In the current study, emotional support was appreciated and emphasised by all but one participant, and certainly was not limited to the one participant who had social, emotional and mental health needs. Participants talked about the TA making them feel happy ('she's the only one who makes me happy') and they often saw their TA as the person they could talk to about their worries and problems, the person who would listen non-judgementally, and the one who could promote emotional coping strategies in the heat-of-the-moment. Discussions about participants' ideal TAs suggested that there is great potential for them to provide a 'counselling' role. This echoes previous pupil-voice research, in that TAs appear to be very effective supporters of children's emotional well-being (Groom and Rose 2005; Woolfson and Truswell 2005). Positive findings regarding pupils' social and emotional outcomes add to quantitative research, which has largely focused on academic outcomes or emotional factors relating to learning, i.e. motivation (e.g. Blatchford, Russell and Webster 2012; Muijs and Reynolds 2003). Perhaps quantitative measures of social inclusion and emotional well-being (e.g. observable behavioural indicators or teacher-ratings) would not gain such accurate and insightful information as seeking participants' own views in this way.

With participants suggesting the significant social-emotional benefits of TA support, schools ought to acknowledge this aspect of the TA role more clearly, and take action to provide TAs with the skills, resources and targets to maximise this impact. By supporting some of the most vulnerable pupils to feel happy, calm and as if they truly belong within their mainstream school, TAs play a significant role in making these schools a more inclusive place.

Conclusion

The child-friendly interview methodology of the study, including the creative activity and toy props, helped to encourage participants' engagement, to support their communication and to build rapport and break down power imbalances between interviewer and interviewee. The flexible semi-structured interview schedule meant that the interviewer had opportunities to follow participants' leads and tangents, allowing them to talk about the issues that were most important/relevant to them. Participants were purposefully the sole interviewees, so that their perspectives and insights were not overshadowed by other stakeholders. However, the lack of triangulation could also be considered a limitation of the study, and gathering the perspectives of teachers, TAs and parents, as well as conducting observations of participants working with their TAs, could have contributed more detail and reliability. A further consideration with regard to limitations is that the SENCOs who responded to the request for participants might have felt more confident about TA practice in their schools, compared with those many SENCOs across the city who did not respond. Future research could extend current findings using a larger sample, more diverse in age, and might seek to look for possible trends amongst pupils with particular types of SEN.

In summary, primary school children with SEN provided insightful and important feedback about the support that they receive from TAs. They felt that TAs supported them to access the curriculum, but also highlighted important issues around separation from the teacher, and about TA practice when they are allocated to work largely one-to-one, having to make pedagogical decisions on-the-spot. Participants' perspectives highlighted a wider impact of TA support than is sometimes recognised, researched and celebrated, by strongly emphasising the power of the TA in promoting pupils' social inclusion and emotional well-being.

Acknowledgements

I would like to thank Professor Melanie Nind (University of Southampton) for supervising this research – providing encouragement, challenge and inspiration each step of the way.

Originally published as Hayley Pinkard (2021) The perspectives and experiences of children with special educational needs in mainstream primary schools regarding their individual teaching assistant support, European Journal of Special Needs Education, 36:2, 248-264, DOI: 10.1080/08856257.2021.1901375.

© Taylor & Francis Ltd (2021), reprinted by permission of the publisher.

References

Alborz, A., D. Pearson, P. Farrell, and A. Howes. 2009. "The Impact of Adult Support Staff on Pupils and Mainstream Schools." Technical Report, London: Institute of Education.

Allen, K., M. L. Kern, D. Vella-Brodick, J. Hattie, and L. Waters. 2016. "What Schools Need to Know about Fostering School Belonging: A Meta-analysis." *Educational Psychology Review* 30: 1–34. doi:10.1007/s10648-016-9389-8.

Bland, K., and S. Sleightholme. 2012. "Researching the Pupil Voice: What Makes a Good Teaching Assistant?" *British Journal of Learning Support* 27 (4): 172–176. doi:10.1111/1467-9604.12000.

Blatchford, P., A. Russell, and R. Webster. 2012. *Reassessing the Impact of Teaching Assistants: How Research Challenges Practice and Policy.* Oxon: Routledge.

Braun, V., and V. Clarke. 2006. "Using Thematic Analysis in Psychology." *Qualitative Research in Psychology* 3 (2): 77–101. doi:10.1191/1478088706qp063oa.

Broer, S. M., M. B. Doyle, and M. F. Giangreco. 2005. "Perspectives of Students with Intellectual Disabilities about Their Experiences with Paraprofessional Support." *Exceptional Children* 71: 415–430.

Clarke, A., and P. Moss. 2001. *Listening to Young Children: The Mosaic Approach.* London: National Children's Bureau.

Clarke, A., and P. Moss. 2005. *Spaces to Play: More Listening to Young Children Using the Mosaic Approach.* London: National Children's Bureau.

DfE (Department for Education). 2014. *Special Educational Needs & Disability Code of Practice: 0 to 25 Years.* London: DfE.

DfE (Department for Education) 2019. *School Workforce Census 2018.* https://assets.publishing.service.gov.uk/government/uploads/system/uploads/attachment_data/file/811622/SWFC_MainText.pdf

DfES (Department for Education and Skills). 2003. *Raising Standards and Tackling Workload: A National Agreement.* London: HMSO.

Eyres, I., C. Cable, R. Hancock, and J. Turner. 2004. "Whoops I Forgot David: Children's Perceptions of the Adults that Work in Their Classrooms." *Early Years* 24 (2): 149–162. doi:10.1080/0957514032000733000.

Farrell, P., M. Balshaw, and F. Polat. 2000. "The Work of Learning Support Assistants in Mainstream Schools: Implications for Educational Psychologists." *Educational & Child Psychology* 17 (2): 66–76.

Fitzgerald, H., A. Jobling, and D. Kirk. 2003. "Listening to the 'Voices' of Students with Severe Learning Difficulties through a Task-based Approach to Research and Learning in Physical Education." *Support for Learning* 18 (3): 123–129. doi:10.1111/1467-9604.00294.

Fraser, C., and S. Meadows. 2008. "Children's Views of Teaching Assistants in Primary Schools." *Education* 36 (4): 351–363.

Giangreco, M. F. 2021. "Maslow's Hammer: Teacher Assistant Research and Inclusive Practices at a Crossroads." *European Journal of Special Needs Education* 36 (2): 278–293

Giangreco, M. F., J. C. Suter, and M. B. Doyle. 2010. "Paraprofessionals in Inclusive Schools: A Review of Recent Research." *Journal of Education and Psychological Consultation* 20 (1): 41–57. doi:10.1080/10474410903535356.

Groom, B., and R. Rose. 2005. "Supporting the Inclusion of Pupils with Social, Emotional and Behavioural Difficulties in the Primary School: The Role of Teaching Assistants." *Journal of Research in Special Educational Needs* 5 (1): 20–30. doi:10.1111/j.1471-3802.2005.00035.x.

Klassen, R. 2001. "After the Statement: Reading Progress Made by Secondary Students with Specific Literacy Difficulty Provision." *Educational Psychology in Practice* 17 (2): 121–133. doi:10.1080/02667360120059337.

Lacey, P. 2001. "The Role of Learning Support Assistants in the Inclusive Learning of Pupils with Severe and Profound Learning Difficulties." *Educational Review* 53 (2): 157–167. doi:10.1080/00131910120055589.

Lamb, B. 2009. *The Lamb Inquiry: Special Needs and Parental Confidence*. Nottingham: DCSF Publications.

Moran, H. 2001. "Who Do You Think You Are? Drawing the Ideal Self: A Technique to Explore A Child's Sense of Self." *Clinical Psychology and Psychiatry* 6: 599–604. doi:10.1177/1359104501006004016.

Muijs, D., and D. Reynolds. 2003. "The Effectiveness of the Use of Learning Support Assistants in Improving the Mathematics Achievement of Low Achieving Pupils in Primary School." *Educational Research* 45: 219–230. doi:10.1080/0013188032000137229.

Newton, C., and D. Wilson. 2011. *Keys to Inclusion*. UK: Inclusive Solutions UK.

Rose, R., and M. Doveston. 2008. "Pupils Talking about Their Learning Mentors: What Can We Learn?" *Educational Studies* 34 (2): 145–155. doi:10.1080/03055690701811222.

Rubie-Davies, C. M., P. Blatchford, R. Webster, M. Koutsoubou, and P. Bassett. 2010. "Enhancing Learning? A Comparison of Teacher and Teaching Assistant Interactions with Pupils." *School Effectiveness and School Improvement* 21 (4): 429–449. doi:10.1080/09243453.2010.512800.

Rutherford, G. 2011. "Doing Right by Teacher Aides, Students with Disabilities and Relational Social Justice." *Harvard Educational Review* 81 (1): 95–118. doi:10.17763/haer.81.1.wu14717488wx2001.

Saddler, H. 2013. "Researching the Influence of Teaching Assistants on the Learning of Pupils Identified with Special Educational Needs in Mainstream Primary Schools: Exploring Social Inclusion." *Journal of Research in Special Educational Needs* 14 (3): 145–152. doi:10.1111/1471-3802.12019.

Shevlin, M., and R. Rose. 2008. "Pupils as Partners in Education Decision-making: Responding to the Legislation in England and Ireland." *European Journal of Special Needs Education* 23 (4): 423–430. doi:10.1080/08856250802387430.

Skipp, A., and V. Hopwood. 2019. *Deployment of Teaching Assistants in Schools: Research Report*. https://assets.publishing.service.gov.uk/government/uploads/system/uploads/attachment_data/file/812507/Deployment_of_teaching_assistants_report.pdf

Tews, L., and J. Lupart. 2008. "Students with Disabilities' Perspectives of the Role and Impact of Paraprofessionals in Inclusive Education Settings." *Journal of Policy & Practice in Intellectual Disabilities* 5: 39–46. doi:10.1111/j.1741-1130.2007.00138.x.

Thomas, N., and C. O'Kane. 1998. "The Ethics of Participatory Research with Children." *Children and Society* 12: 336–348. doi:10.1111/j.1099-0860.1998.tb00090.x.

United Nations. 1989. *The United Nations Convention on the Rights of the Child.* https://www.unicef.org.uk/what-we-do/un-convention-child-rights/

Vollet, J. D., T. A. Kindermann, and E. A. Skinner. 2017. "In Peer Matters, Teachers Matter: Peer Group Influences on Students' Engagement Depend on Teacher Involvement." *Journal of Educational Psychology* 109 (5): 635–652. doi:10.1037/edu0000172.

Warhurst, C., D. Nickson, J. Commander, and K. Gilbert. 2014. "'Role Stretch': Assessing the Blurring of Teaching and Non-teaching in the Classroom Assistant Role in Scotland." *British Educational Research Journal* 40 (1): 170–186. doi:10.1002/berj.3036.

Webster, R. 2014. "2014 Code of Practice: How Research Evidence on the Role and Impact of Teaching Assistants Can Inform Professional Practice." *Educational Psychology in Practice* 30 (3): 232–237. doi:10.1080/02667363.2014.917401.

Webster, R., and P. Blatchford. 2013. "The Educational Experiences of Pupils with a Statement for Special Educational Needs in Mainstream Primary Schools. Results from a Systematic Observation Study." *European Journal of Special Needs Education* 28 (4): 463–479. doi:10.1080/08856257.2013.820459.

Webster, R., and P. Blatchford. 2019. "Making Sense of 'Teaching', 'Support' and 'Differentiation': The Educational Experiences of Pupils with Education, Health and Care Plans and Statements in Mainstream Secondary Schools." *European Journal of Special Needs* 34 (1): 98–113. doi:10.1080/08856257.2018.1458474.

Webster, R., P. Blatchford, P. Bassett, P. Brown, C. Martin, and A. Russell. 2010. "Double Standards and First Principles: Framing Teaching Assistant Support for Pupils with Special Educational Needs." *European Journal of Special Educational Needs* 25 (4): 319–336. doi:10.1080/08856257.2010.513533.

Webster, R., P. Blatchford, P. Bassett, P. Brown, C. Martin, and A. Russell. 2011. "The Wider Pedagogical Role of Teaching Assistants." *School Leadership & Management* 31 (1): 3–20. doi:10.1080/13632434.2010.540562.

Woolfson, R. C., and E. Truswell. 2005. "Do Classroom Assistants Work?" *Educational Research* 47: 63–75. doi:10.1080/0013188042000337569.

Part III
Teaching assistants and teachers

7 Teaching assistants and teachers providing instructional support for pupils with SEN

Results from a video study in Swiss classrooms

Franziska Vogt, Annette Koechlin, Annina Truniger and Bea Zumwald

Introduction: Policy background

Whereas teaching assistants (TAs) have been part of school provision in mainstream schools in some countries for a more than two decades (Webster et al. 2010), the employment of TAs in mainstream schools in Switzerland was unknown until ten years ago. Within the wider context of policy changes for special educational needs (SEN) education, TAs were introduced at the local level in school in the last decade. Two different models are stipulated. Swiss schools explicitly distinguish between TA employment for supporting the whole class as a general aide and TA employment for a specific pupil with SEN. The chapter therefore begins with a discussion of the policy context and the regulations regarding the two models in Switzerland.

Recent introduction of TAs in mainstream schools in Switzerland

Switzerland has a long tradition of flat hierarchies in schools (Vogt 2003), with the teacher mostly being the only adult in the classroom. In the last two decades a variety of forms of professional cooperation between teachers and SEN-teachers have emerged (Baumann 2019). However, TAs are a more recent phenomenon.

Compared to other European countries, Switzerland continues to have high numbers of pupils with SEN attending fully separate educational settings (either special schools or separate classes within schools); 3.86% of all pupils are in separate provision compared to the 1.55% average in more than 23 European countries (EASIE 2020; indicator 2.3b.5). Inclusion of pupils with SEN in mainstream classrooms is supported through SEN-teachers, generally qualified with a specialist master's degree. They prepare materials and programmes tailored to the needs of the SEN pupils in defining an 'individual educational plan' (Paccaud and Luder 2017). On average, SEN-teachers are present during three lessons per week in a given class,

DOI: 10.4324/9781003265580-11

team-teaching with the main classroom teacher. Much of the time, the teachers are responsible for teaching the whole class without the support of the SEN-teacher. The challenges of meeting diverse students' needs, especially the needs of pupils with SEN, together with the need to work together with a specialist, are perceived as burdensome by some teachers (Sandmeier et al. 2017). TAs, in contrast, are often regarded as welcome support for teachers (PHSG 2020). The increasing establishment of inclusive classrooms in Switzerland since the 2010s has led to the rapid growth in the number of TAs in mainstream schools. This trend is comparable to the rise of TAs in mainstream classrooms in the UK more than a decade earlier (Webster et al. 2010).

Within Switzerland, policy and practice regarding TAs vary widely as cantons (comparable to counties) are responsible for education policy. TAs are not required to have a professional pedagogical qualification. Most Swiss cantons list general criteria for TA recruitment such as good skills in the language of schooling, patience, the ability to cope with pressure and having attained an occupational qualification of some sort. The cantonal recommendations on the employment of TAs emphasise that TAs should provide administrative and organisational support, but that they should not take on instruction, as they are not qualified. Within Switzerland, the employment of TAs continues to attract strong criticism and public debate. The Teachers' Association fears that the increase in TAs might lead to the 'deprofessionalisation' and replacement of SEN teachers (LCH 2017).

Two models: TAs supporting either the whole class or a specific pupil with SEN

TAs are either employed 'for the whole class', as a general aide or are deployed to support the inclusion of a specific pupil with SEN. It is left to the discretion of the individual schools to decide how TAs, as general aides, are to be employed. No regulations exist as to qualifications, scope of work time or joint preparation time. It is up to the teacher and the decision of the head teacher as to whether or not a class is supported by a TA and for how many lessons per week. TAs are also deployed to support the inclusion of a specific pupil with SEN. These TAs are also employed by the local school and their work is equally unregulated. Compared to other countries, the model of TA employed for the whole class corresponds to the 'class support model' and the model employed for a pupil with SEN is similar to the 'one-on-one-model' (Butt 2016, 997).

The role of the TA in both models is embedded with tensions: TAs need to be effective and invisible helpers in often precarious, hourly paid employment (Heinrich and Lübeck 2013). Their role often involves emotional labour within the context of contradictory expectations (Zumwald 2014), i.e. supporting learning but not taking a similar role to the teacher: they should not 'teach', as they are not to substitute the teacher, but provide support in the classroom.

Research on TAs' instructional support and effects on pupils with SEN

A study involving a large sample of classes across school years in the UK raised concerns about the negative effects of TAs on pupils' learning (Blatchford, Russell and Webster 2012). Those pupils who received the most support by a TA made less progress in English and mathematics than pupils not supported by a TA. As for science, no effects or negative effects were found (Webster, Blatchford and Russell 2012, 324). Interestingly, there was a positive effect of TAs noted on pupils' time-on-task (Blatchford et al. 2009). This could be interpreted as the TA providing instructional support in attention guiding. However, the increased time-on-task did not result in higher learning gains (Blatchford, Russell and Webster 2012). The negative effects may be due to: (i) the quality of instructional support provided by the TAs and teachers, and (ii) the risk of insular relationships between TA and pupil.

Instructional support during individual seatwork

The co-constructivist theory of learning with its emphasis on learners actively constructing understanding within a social process led to a focus on how teachers provide instructional support in such ways that individual pupils be enabled to actively build up understanding (Pauli, Reusser and Grob 2007). Constructivist teaching would, for example, involve scaffolding, whereby the teacher highlights the relevant characteristics of a task and models the problem-solving in such a way that the pupil is able to solve the task (Van De Pol, Volman and Beishuizen 2010; Wood, Bruner and Ross 1976). As Radford et al. (2015, 9) puts it: 'the ultimate aim ... is for learners to be able to self-scaffold'. Constructivist teaching can be distinguished from transmission, which involves 'telling how to' and 'giving verbal explanations' (Kleickmann, Vehmeyer and Möller 2010). In order to provide individual support in such a way that constructivist learning is possible, teaching adaptively to the diverse learning needs of the pupils is essential (Bruehwiler and Vogt 2020; Vogt 2013).

Such individual support often occurs during individual seatwork. A large-scale study in secondary schools revealed that phases of individual seatwork are more extensive in Switzerland than in other countries (Krammer, Reusser and Pauli 2010, 108). Individual seatwork is highly relevant for the role of TAs. Swiss policy documents state that TAs should neither take on the role of teachers nor provide instruction but solely assist. During individual seatwork, it is common practice, however, that both TAs and teachers provide support for pupils. The question arises about the quality of support provided by TAs and teachers for pupils during individual seatwork.

By using conversation analysis the main differences between the instructional support provided by teachers and that of TAs could be pinpointed: the support provided by teachers includes more 'opening up', i.e. providing open invitations to elicit pupils' thoughts on a particular topic and enhance understanding, whereas TAs tend to 'close down', i.e. ask closed questions and supply answers (Radford, Blatchford and Webster 2011, 625). Furthermore, TAs' quality of interactions with pupils has been described as focusing on task completion rather than on understanding (Rubie-Davies et al. 2010). Webster et al. (2011) argue that pupils with SEN should have more access to teachers' support, as teachers' qualifications are higher than TAs'.

Impact on inclusion for pupils with SEN

The international research literature shows that the deployment of TAs for pupils with SEN often leads to an increase of one-to-one instruction between TA and pupil with SEN, thereby undermining both the inclusion and independence of the pupils with SEN (Sharma and Salend 2016). TAs are often employed to give direct support to these pupils (Egilson and Traustadottir 2009; Lacey 2001). Pupils with SEN experience fewer interactions with their teacher when assisted by a TA (Butt 2016; Webster et al. 2010). Wendelborg and Tøssebro (Wendelborg and Tøssebro 2010, 712) use the term 'covert segregation process' to describe the practices of delegating responsibilities to special education teachers or TAs.

TAs sitting next to a pupil and providing support are described as 'excessive proximity' which can lead to an insular relationship between TA-supported pupils and their TAs (Giangreco 2013, 6). Insular relationships result in reduced interactions with the teacher (Butt 2016), as well as with peers: Malmgren and Causton-Theoharis (2006) observed the interactions of TA-supported pupils with their classmates and found that peer interactions occur almost exclusively (i.e. 90% of the interactions) when the pupils were not in proximity to their TA. Tews and Lupart (2008) interviewed TA-supported pupils who reported that they mainly interact with their assigned TA, but rarely with their classmates. However, the marginalisation of pupils with SEN is also found in studies where no TAs are involved (Asbjørnslett, Engelsrud and Helseth 2015; Simeonsson et al. 2001). Rubie-Davies et al. (2010) report that TAs interact more often with pupils of lower attainment, whereas teachers support medium to high attainment levels.

Research questions

The research hitherto discussed highlights the importance of the quality of interactions for learning, i.e. scaffolding interactions during individual seatwork, as well as the risk of pupils with SEN, who are supported by TAs, having fewer interactions with their teacher and peers during class. The purpose of the study presented in this chapter is to examine the teachers' and TAs' interactions with pupils based on observational data in order to analyse how these interactions compare and how they reflect the roles foreseen for TAs and teachers in the two models. Drawing on research, which reveals that the continuous presence of a TA at the side of a pupil with SEN can hinder the inclusion of that pupil (Butt 2016; Giangreco 2013) by creating an insular relationship, this chapter, focuses on individual seatwork. In these sequences, the apparent roles of the TAs and teachers are found to be more similar, whereas during whole class teaching sequences, the teacher is clearly more active and the TA assumes a more passive role, observing and waiting (Koechlin et al. 2019).

The chapter addresses the overall research question: How do teachers' and TAs' interactions with pupils during individual seatwork compare, in relation to support provided for the class as a whole and for pupils with SEN? In order to address the overall research question, the following three sub-questions are posed:

(i) How do the types of individual support provided by the TA and the teacher during individual seatwork compare in relation to the two models common in Switzerland? The first research sub-question is posed against the background of Swiss education policy, which distinguishes TAs as support for the whole class and TAs as support for pupils with SEN and insists that TAs are there to assist with organisational matters and not teach. Research has, however, raised concerns about the role of non-qualified staff providing instructional support.

(ii) How does the content of instructional support given to pupils with SEN by TAs and the teachers compare? The second research sub-question takes into account that international research has highlighted that pupils with SEN often experience insular relationships with the TA, thus receive lower quality of instructional support (for example, focused on task completion rather than scaffolding) from the TA and less support from their teacher. Therefore, the content of the support for pupils with SEN needs to be examined in detail in order to assess the role of TAs for inclusion in Swiss mainstream schools.

(iii) How do TAs and teachers share the instructional support amongst higher-, medium- and lower-attaining pupils? The third research sub-question is informed by international research findings, stipulating that TAs interact more with lower achieving pupils and teachers with medium- to high-achieving pupils. As Swiss policy foresees a model whereby the TA is employed as a general aide to the class, it is of interest, who the TA and teacher support when the TA is employed for the whole class.

Methods

Research design

These questions are at the centre of the research project 'the cooperative practices of teaching assistants and teachers'. It is the first research project in

130 *Franziska Vogt et al.*

Switzerland to focus on TAs and teachers working together in mainstream primary school classrooms. Data-gathering took place between January 2017 and June 2018 and included (i) a video recording of 90 minutes shared classroom practice; (ii) individual semi-structured interviews with TAs and teachers after the video-recording; and (iii) a short written questionnaire on demographic information and information about the class (SEN-status, attainment levels, etc.). This chapter focuses on video data of teachers' and TAs' classroom interactions while both support pupils during individual seatwork at the same time in class.

Sample

Thirty-one classes in 31 different primary schools in German-speaking Switzerland took part in the research. Participants were recruited through newsletters, mailing lists and professional contacts. The two models for deployment of TAs suggested in Swiss education policy were represented in the sample: 16 classes were following the model of the TA being deployed as a general aide for the whole class and 15 classes had TAs deployed for one specific pupil with SEN. The lessons per week in which the TA worked in the participating class and with the participating teacher varied: On average, TAs were working during 8.5 lessons per week in the participating class (min = 3, max = 30). All classes were primary school classes, grade 1 to 6, with children's aged between 6 and 12 years. Classes videographed included an average of 18.3 pupils per class, similar to the average Swiss class size in primary school of 19.2 pupils (bfs 2020). Teachers, TAs and pupils' guardians were asked to give informed consent to participating in the research and to being videographed, all 31 teachers and 31 TAs, as well as 91.4% of pupils (n = 529) took part.

Data collection

Video observation

The video observation was carried out using two cameras in order to observe classroom interactions from two different angles: one camera taking in the whole of the classroom, being linked with the wireless microphone of the teacher, the second camera being moved when needed to capture the TA and being linked to the wireless microphone of the TA. Two consecutive lessons, a total of 90 minutes per class, were observed in order to ensure that for each teacher and TA, different settings such as individual seatwork and whole-class-teaching could be observed.

Teachers were asked to identify the pupils with SEN and the TAs who were employed to support them from a photograph of the class. They were also asked to indicate the identified pupils' attainment level in German and mathematics. Three very basic categories were provided – 'lower-attaining', 'average-attaining' and 'higher-attaining' – thus representing a basic ranking

(Schrader 2013). As this was given at the time of data collection, it represents the teacher's judgement of the pupil's attainment levels at that moment in time and it is likely that they would also provide support according to their judgement. Teachers rated 24.5% of the pupils as lower-attaining', 51.9% as 'average-attaining' and 23.5% as 'higher-attaining'. The identifications of SEN and attainment level were referred to during the coding of the videos.

Data analysis

The two audio and video recordings were combined to one video with split screen and two audio lines so that the coding of any given moment could be assessed for both, the activity of the TA and the teacher. Using MAXQDA (VERBI Software 2018), the 31 videos (average length = 91.5 minutes, min = 72.5 minutes, max = 112 minutes) were coded throughout, thus enabling codes to be analysed regarding frequency and duration (Appel and Rauin 2016). The setting was coded first. Settings differentiated between whole class instruction (i.e. teacher addressing the whole class collectively), group work and individual seatwork. For this chapter, all recordings of individual seatwork are used for data analysis.

Interrater reliability between the three raters was examined for all the codings in a random selection of a minimum of a quarter of the videos using MAXQDA's features, performing an examination of the percentage match. Percentage match overall was good (>70%); the analysis of interrater differences revealed that the interrater match was difficult in particular for very short sequences (i.e. shorter than 5 seconds).

Coding individual support regarding type

Within sequences of individual seatwork, all observable and audible individual interactions of TAs and teachers with all pupils were coded as 'individual support'. For each of the sequences of individual support the coding differentiated between organisational, attention-guiding and instructional support. This differentiation was adapted from coding schemes used by Krammer, Reusser and Pauli (2010), Radford et al. (2015) and Rubie-Davies et al. (2010). Descriptions of these types of support as well as coding examples are listed in Table 7.1.

This coding scheme was used for analysing all instructional support during individual seatwork with all pupils. Further, these codes were examined in relation to pupils' attainment levels in classes where the TA is employed for the whole class.

Coding the content of instructional support for pupils with SEN

In order to compare the kind of instructional support provided by TAs and teachers during individual seatwork, a coding scheme was developed

132 *Franziska Vogt et al.*

Table 7.1 Types of individual support, coding scheme and examples

Type of support	Description of interaction focus	Coding examples (translated from German)
Organisational	Solely on organisational aspects	Helping a pupil to find materials for work: 'You need a blue pen for this. Look, here it is' Opening a book on the right page for a pupil: 'It's on page 31'
Attention-guiding	Fostering on-task behaviour or discipline	'Keep on working, please' 'Shh ... listen carefully now'
Instructional	Relating to the learning task (explanations, hints, strategies, questions, evaluation of the task)	'How do we write the first word in a sentence?' 'Look, when subtracting, you always have to put the bigger number first' 'That's correct, well done'

Adapted from Krammer, Reusser and Pauli (2010); Radford et al. (2015); Rubie-Davies et al. (2010).

based on established coding schemes used to elicit teacher–pupil interaction in primary school regarding cognitive apprenticeship, scaffolding and co-construction. The coding scheme developed by Krammer (2009) was used for mathematics lessons, whereas Schnebel and Wagner (2016) developed their scheme to rate instructional support in physics. As subjects varied in this study, these coding schemes were adapted to be less subject-specific. Further, the coding scheme used for TA–pupil and teacher–pupil interaction by Rubie-Davies et al. (2010) also was consulted. Table 7.2 provides the codes used to analyse the content of individual instructional support, aiming at distinguishing instructional support of a more transmissive character from a co-constructivist support.

This coding scheme was applied to all instructional support provided by either teacher or TA for the pupil with SEN in those classes, where the TA was deployed for this specific pupil with SEN.

Statistical analysis

All codes from the video analysis in MAXQDA (VERBI Software 2018) were exported regarding duration (seconds of a code) or occurrences (how often was this code given). The tool MAXQDA also allows for data retrieval combining several categories (i.e. organisational support for higher-attaining pupils by the teacher). Codes were exported to SPSS 25 (IBM Statistical Package for Social Sciences) for quantitative data analysis. In the analysis, non-parametric tests were used, as the variables did not meet the criteria of normal distribution. For comparing the two models, the Mann-Whitney-U-Test was used. For the comparison between the instructional support by the TA or the teacher, Wilcoxon for paired samples was chosen.

Table 7.2 Content of instructional support, coding scheme and examples

Content of instructional support	Description	Coding examples (translated from German)
Explanations oriented towards understanding	Focus on supporting understanding though providing an explanation, without involving the pupil deeply	'The beaver gets branches to build a nest' 'You need to put glue at three places in order for it to hold'
Dialogic explanations	Focus on building understanding with eliciting the pupil's explanations (co-constructivist teaching)	'What do you already know about … ?' 'How do you approach solving the task today?'
Transmission of facts	Knowledge, keywords, hints, step by step procedures	'Write … here again, come on' 'next we need to know, whether … '
Transmission: solving the task for the pupil	Telling the correct result, write for the pupil	Writes on the pupil's work sheet, uses scissors instead of pupil
Feedback related to the task	Task and content is referred to, the evaluation is related to the content of the task.	'Watch closely' 'Focus on this calculation task. Do you notice anything?'
General feedback	General praise or critique regarding the solution provided	'good', 'well done' 'mmmh' (approving) 'stop it!'
Motivation related to task	Motivating to solve or complete the task	'Just this one task, after that we play' 'You will succeed'
General motivation	Motivating, showing understanding for the pupil	'I am coming to help you right after this' 'Are you tired?'
Observing, listening, waiting	Observe, what the pupil does, listening to the pupil,	sits next to the pupil and waits, listens to the pupil reading aloud
No allocation	Categories do not fit	

Adapted from Rubie-Davies et al. (2010), Schnebel and Wagner (2016) and Krammer (2009).

Results

In order to investigate the support provided by TAs and teachers during individual seatwork, the analysis focuses on the three research sub-questions. First, an overview is provided of the type of support given during individual seatwork in the whole sample ($N = 31$ classes), comparing TAs and teachers in the two models. Second, the focus is on the content of the instructional support provided by TAs and teacher for pupils with SEN. To this end, 15 classes with TAs being employed for a specific pupil with SEN will be used. Third, it is investigated, whether the TAs being deployed for the whole class ($n = 16$) provide instructional support for all pupils regardless of their attainment levels during individual seatwork, or whether there are differences between TAs and teachers regarding the pupils they support.

Individual support during individual seatwork

Individual seatwork occurred on average two-thirds of the time videographed, on average 63 minutes per class. Table 7.3 shows the overall mean length of individual support provided by TAs and teachers, as well as the duration for the three different types of support: organisational, attention-guiding support and instructional.

From the three types of individual support distinguished, instructional support is by far the most common for both, teachers and TAs. TAs have longer interactions than teachers providing individual support (total) and instructional support. This is the case for both models. Furthermore, in the model where the TA is deployed for a specific pupil with SEN, the teacher is providing more organisational support than the TA.

Instructional support for pupils with SEN during individual seatwork

In order to describe the kind of instructional support which pupils with SEN receive from the TA and the teacher, all interactions which were coded as instructional support were analysed in more detail, taking the content, i.e. explanations, transmission of facts, feedback, into account. Table 7.4 provides the descriptives for TAs and teachers.

The pupils with SEN receive significantly more often and longer instructional support from the TA than from the teacher; the difference between TA and teacher using the Wilcoxon test for paired sample is significant for occurrence and duration for all the codes, except for the duration of dialogic explanation, with only a tendency. The mean of the total duration of instructional support for pupils with SEN during individual seatwork is for TAs at 25.54 minutes, for teachers at 1.86 minutes. The teachers in general have very short interactions of instructional support with the pupils with SEN, whilst the TAs more often stay in the interaction, with more time observing,

Table 7.3 Individual support distinguished in minutes by type and TA versus teacher in the two models and in total

Mean duration (minutes) per type of individual support	Model TA for SEN n = 15 classes		Model TA as general aide for the class n = 16 classes		Total sample N = 31 classes	
	TA	Teacher	TA	Teacher	TA	Teacher
Organisational	3.62*	7.69*	5.72	5.89	4.71	6.76
Attention-guiding	0.38	0.50	0.33	0.53	0.35	0.52
Instructional	35.32*	15.78*	27.68*	17.33*	31.37***	16.58***
Total	39.33*	23.97*	33.73*	23.75*	36.43***	23.85***

(significant differences between TA and teacher mean duration *$p < .05$; ***$p < .001$ Wilcoxon for paired sample).

Table 7.4 Content of instructional support for pupils with SEN, descriptives and differences

Content of instructional support for pupils with SEN during individual seatwork	TA (n = 15) Mean occurrence	TA (n = 15) Mean duration minutes	Teacher (n = 15) Mean occurrence	Teacher (n = 15) Mean duration minutes
Explanations oriented towards understanding	4.79	1.25	.53	0.15
Dialogic explanations	2.00	1.75	.67	0.37
Transmission of facts	32.33	8.47	2.53	0.47
Transmission: solving the task for the pupil	10.87	2.89	.40	0.06
Feedback related to the task	6.67	1.07	1.20	0.29
General feedback	7.33	0.85	.93	0.08
Motivation related to task	4.33	0.95	.13	0.02
General motivation	1.60	0.31	.07	0.01
Observing, listening, waiting	26.07	7.83	2.27	0.41
No allocation	1.07	0.17	.00	.00
Total	97.06	25.54	8.73	1.86

All comparisons between TA and teachers using the paired Wilcoxon test were significant, with the exception of dialogic explanations, which showed a tendency ($p = .055$).

listening and waiting. When providing instructional support, TAs on average wait, listen and observe the pupil during 7.83 minutes with an occurrence of 26.07 times.

The TAs are transmitting facts most of the time when providing instructional support: Transmitting facts occur on average 32.33 times with a mean duration of 8.47 minutes – approximately a third of the time of their support. Quite often, on average 10.87 times, the TA tells the pupil the correct result or solves the task for the pupil. Teachers are providing the correct results much less than the TA. When comparing the type of instructional support, a more transmissive way of instructional support provided by the TAs becomes apparent.

The analysis of the content of instructional support provided for the pupil with SEN by the TA and the teacher shows very clearly that the teacher only has very few very short interactions with the pupil with SEN, whilst the TA provides much instructional support and stays in interaction with the SEN pupil longer. The content of the TAs' instructional support focuses on transmission. Indeed, they very often just provide the result, or tell facts. Explanations focused on understanding and dialogue are relatively rare.

Instructional support provided in classes with TAs employed as general aide

For the classes where TAs are employed for the whole class it is analysed as to whether TA and teacher also differ regarding the instructional support they provide for pupils. A proximate indication of the attainment level of the

Table 7.5 Instructional support provided by TA and teacher for different attainment groups during individual seatwork in classes where TAs are employed for the whole class

Instructional support during individual seatwork provided for	Mean duration (minutes)	
	TA (n = 16)	Teacher (n = 16)
Lower-attaining pupils	14.02*	7.32*
Average-attaining pupils	16.13	10.14
Higher-attaining pupils	2.35	2.49
Total	32.50*	19.95*

(*significant Wilcoxon paired sample $p < .05$).

children is used: the teachers were rating the overall performance in school of the pupils as low, average or high. Table 7.5 provides the results of the instructional support provided for pupils in relation to the three attainment levels by TAs and teachers.

During individual seatwork, higher-attaining pupils receive little instructional support from TA and teacher, as they might not have any problems with the tasks they are given to work on. Lower-attaining pupils receive significantly longer instructional support from TAs than from teachers. With regard to the average-attaining pupils, who generally form the largest group within the class, the instructional support provided by TAs and teachers is of similar duration.

Discussion

The research study aimed at examining the teachers' and TAs' interactions with pupils based on observational data in order to analyse how these interactions compare and how they reflect the roles foreseen for TAs and teachers in the two models. In the results presented, comparisons between TA–pupil interactions and teacher–pupil interactions are made, as well as comparison of the two models.

The first research sub-question sought to discern whether TAs and teachers support differs, as is foreseen in Swiss policy. The analysis of the support provided by TAs or teachers during individual seatwork reveals that instructional support is more prevalent than organisational and attention-guiding support. The focus on instructional support does not differ between the two models of deployment of TAs nor between TAs and teachers. The findings tie in with research results showing that TAs are as much engaged in instruction as teachers (Webster, Blatchford and Russell 2012). Clearly, this contradicts policy claims that TAs should provide administrative support to the teacher but not 'teach' (LCH 2017). The high amount of instructional support provided by both TAs and teachers during individual seatwork compared with the low amount of organisational and attention-guiding support raises the question as to whether the distinction implied in policies on TA deployment is appropriate. Heinrich (2016) claims, based on theoretical considerations, that pedagogical and non-pedagogical activities can never be totally separated. Further research could, therefore, examine whether the support required during individual seatwork is above all instructional and in what ways pupils' learning could best be supported. Regarding policy development, it needs to be discussed whether policy claims to distinguish the type of support provided by TAs and teachers are feasible.

The second research sub-question focused on pupils with SEN, comparing the content of the instructional support they receive by the TA and the teacher. The analysis revealed that TAs who were deployed to support inclusion of a specific pupil with SEN provided instructional support far more extensively for the specific pupil than the teachers were. Not only did teachers engage considerably less with the pupil with SEN, some of the observed teachers had no individual interaction with the pupil with SEN during individual seatwork. This finding mirrors results from other research, raising concerns that the reliance on TAs for inclusion of pupils which SEN can lead to insular relationships and a reduction of learning support through the teacher (Butt 2016; Giangreco, Broer and Edelman 2001; Webster et al. 2011).

The detailed analysis of the content of instructional support provided to the pupil with SEN reveals that TAs provide instructional support in a more transmissive way. On average, 11 interactions of a total of 97 are such that the TA gives the correct result or does the task for the pupil. This could be interpreted as a concern of the TA to help the pupil of SEN to fulfil the task somehow (Radford, Blatchford and Webster 2011; Rubie-Davies et al. 2010) and as an indicator of the delegation of the teacher's responsibility for the learning processes of pupils with SEN to the TA (Wendelborg and Tøssebro 2010). The rare occurrence of dialogic explanation shows that scaffolding is difficult for TAs to provide, possibly due to a lack of diagnostic competencies needed to provide contingent learning support (Van De Pol, Volman and Beishuizen 2010). However, from a coconstructivist perspective, scaffolding and learning aimed at understanding are very important for learning. This raises questions about the quality of learning support, as pupils with learning difficulties have an enhanced need to receive support from a qualified professional (Webster et al. 2011). Based on international research (Demmer, Heinrich and Anika 2017; Giangreco 2021) it has to be assumed that the problem cannot be met by an increase of TAs' training but that it should be understood as a structural problem of relying on TAs for inclusion.

The third research sub-question focused on the model of deployment of a TA as a general aide to the whole class, examining whether the TA is providing instructional support to all pupils regardless of their attainment-level. The results show that when a TA is not employed for a specific pupil with SEN but for the class as a whole, the TA nonetheless spends more time providing instructional support for the lower-attaining pupils than the teacher does. This raises concerns whether lower-attaining pupils are as a result receiving less support from the teacher. Whilst it has been advised that TAs could be deployed to support the class as a whole to free up the teacher to provide focused support for lower-attaining pupils (Zumwald 2014), this practice has not been implemented in the classes participating in this study. The results reported here reveal that the problem of insular relationships arises not only when TAs are deployed for a specific pupil with SEN but also when TAs are deployed as a general aide to the whole class.

The use of observational data on the cooperation of TAs and teachers has proved very advantageous as the method allowed the simultaneous comparison of the activities of TAs and the teachers. It has, however, to be noted, that the audio quality was such that only the utterances of the TAs and teachers could be analysed, but not that of the pupils. In order to evaluate the effects of the type and content of instructional support provided by the TAs and teachers on the learning process of the pupil, research focusing on the coconstructive learning process is needed.

Conclusion

The findings of this study lead to the conclusion that the deployment of TAs in general and the reliance on TAs for the inclusion of pupils with SEN in particular is not unproblematic. The analysis of the content of instructional support provided for pupils with SEN revealed long durations provided by the TAs with a more transmissive, rather than co-constructivist, approach, thus raising concerns about insular relationships and excessive proximity (Giangreco 2013). As Zumwald (2015) suggests, professional development for the teachers is needed for the teachers concerning the effective deployment of TAs in order to reduce these negative effects. There are also repercussions for policy development. Whilst the deployment of TAs as general aides for the whole class might reduce some of the negative effects, the research presented here reveals that the difference between the two models is not considerable. Also, TAs deployed as a general aide provide more instructional support to the lower-attaining pupils than the teachers. In conclusion, the heavy reliance on TAs for inclusive education needs to be fundamentally questioned. Despite formulating policies such as 'TAs should not teach' and differentiating between two models of TAs' deployment, the same problems of insular relationships and more transmissive instructional support have been identified in this study, in line with international research. As Giangreco (2021) argues, too often the underlying assumption goes unchallenged that the deployment of TAs is *the* answer to inclusion-related pedagogical challenges. As Switzerland has only recently introduced TAs into mainstream schools, it could be questioned as to whether the employment of TAs is the optimal policy to enhance inclusion.

Acknowledgements

We are very grateful to the teachers, teaching assistants and the pupils who gave their time to take part in this research.

We also wish to thank the reviewers of the *European Journal of Special Needs Education* for their most valuable remarks.

Originally published as Franziska Vogt, Annette Koechlin, Annina Truniger & Bea Zumwald (2021) Teaching assistants and teachers providing instructional support for pupils with SEN: results from a video study in Swiss classrooms, European Journal of Special Needs Education, 36:2, 215-230, DOI: 10.1080/08856257.2021.1901373.

© Taylor & Francis Ltd (2021), reprinted by permission of the publisher.

Funding

The present study is based on the research project 'The cooperative practices of teaching assistants and teachers' funded by the Swiss National Science Foundation (Project number 165967, PI Bea Zumwald). The Open Access Publication of this chapter was funded by the Open Access Publication Fund of the St.Gallen University of Teacher Education (PHSG).

References

Appel, J., and U. Rauin. 2016. "Quantiative Analyseverfahren in der Videobasierten Unterrichtsforschung." In *Videoanalysen in der Unterrichtsforschung: Methodische Vorgehensweisen und Anwendungsbeispiele*, edited by U. Rauin, M. Herrle, and T. Engartner, 130–152. Weinheim: Beltz Juventa.

Asbjørnslett, M., G. H. Engelsrud, and S. Helseth. 2015. "Inclusion and Participation in Everyday School Life: Experiences of Children With Physical (Dis)abilities." *International Journal of Inclusive Education* 19 (2): 199–212. doi:10.1080/13603116.2014.916353.

Baumann, B. 2019. "Integrativen Unterricht gemeinsam planen, durchführen und reflektieren: Unterrichtsbezogene Kooperation zwischen Regellehrpersonen und Schulischen Heilpädagoginnen und Heilpädagogen." *Schweizerische Zeitschrift für Heilpädagogik* 25 (10): 28–33.

bfs (2020) "Klassengrösse." Accessed 24.02.2021 https://www.bfs.admin.ch/bfs/de/home/statistiken/bildung-wissenschaft/bildungsindikatoren/themen/ressourcen-betreuung/klassengroesse.assetdetail.12527161.html

Blatchford, P., P. Bassett, P. Brown, and R. Webster. 2009. "The Effect of Support Staff on Pupil Engagement and Individual Attention." *British Educational Research Journal* 35 (5): 661–686. doi:10.1080/01411920902878917.

Blatchford, P., A. Russell, and R. Webster. 2012. *Reassessing the Impact of Teaching Assistants. How Research Challenges Practice and Policy*. London: Routledge.

Bruehwiler, C., and F. Vogt. 2020. "Adaptive Teaching Competency. Effects on Quality of Instruction and Learning Outcomes." *Journal for Educational Research Online* 12 (1): 119–142.

Butt, R. 2016. "Teacher Assistant Support and Deployment in Mainstream Schools." *International Journal of Inclusive Education* 20 (9): 995–1007. doi:10.1080/13603116.2016.1145260.

Demmer, C., M. Heinrich, and L. Anika. 2017. "Rollenklärung als zentrale Professionalisierungsherausforderung im Berufsfeld Schule angesichts von Inklusion: Zur Gegenstandsorientierten Konzeption einer Lehrerfortbildung am Beispiel von Schulbegleitungen." *Die Deutsche Schule* 109 (1): 28–42.

EASIE. 2020. "European Agency Statistics on Inclusive Education: 2018 Dataset Cross-Country Report." Odense, European Agency for Special Needs and Inclusive Education (EASIE). Accessed 24.02.2021 https://www.european-agency.org/sites/default/files/easie_2018_dataset_cross-country_report.docx

Egilson, S. T., and R. Traustadottir. 2009. "Assistance to Pupils with Physical Disabilities in Regular Schools: Promoting Inclusion or Creating Dependency?" *European Journal of Special Needs Education* 24 (1): 21–36. doi:10.1080/08856250802596766.

Giangreco, M. F. 2013. "Teacher Assistant Supports in Inclusive Schools: Research, Practices and Alternatives." *Australasian Journal of Special Education* 37 (2): 93–106. doi:10.1017/jse.2013.1.

Giangreco, M. F. 2021. "Maslow's Hammer. Teacher Assistant Research and Inclusive Practices at Crossroads." *European Journal of Special Needs Education* 36: 2.

Giangreco, M. F., S. M. Broer, and S. W. Edelman. 2001. "Teacher Engagement with Students with Disabilities: Differences between Paraprofessional Service Delivery Models." *Journal of the Association for Persons with Severe Handicaps* 26 (2): 75–86. doi:10.2511/rpsd.26.2.75.

Heinrich, M., and Lübeck, A. (2013). "Hilflose häkelnde Helfer? Zur pädagogischen Rationalität von Integrationshelfer/inne/n im inklusiven Unterricht." *Bildungsforschung* 10(1): S. 91–110 doi: 10.25656/01:8539.

Heinrich, M. 2016. "Unpädagogische Schulbegleitung? Professionstheoretische Interpretation der Befunde zur Nicht-Professionalisierbarkeit einer pädagogischen Tätigkeit." In *Schulbegleitung im Professionalisierungsdilemma. Rekonstruktionen zur inklusiven Beschulung*, edited by A. Lübeck and M. Heinrich, 129–143. Münster: Monsenstein und Vannerdat.

Kleickmann, T., J. Vehmeyer, and K. Möller. 2010. "Zusammenhänge zwischen Lehrervorstellungen und kognitivem Strukturieren von Unterricht am Beispiel von Scaffolding-Massnahmen." *Unterrichtswissenschaft* 38 (3): 210–228.

Koechlin, A., A. Truniger, B. Zumwald, and F. Vogt. 2019. "Koordination von Lehrund Assistenzpersonen im gemeinsamen Unterricht." Paper presented at *DGfE Jahrestagung der Kommission Professionsforschung und Lehrerbildung*. Göttingen, September, 23–25.

Krammer, K. 2009. *Individuelle Lernunterstützung in Schülerarbeitsphasen*. Münster: Waxmann.

Krammer, K., K. Reusser, and C. Pauli. 2010. "Individuelle Unterstützung der Schülerinnen und Schüler durch die Lehrperson während der Schülerarbeitsphasen." In *Unterrichtsgestaltung und Unterrichtsqualität*, edited by K. Reusser, C. Pauli, and M. Waldis, 107–122. Münster: Waxmann.

Lacey, P. 2001. "The Role of Learning Support Assistants in the Inclusive Learning of Pupils with Severe and Profound Learning Difficulties." *Educational Review* 53 (2): 157–167. doi:10.1080/00131910124783.

LCH. 2017. "Kein missbräuchlicher Einsatz von Assistenzpersonal an Schulen. Positionspapier." Dachverband Lehrerinnen und Lehrer Schweiz. Accessed 24.02.2021. https://www.lch.ch/themen/thema/detail/kein-missbraeuchlicher-einsatz-von-assistenzpersonal-an-schulen-1

Malmgren, K. W., and J. Causton-Theoharis. 2006. "Boy in the Bubble: Effects of Paraprofessional Proximity and Other Pedagogical Decisions on the Interactions of a Student with Behavioral Disorders." *Journal of Research in Childhood Education* 20 (4): 301–312. doi:10.1080/02568540609594569.

Paccaud, A., and R. Luder. 2017. "Participation versus Individual Support: Individual Goals and Curricular Access in Inclusive Special Needs Education." *Journal of Cognitive Education and Psychology* 16 (2): 205–224. doi:10.1891/1945-8959.16.2.205.

Pauli, C., K. Reusser, and U. Grob. 2007. "Teaching for Understanding And/or Self-regulated Learning? A Video-based Analysis of Reform-Oriented Mathematics in Instruction in Switzerland." *International Journal of Educational Research* 46 (5): 294–305. doi:10.1016/j.ijer.2007.10.004.

PHSG 2020. "Klassenassistenz: Ihr Einsatz muss gut überlegt sein." Medienmitteilung der Pädagogischen Hochschule St. Gallen (2.7.2020) Accessed 24.04.2021. https://www.phsg.ch/sites/default/files/cms/Ueber-uns/Medien/Downloads/Medienmitteilungen/2020/E_Thema%203_Klassenassistenzen.pdf

Radford, J., P. Blatchford, and R. Webster. 2011. "Opening up and Closing Down: How Teachers and TAs Manage Turn-Taking, Topic and Repair in Mathematics Lessons." *Learning and Instruction* 21 (5): 625–635. doi:10.1016/j.learninstruc.2011.01.004.

Radford, J., P. Bosanquet, R. Webster, and P. Blatchford. 2015. "Scaffolding Learning for Independence: Clarifying Teacher and Teaching Assistant Roles for Children With Special Educational Needs." *Learning and Instruction* 36: 1–10. doi:10.1016/j.learninstruc.2014.10.005.

Rubie-Davies, C. M., P. Blatchford, R. Webster, M. Koutsoubou, and P. Bassett. 2010. "Enhancing Learning? A Comparison of Teacher and Teaching Assistant Interactions with Pupils." *School Effectiveness and School Improvement* 21 (4): 429–449. doi:10.1080/09243453.2010.512800.

Sandmeier, A., D. K. Heim, B. Windlin, and A. Krause. 2017. "Negative Beanspruchung von Schweizer Lehrpersonen. Trends von 2006 bis 2014." *Schweizerische Zeitschrift für Bildungswissenschaften* 39 (1): 75–94. doi:10.24452/sjer.39.1.5000.

Schnebel, S., and S. Wagner. 2016. "Muster im Handeln von Lehrpersonen – Eine videobasierte Untersuchung von Lernunterstützung auf Mikroebene." *Lehrerbildung auf dem Prüfstand* 9 (2): 157–178.

Schrader, F.-W. 2013. "Diagnostische Kompetenz von Lehrpersonen." *Beiträge zur Lehrerinnenund Lehrerbildung* 31 (2): 154–165.

Sharma, U., and S. Salend. 2016. "Teaching Assistants in Inclusive Classrooms: A Systematic Analysis of the International Research." *Australian Journal of Teacher Education* 41 (8): 118–134. doi:10.14221/ajte.2016v41n8.7.

Simeonsson, R. J., G. S. Dawn Carlson, J. S. M. Huntington, and J. Lytle Brent. 2001. "Students with Disabilities: A National Survey of Participation in School Activities." *Disability and Rehabilitation* 23 (2): 49–63. doi:10.1080/096382801750058134.

Tews, L., and J. Lupart. 2008. "Students with Disabilities: Perspectives of the Role and Impact of Paraprofessionals in Inclusive Education Settings." *Journal of Policy and Practice in Intellectual Disabilities* 5 (1): 39–46. doi:10.1111/j.1741-1130.2007.00138.x.

Van De Pol, J., M. Volman, and J. Beishuizen. 2010. "Scaffolding in Teacher–Student Interaction: A Decade of Research." *Educational Psychology Review* 22 (3): 271–296. doi:10.1007/s10648-010-9127-6.

VERBI Software. 2018. *MAXQDA 2018* [Computer Software]. Berlin, Germany: VERBI Software.

Vogt, F. 2003. "New Managerialism and Primary Teachers' Collegiality and Teamwork." In *Leading People and Teams in Education*, edited by L. Kydd, L. Anderson, and W. Newton, 245–260. London: Paul Chapman.

Vogt, F. 2013. "Kompetenzen für eine adaptive Didaktik." In *Jahrbuch für Allgemeine Didaktik*, edited by K. Zierer, 196–202. Baltmannsweiler: Schneider Verlag Hohengehren. doi:10.18747/PHSG-coll3/id/750.

Webster, R., P. Blatchford, P. Bassett, P. Brown, C. Martin, and A. Russell. 2010. "Double Standards and First Principles: Framing Teaching Assistant Support for Pupils with Special Educational Needs." *European Journal of Special Needs Education* 25 (4): 319–336. doi:10.1080/08856257.2010.513533.

Webster, R., P. Blatchford, P. Bassett, P. Brown, C. Martin, and A. Russell. 2011. "The Wider Pedagogical Role of Teaching Assistants." *School Leadership & Management* 31 (1): 3–20. doi:10.1080/13632434.2010.540562.

Webster, R., P. Blatchford, and A. Russell. 2012. "Challenging and Changing How Schools Use Teaching Assistants: Findings from the Effective Deployment of Teaching Assistants Project." *School Leadership & Management* 1–19. doi:10.1080/13632434.2012.724672.

Wendelborg, C., and Tøssebro Jan. 2010. "Marginalisation Processes in Inclusive Education in Norway: A Longitudinal Study of Classroom Participation." *Disability & Society* 25 (6): 701–714. doi:10.1080/09687599.2010.505744.

Wood, D., J. S. Bruner, and G. Ross. 1976. "The Role of Tutoring in Problem Solving." *Journal of Child Psychology and Psychiatry* 17 (2): 89–100. doi:10.1111/j.1469-7610.1976.tb00381.x.

Zumwald, B. 2014. "Spannungsfelder beim Einsatz von Klassenassistenzen." *Schweizerische Zeitschrift für Heilpädagogik* 20 (4): 21–27.

Zumwald, B. 2015. "Professionalisierung von Lehrpersonen und Fachpersonen Sonderpädagogik für den Einsatz von Assistenzpersonal in inklusiven Schulmodellen." In *Veränderungen und Beständigkeit in Zeiten der Inklusion. Perspektiven sonderpädagogischer Professionalisierung*, edited by H. Redlich, L. Schäfer, G. Wachtel, K. Zehbe, and V. Moser, 44–54. Bad Heilbrunn: Klinkhardt.

8 The role of teaching assistants in managing behaviour in inclusive Catalan schools

Andrea Jardí, Ignasi Puigdellívol, Cristina Petreñas and Dorys Sabando

Introduction

One of the support measures various education systems (e.g. in the USA, the UK, Australia, New Zealand, Ireland, Canada, Cyprus, Finland, Iceland, Italy, Norway, Austria, Bulgaria, Portugal, Slovakia and Spain) have implemented to facilitate the presence of students in mainstream schools is the provision of teaching assistants (TAs) (Breyer, Lederer and Gasteiger-Klicpera 2020; Jardí, Puigdellívol and Petreñas 2018; Sharma and Salend 2016). The progressive transfer of students from special education schools to mainstream schools, which involves hiring non-teaching support personnel (Blatchford et al. 2009; Butt 2016), has also led to TAs becoming a key stakeholder in inclusion. Once students are present within classrooms, TAs and teachers have an important role to ensure the other two main principles of inclusion: participation and achievement (UNESCO 2009).

Much of the literature on TAs concerns their role relating to teaching and learning, and addresses matters such as the role and responsibilities of TAs and their training and supervision (Giangreco, Suter and Doyle 2010; Sharma and Salend 2016). Webster et al. (2011) proposed the wider pedagogical role which considers contextual factors, such as contract terms, preparation, provision of support and practices, which affect how TAs are deployed in instructional roles, but over which they have little or no control. High-intensity support for learning from a TA can restrict peer interactions and perpetuates a sense of the TA as the main person responsible for the student. Researchers recommend the sharing and exchange of roles, avoiding an over-reliance on TAs (Biggs, Gilson and Carter 2016; Butt 2016; Giangreco et al. 2005). The heavily reported 'Velcro effect' – whereby a student receives high amounts of intense one-to-one support from a TA – can be mitigated by not allocating a TA to a particular student (Giangreco et al. 2005). Butt (2016) proposes the Teacher Assistant As Facilitator (TAAF) model, whereby TAs help relatively more autonomous students in order to release teachers to support students who require more specialised or intensive forms of support.

DOI: 10.4324/9781003265580-12

Sharma and Salend's (2016) systematic review showed that the main instructional roles of TAs are academic support for students with disabilities and behaviour management. TAs assume this role in educational stages from pre-kindergarten classrooms to secondary school. Their contributions have been reported as helping to reduce the number of challenging behaviours (e.g. Walker and Snell 2017). A survey by Gibson, Paatsch and Toe (2016) found that both TAs and teachers had similar perception of behaviour-related roles. In an exploratory study conducted in Catalonia by Jardí, Puigdellívol and Petreñas (2018) contrasted the perceptions of the role TA should perform with the role they actually perform. They observed that a high percentage of TAs believed that they had been hired to deal with the students' behavioural problems, with even more TAs stating they were doing just that in practice. Moreover, almost one-fifth of the TAs questioned were solely responsible for the behaviour of the students.

Despite the fact that TAs take on behaviour management responsibilities, few descriptive studies have shown what they specifically do to manage student behaviour. Harris and Aprile (2015) found that as well as supervising students for behaviour reasons, TAs recorded behaviour-related information and participated in school committees and programmes on behaviour. McConkey and Abbott (2011) described TA participation in behaviour support teams (debating and making suggestions). While they stated that the primary responsibility for managing behaviour lies with the teacher, Radford et al. (2015) included behaviour management as part of the 'support role' for TAs. They proposed three functions: *recruitment* to get students involved, encouraging and engaging them in the main classroom activities; *direction maintenance* to guide students back to being on-task; and *contingency management/frustration control* which encompasses actions to help reduce anxiety or discomfort in students.

Rubie-Davies et al. (2010) showed that behaviour management by TAs is more reactive than when done by teachers. This suggests that teachers use strategies to prevent misbehaviours, perhaps handling them in a more inclusive way. Madden and Senior's (2017) mixed method study showed that training has a positive impact on the use of more effective proactive strategies among teachers. However, Clunies-Ross, Little and Kienhuis (2008) observe that the use of proactive strategies is not significantly associated with increased on-task behaviour. Although the use of reactive strategies is strongly associated with decreased on-task behaviour, they argue this is less due to using proactive strategies but rather replacing reactive strategies.

Beyond the integration of on-task management techniques within TAs' everyday classroom practice, some TAs implement specific behaviour regulation programmes and interventions. Examples include: *function-based classroom interventions* – which consist of understanding patterns of challenging behaviour and selecting effective strategies (Walker and Snell 2017); and *response interruption and redirection* – based on interrupting the target behaviour and redirecting it to a non-harmful response – (Giles et al. 2018). When TAs are specifically trained to deliver such interventions, they are reported to be effective; however, there are limitations insofar as the transferability of single-case designs, as well as no data tracking of the long-term maintenance and generalisation of these interventions.

That said, outside this context, there seems to be a persistent problem in that TAs are not generally trained for specialised behaviour interventions (Cardinal et al. 2017). Gibson's (2015) descriptive study noticed that implementing behaviour management programmes is one of the three tasks for which TAs feel least prepared. In a Northern Ireland study, behaviour management was identified as the greatest challenges by 84% of TAs (McConkey and Abbott 2011).

Managing student behaviour is not exclusive to TAs, but rather the responsibility of the whole school community. Giangreco (2021) emphasises that the roles of TAs must not be determined in an isolated manner and that teacher roles must first be established to then create opportunities for teacher–student collaboration and support. Yet, as Hendrix et al. (2018) mentioned, most research into behaviour interventions focuses on teachers, which means further study on how other stakeholders, including TAs, contribute to behaviour regulation is needed. The aim of the work reported in this chapter, therefore, is to address this gap by describing how TA-teacher teams manage disruptive behaviour in inclusive schools.

The Catalan context

Education in Spain is delegated to the 17 autonomous regions. Each region has its own education laws. In the Catalan education system, there are four types of TA role hired by the Department-of-Education: Preschool Education Specialists (PES), Social Integration Specialists (SIS), Special Education Educators (SEE) and Special Education Assistants (SEA). The SEEs and SEAs along with carers (subcontracted TAs) provide direct attention for students with disabilities or behaviour difficulties. The roles of SEEs, SEAs and Carers align with those internationally attributed to TAs. PESs are assigned in the first year of preschool (3 years old) in public schools, while SISs work support students in at-risk situations by intervening directly with them, their families and other social agents in the education community (Department-of-Education 2019).

Methods

The research reported in this chapter used a qualitative phenomenological approach in order to understand the qualities of a phenomenon within a particular context by studying the meaning people attribute to their experiences (Brantlinger et al. 2005).

Participants

Schools were selected on the basis of achieving high scores on the 'Survey on the Inclusive Profiles of Primary Schools in Catalonia' (Sabando, Puigdellívol and Torrado 2019). The survey identifies the degree of inclusion at each school based on six dimensions: school organisation; inclusive school climate; classroom organisation; educational support; and community involvement and lifelong learning.

TA-teacher teams in 14 Early and Primary schools took part in the study. Each participating TA was asked to identify the teacher with whom they felt they worked most effectively. These teachers were then approached to participate in the study. In some cases, more than one TA identified the same teacher. In total, the study recruited 17 TAs (94.12% women, aged 22–58, M = 41.35 SD = 11.06 years) and 12 form teachers (100% women, aged 31–49, M = 39.58, SD = 5.78).

Interviews

Semi-structured interviews were conducted with the participants on a one-to-one basis. Questions were structured around four themes: roles (including behaviour management); communication; interpersonal interaction; and professional identity. The average duration of the interviews was 43:30 minutes (range = 39–68).

Procedure

Authorisation was requested from the Consell d'Avaluació Superior (Catalan Government) to contact the most inclusive urban schools. They were informed of the aims of the research and the ethical aspects (European Commission 2013), ensuring their anonymity, confidentiality, feedback and the possibility of withdrawing consent at any time during the research. Participants agreed with the ethical aspects and signed an informed consent sheet. Interviews were recorded, transcribed and transcripts sent to each stakeholder to verify that their perspective was accurately represented, and provide any clarifications (e.g. nuances in vocabulary or expressions).

Data analysis

The interview data were subjected to an inductive thematic analysis. The analytical strategy for this multi-perspective design was the identification of the reciprocity of concepts (Larkin, Shaw and Flowers 2019), whereby the perceptions of and points raised by the different stakeholders (TAs and teachers) are shared in a complementary way.

A coding scheme relating to the experiences of disruptive behaviours was developed on the basis of a complete reading of all the interview transcripts. Themes and findings from prior research (e.g. Clarke and Visser 2016; Harris and Aprile 2015; Rubie-Davies et al. 2010; Walker and Snell 2017) were additionally considered in the development of the coding scheme. Consensus on the final coding scheme, shown in Table 8.1, was reached via a process of debate and validation among members of the research team. The interview data were analysed thematically using NVivo Plus 11.

Table 8.1 Coding categories and sub-codes

Code	Sub-code
Roles in behaviour management	Need for more adults
Coordination in behaviour management	Responsibilities
	Rules
Behaviour management procedures	Teamwork
	Teaching method
	Background identification
	Anticipation
	Systematic intervention procedures Strategies

Results

The presentation of the results of the analyses of the interview data on how TAs and teachers manage disruptive behaviour in inclusive Catalan schools is structured using the three main coding categories.

Roles in behaviour management

Participants described the externalisation of behaviours they considered disruptive. These ranged from screaming to physical aggression against classmates and/or materials. Schools assigned TAs to address disruptive behaviour even if their role was legally associated with supporting another student. This was due to the need to guarantee all students' safety and well-being. Teacher-1 explained the difficulty of managing behaviour incidences when there was only one adult in the classroom:

> I think we need many aides in mainstream classrooms. He can be so calm and then suddenly two minutes later, bam! You know? So, what am I supposed to do with him and 23 more? I want him to be just another student. If he takes off running, what do I do? Do I leave the 23 inside and go running after him? What am I supposed to do? [TAs] are absolutely important in schools.

All the teachers interviewed mentioned how important TAs are to working inclusively. As Teacher-12 articulated, they were essential to schools being able to offer a proactive and good quality response to disruptive behaviour incidents:

> Last Monday, I had to engage in real physical restraint. We were doing a group activity he didn't want to do. I gave him one opportunity after another and he continued bothering everyone, interrupting and increasing [. . .] we warned him, he got angry and that's when we had to engage in physical restraint because he was super angry, was spitting, biting, scratching and everything. But those things happen a lot more

when you're alone in a classroom. If a carer is there, we can anticipate it all and the carer just says, "Let's go out to the playground" and there's no conflict because someone was able to calmly and peacefully offer such a solution. This really minimized these behaviours. When there's just one person in a classroom, we're much more likely to end up with disruptive behaviour in the same situation.

Having two adults in the classroom allowed one to proceed with classroom activities and routines, while the other was free to intervene in the early stages of a disruptive, or potentially disruptive, incident. This complementarity had an effect on professionals' well-being. Teacher-7 mentioned feeling relaxed when two people were in the classroom as there was a sense of peace. Teacher-3 and Teacher-14 described how TAs calmed students outside of the room so that they were able to rejoin the group. Carer TA-18 explained how the educational attention students received was dependent on the teacher's attitude and their involvement in behaviour management to ensure students spend more time in the classroom.

The responsibilities TAs and teachers perceived as being attributed to TAs with respect to disruptive behaviour management depended on each teacher and the school's organisation. In general, TAs felt responsible for the students they had been employed to support, yet recognised that the teacher had the greater authority. Some professionals believed behaviour management was a shared task. There was a pragmatic dimension to this, insofar as 'whoever is closest' to the incident (Teacher-15; TA-15), or which adult had the stronger skills or better knowledge of the student (TA-21), responded first. In other cases, managing disruptive behaviour was delegated to the TA. Some participants (Teacher-9; TA-7) felt that teachers had given too much responsibility to TAs. TA-22 described how TAs had taken on the role of 'trouble-shooters':

> Well, we've always got a phone on hand because the form teachers can call us at any time. They'll say "hey, Sara's really edgy or José's..." They call us for everything. [. . .] We feel quite responsible. I mean, they make us feel responsible. If there's any kind of problem, they call us. [. . .] In this case, that's the way it is. I feel that's what it's like and the special education teacher does too. If the head teacher needs to speak to someone about those kids because there's been an issue, they talk to us, not the form teacher.

Teacher-15 described how TAs helped with behaviour in a broader sense. For example, the SIS (TA-8) was responsible for dealing with certain disruptive behaviours (e.g. disrespect, insults, threats) before (or to prevent) escalation to the head teacher. The SIS also provided mediation between students and held individual guidance sessions to identify causes of their troubles; for instance, problematic situations at home or social shyness. TAs in the SIS role also acted as a communication link with families.

Coordination in behaviour management

Teachers mentioned the existence of and adherence to basic school rules and routines, and some modelled these for students in their everyday practice. However, as one TA described, students with an intermittent record of attendance (e.g. for medical reasons) had difficulty retaining these routines.

Participants talked of the need to co-create and share rules and routines with students, and ensuring a consistent approach when teachers and TAs work alongside each other in the classroom. Teacher-14 remarked how it was considered important for adults to project unity and consistency to the students. TA-21 described the need for prior agreement on rules and coherent consequences in order to guarantee coexistence in the classroom:

> I think communication among everyone, teachers and non-teaching staff working with these students, is very important to uniting efforts. What I mean is that everyone should work in the same way. Agreeing "we're going to do it like this if there are certain behaviours" in the case of behaviour disorders is very important to setting up certain frameworks, you know? "If this happens, everyone has to do the same thing," talk about what can be allowed when the child may not be doing something on purpose but rather just can't control themselves and determine to what extent "this is allowable yet this should never be accepted". Communication is essential in these cases as is reaching an agreement on how to work.

Depending on the specific instance, some adults may deliberately ignore certain behaviours. This again required agreement between teachers and TAs in terms of which behaviours could be ignored and which could not. In Catalan schools, TAs often move from classroom to classroom, which means teachers must build consistent relationships with several TAs, and vice versa. Teacher-14 explained that this may lead to discrepancies and differences between teacher–TA teams within the same school.

Participants described the need to avoid the perception of a hierarchical relationship, where one adult gave orders to the other or was at risk of undermining them. Through their interactions with one another in the classroom, teachers and TAs wanted to ensure that students did not perceive one adult having less authority than the other. As TA-17 put it, practitioners did not want to appear as playing 'good cop/bad cop'. Teachers and TAs gave one another space to complete a behaviour correction, and not intervene.

Teacher-5, Teacher-18 and TA-8 mentioned *Attention to Diversity Committees*[1] as a formal meeting space to discuss student behaviours and effective responses. These meetings were described as useful in preventing instances disruptive behaviour (TA-8). The SEA (TA-7) and SEE (TA-10) explained how they made notes based on observations to discuss at these meetings. Less informal exchanges of information were also important to day-to-day operation.

Teacher-8 highlighted the importance of involving students in management and support processes and reminding them of their responsibilities, as a way of ensuring coherence and maintaining good classroom order. TA-8 mentioned the importance of involving other school staff in behaviour process and routines, such as in the canteen, and how effective communication is key to ensuring consistency:

> I normally stay for lunch and am around. If there's a conflict they can't handle or if children I normally work with are involved, they come get me. It happened a lot last year; this year not as much. But, we all have to work together. It doesn't matter if you're leading an extracurricular activity, monitoring the canteen or whatever. And it's important for the kids to know that. I see it like that and think if the children know we're all communicating, that I talk with the canteen supervisor, the girl who gives homework help ... Then, they say, my goodness everyone knows everything around here and we can also later talk about it more easily. I think communication is so very important. Good communication and always in a positive way. Of course, I'm always working with problems and you have to try to see the positive side of it all!

Behaviour management procedures

Participants mentioned the importance of the approach to teaching (teaching method) and the design of lesson activities as a strategy for minimising the potential for disruptive behaviour by maximising students' engagement (TA-7):

> His attention span is quite low, possibly three or four minutes when the others can concentrate for 20 minutes. So, when he gets bored, I tell him to do something else and this is the way it is all the time. You really need a lot of imagination or a whole lot of resources. They need double the material the others do. Why? Well, because they get tired and their boredom can turn into aggression or disconnection (sleeping).

Carer TA-5 believed it was important to have an adult nearby who encourages students to remain focussed on tasks and to persist with them. Teacher-3 indicated that it was necessary to anticipate how disruptive behaviour might affect a lesson, and make changes, if a particular activity was not going well. Designing suitable activities that best ensured student participation and engagement was a first prevention measure. TA-8 explained that supported students need activities that were similar to tasks given to the rest of the class, so supported students feel included.

Participants talked about how TAs were timetabled. The allocation of TAs' hours – and consequently how they were timetabled – was specified in a student's individual plans (Teacher-4). Teachers emphasised the importance of arranging TA support around the subjects and locations that caused students to be anxious (Teacher-1; Teacher-15), while being flexible and amenable to change part way through a course of study (Teacher-18). Teacher-15 mentioned the importance of avoiding grouping particular students with particular needs (e.g. relating to self-regulation) together.

Another element of effective behaviour management mentioned by participants was good knowledge of the students and the situations that can trigger disruptive behaviour, and which behaviour mitigation strategies they responded to (TA-13; TA-16). Carer (TA-5) explained the case of a student whose mood can be determined from the moment he enters the school, so welcoming him at the door in the morning, assessing his support needs throughout the day, and supporting basic needs such as sleep and physical well-being all helped to stabilise his behaviour.

Relatedly, participants talked about 'warning signs': the signals that indicate when students' behaviour is escalating. In such instances, practitioners could manage the situation and prevent negative behaviour by supporting verbal regulation (TA-1) or by deploying de-escalation strategies (Teacher-14; Teacher-8; Teacher-12; Teacher-3). Carer (TA-17) talked about a de-escalation strategy that required cooperation with the teacher and administrative personnel:

> When I would see her getting really distressed, I learnt to anticipate her actions. So, when I would see her getting angry for any reason: because her pencil was too short and she wanted another one or she would demand the tallest chair, I'd say "I have to go get something from the photocopier. Shall we go? Will you come with me?" and I'd take her to the porter: "We've come to get a paper from the photocopier" and, of course, she'd say "Yeah, this is it" and would give me a sheet from the recycling paper. "OK, this is what I needed" and while going down a floor in the building and going back up, she would change and could return to the class.

When there are serious cases of disruptive behaviour, school-wide agreements were reached on how to proceed by systematising intervention procedures. For example, TA-1 explained a process whereby a student is removed from the classroom (to protect him or her as well as the rest of the class) if prior steps to managing disruptive behaviour (e.g. talking to the student) are unsuccessful. The student returns to the class when they feel calm and their behaviour had stabilised. TA-22 said staff used mobile phones to call colleagues for support, while the teacher spoke with the student outside the classroom.

Discussion

The present study has provided evidence of TAs taking on specific roles in student behaviour management in Catalan schools, which is reflected in the broader international literature (Sharma and Salend 2016). Although the teacher is legally the main professional responsible for managing student behaviour, our data show that, in practice, TAs take on at least responsibility for behaviour management. Our study found experiences where there was a high level of reciprocity and equity, as well as others with an excessive delegation of responsibilities.

The literature on the role and impact of TAs has consistently shown that if TAs are not appropriately supported and trained, their interactions tend to be of lower quality than that of teachers (Rubie-Davies et al. 2010), and that the effects of this are greatest for the students most in need (Blatchford et al. 2009; Giangreco, Suter and Doyle 2010). Teamwork leads to better professional experiences for teachers and TAs, and the inclusive experiences for the students they teach and support (Ainscow 2001).

In the Catalan context, there is one type of TA role, the SIS, who has a specific role in managing co-existence in the school. Despite being trained in social integration (non-tertiary education) (Department-of-Education 2019), questions still remain as to the degree of responsibility and competencies with regard to certain behaviour-related practices. They are not 'miracle workers' (Lim, Wong and Tan 2014), however, and their work requires close collaboration with teachers, and so ought to be coordinated by support specialists with whom they can better overcome the barriers and foster inclusive education (Gómez-Zepeda et al. 2017).

Despite this, and contrary to some evidence (e.g. Walker and Snell 2017), our study found that TAs do not engage in behavioural interventions beyond the application of some protocol-based prevention strategies. The roles described here were more in line with Wilson, Schlapp and Davidson's (2003) description of providing an extra 'set of hands' in situations that can be more difficult to manage by one adult (the teacher) in the classroom. The presence of the TA makes proactive responses more achievable, which can prevent behaviour escalation (Webster-Stratton 2012) and the stigmatisation of students for whom regulating their behaviour is a particular challenge. Participants stated that preventive action to minimise disruptive behaviour contributes to all students' engagement and participation within classrooms, and avoids more restrictive and less inclusive measures. Prevention was considered essential for dealing with behaviour problems in an inclusive way, whenever they did arise.

Participants highlighted the importance of rules, routines and responses being consensual, coherent, contextualised and consistent. Professionals must analyse the behaviours, classify them, study measures and generalise them in appropriate contexts. *Attention to Diversity Committees* appears to provide a useful space for this. This practice is consistent with *consultation groups* (Hayes and Stringer 2016) in which teachers can raise opportunities for reflection, mutual support and generate and discuss strategies in order to improve their behaviour management skills. We argue that there is much to be gained from TAs also participating in these meetings.

Students must develop a system of values with socially accepted rules that help them choose more acceptable behaviours (Rokeach 1973). Professionals must not take these rules and functional routines for granted. Restorative practices can help to this end by putting students at the centre of behaviour management and co-existence (Bob, Wachtel and Wachtel 2010). Students must be sensitive to diversity and understand that in order to ensure overall compliance with the school's behaviour standards, some degree of flexibility is required. In the experiences reported, we observed that certain management situations involve turning the rest of the group into accomplices, and thereby turning peers into support agents. Beyond this, coherence and complicity must be guaranteed in all contexts, meaning communication with other stakeholders (e.g. families; canteen supervisors) is key to operating as a real support network (Puigdellívol et al. 2017) fostering inclusive education.

In addition to clarifying roles, responsibilities and expectations regarding behaviour, the findings reported here highlight the importance of the teaching approach to behaviour management. Planning and designing teaching sessions can help eliminate some of the barriers participants perceived as stimulating disruptive behaviours. In other words, prevention involves considering all students from the beginning as reflected by UDL (CAST 2011). Some of the strategies reported by the participants contributed to a decrease in absenteeism, sensitising students and other stakeholders, providing strategies and areas for mediation and conflict resolution and engaging the whole community as support stakeholders, as more inclusive and universal measures.

Participants highlighted the significance of anticipating behaviours in prevention; therefore, it is important to acknowledge precedents so as to improve the context in which they occur and study their functionality, so as to avoid them (Walker and Snell 2017). Participants described how identifying the warning signs of escalating behaviour helped minimise incidents. Although TAs and teachers in our study reported that challenging behaviours could not always be de-escalated, in such cases, they removed students from the class and worked with them outside the room in order to facilitate a safe return. As a last resort, some participants described having to use physical restraint, which is a widely debated responsive strategy requiring caution, consent and specific training (Madden and Senior 2017). Beyond the negative impact of reactive strategies (Clunies-Ross, Little and Kienhuis 2008), our participants agreed on the usefulness of sharing systematic intervention procedures, whether they are proactive or reactive, always maintaining inclusion as the goal.

Conclusions

Our findings have implications for school administrators since the presence of more than one adult within classrooms can help in preventing disruptive behaviours and assisting all students in a more inclusive way. Administrators should provide teamwork time to ensure reflection, discussion, learning and the implementation of consistent measures. TAs and other stakeholders who work with students should be included. Furthermore, schools should involve students considering them as support agents to ensure a good coexistence. The detailed first-hand experiences and strategies shared by TAs and teachers from inclusive-oriented schools may have implications for practices in other schools.

Acknowledgements

We would like to thank the reviewers; their suggestions strengthened the chapter. We would also thank the stakeholders involved in this investigation as well as the Consell Superior d'Avaluació del Sistema Educatiu for contacting the schools.

Originally published as Andrea Jardí, Ignasi Puigdellívol, Cristina Petreñas & Dorys Sabando (2021) The role of teaching assistants in managing behaviour in inclusive Catalan schools, European Journal of Special Needs Education, 36:2, 265-277, DOI: 10.1080/08856257.2021.1901376.

© Taylor & Francis Ltd (2021), reprinted by permission of the publisher.

Funding

The authors are grateful for the funding received from the Agency for Management of University and Research Grants – AGAUR (2017 ARMIF 0009 and 2017 SGR 322); the Institute of Education Sciences (REDICE 18-2061); and the fellowship of the Ministry of Education and Vocational Training (FPU16/00284) awarded to the first author.

Note

1 A multi-professional body that proposes, monitors, assesses and adjusts supports (Department-of-Education 2019).

References

Ainscow, M. 2001. *Desarrollo de escuelas inclusivas.* Madrid: Narcea.
Biggs, E. E., C. B. Gilson, and E. W. Carter. 2016. "Accomplishing More Together: Influences to the Quality of Professional Relationships between Special Educators and Paraprofessionals." *Research and Practice for Persons with Severe Disabilities* 41 (4): 256–272. doi:10.1177/1540796916665604.
Blatchford, P., P. Bassett, P. Brown, M. Koutsoubou, C. Martin, A. Russell, R. Webster, and C. Rubie-Davis. 2009. "Deployment and Impact of Support Staff in Schools: The Impact of Support Staff in Schools (Results from Strand 2, Wave-2)." Institute of Education, University of London. http://discovery.ucl.ac.uk/10001336/1/Blatchford2008Deployment.pdf
Bob, C., J. Wachtel, and T. Wachtel. 2010. *Manual dePrácticas Restaurativas para docentes, personal responsable de la disciplina y administradores de instituciones educativas.* Bethlehem, Pennsylvania: International Institute for Restorative Practices.

Brantlinger, E., R. Jimenez, J. Klingner, M. Pugach, and V. Richardson. 2005. "Qualitative Studies in Special Education." *Exceptional Children* 71 (2): 195–207. doi:10.1177/001440290507100205.

Breyer, C., J. Lederer, and B. Gasteiger-Klicpera. 2020. "Learning and Support Assistants in Inclusive Education: A Transnational Analysis of Assistance Services in Europe." *European Journal of Special Needs Education* 1–14. doi:10.1080/08856257.2020.1754546.

Butt, R. 2016. "Teacher Assistant Support and Deployment in Mainstream Schools." *International Journal of Inclusive Education* 20 (9): 995–1007. doi:10.1080/13603116.2016.1145260.

Cardinal, J. R., T. P. Gabrielsen, E. L. Young, B. D. Hansen, R. Kellems, H. Hoch, T. Nicksic-Springer, and J. Knorr. 2017. "Discrete Trial Teaching Interventions for Students with Autism: Web-Based Video Modeling for Paraprofessionals." *Journal of Special Education Technology* 32 (3): 138–148. doi:10.1214/16-BA971REJ.

CAST. 2011. *Universal Design for Learning Guidelines Version 2.0*. Wakeeld, MA: Author.

Clarke, E., and J. Visser. 2016. "Teaching Assistants Managing Behaviour – Who Knows How They Do It? A Review of Literature." *Support for Learning* 31 (4): 266–280. doi:10.1111/1467-9604.12137.

Clunies-Ross, P., E. Little, and M. Kienhuis. 2008. "Self-reported and Actual Use of Proactive and Reactive Classroom Management Strategies and Their Relationship with Teacher Stress and Student Behaviour." *Educational Psychology: An International Journal of Experimental Educational Psychology* 28 (6): 693–710. doi:10.1080/01443410802206700.

Department-of-Education. 2019. *Document per a L'organitzatió I La Gestió Dels Centres 2019–20*. Barcelona: Generalitat de Catalunya.

European Commission. 2013. *Ethics for Researchers: Facilitating Research Excellence in FP7*. Brussels: European Union. doi:10.2777/7491.

Giangreco, M. F. 2021. "Maslow's Hammer: Teacher Assistant Research and Inclusive Practices at a Crossroads." *European Journal of Special Needs Education*.

Giangreco, M. F., J. C. Suter, and M. B. Doyle. 2010. "Paraprofessionals in Inclusive Schools: A Review of Recent Research." *Journal of Educational and Psychological Consultation* 20 (1): 41–57. doi:10.1080/10474410903535356.

Giangreco, M. F., S. Yuan, B. McKenzie, P. Cameron, and J. Fialka. 2005. "'Be Careful What You Wish for…': Five Reasons to Be Concerned about the Assignment of 'Individual' Paraprofessionals." *Teaching Exceptional Children* 37 (5): 28. doi:10.1177/004005990503700504.

Gibson, D. 2015. "Teachers' Aides' Perceptions of Their Training Needs in Relation to Their Roles in State Secondary Schools in Victoria." *Disability Studies* 23–41. doi:10.1007/978-94-6300-199-1_2.

Gibson, D., L. Paatsch, and D. Toe. 2016. "An Analysis of the Role of Teachers' Aides in a State Secondary School: Perceptions of Teaching Staff and Teachers' Aides." *Australasian Journal of Special Education* 40 (1): 1–20. doi:10.1017/jse.2015.11.

Giles, A., S. Swain, L. Quinn, and B. Weifenbach. 2018. "Teacher-Implemented Response Interruption and Redirection: Training, Evaluation, and Descriptive Analysis of Treatment Integrity." *Behavior Modification* 42 (1): 148–169. doi:10.1177/0145445517731061.

Gómez-Zepeda, G., C. Petreñas, D. Sabando, and I. Puigdellívol. 2017. "The Role of the Support and Attention to Diversity Teacher (SADT) from a Community-Based Perspective: Promoting Educational Success and Educational Inclusion for All." *Teaching and Teacher Education* 64: 127–138. doi:10.1016/j.tate.2017.02.002.

Harris, L. R., and K. T. Aprile. 2015. "'I Can Sort of Slot into Many Different Roles': Examining Teacher Aide Roles and Their Implications for Practice." *School Leadership & Management* 35 (2): 140–162. doi:10.1080/13632434.2014.992774.

Hayes, M., and P. Stringer. 2016. "Introducing Farouk's Process Consultation Group Approach in Irish Primary Schools." *Educational Psychology in Practice Theory* 32 (2): 145–162. doi:10.1080/02667363.2015.1129939.

Hendrix, N. M., S. M. Vancel, A. L. Bruhn, S. Wise, and S. Kang. 2018. "Paraprofessional Support and Perceptions of a Function-Based Classroom Intervention." *Preventing School Failure: Alternative Education for Children and Youth* 62 (3): 214–228. doi:10.1080/1045988X.2018.1425974.

Jardí, A., I. Puigdellívol, and C. Petreñas. 2018. "Teacher Assistants' Roles in Catalan Classrooms: Promoting Fair and Inclusion-Oriented Support for All." *International Journal of Inclusive Education* 1–16. doi:10.1080/13603116.2018.1545876.

Larkin, M., R. Shaw, and P. Flowers. 2019. "Multiperspectival Designs and Processes in Interpretative Phenomenological Analysis Research Phenomenological Analysis Research." *Qualitative Research in Psychology* 16 (2): 182–198. doi:10.1080/14780887.2018.1540655.

Lim, S. M.-Y., M. E. Wong, and D. Tan. 2014. "Allied Educators (Learning and Behavioural Support) in Singapore's Mainstream Schools: First Steps Towards Inclusivity?" *International Journal of Inclusive Education* 18 (2): 123–139. doi:10.1080/13603116.2012.758321.

Madden, L. O. B., and J. Senior. 2017. "A Proactive and Responsive Bio-Psychosocial Approach to Managing Challenging Behaviour in Mainstream Primary Classrooms Challenging Behaviour in Mainstream Primary Classrooms." *Emotional and Behavioural Difficulties* 1–17. doi:10.1080/13632752.2017.1413525.

McConkey, R., and L. Abbott. 2011. "Meeting the Professional Needs of Learning Support Assistants for Pupils with Complex Needs." *Procedia-Social and Behavioral Sciences* 15: 1419–1424. doi:10.1016/j.sbspro.2011.03.305.

Puigdellívol, I., S. Molina, D. Sabando, G. Gómez, and C. Petreñas. 2017. "When Community Becomes an Agent of Educational Support: Communicative Research on Learning Communities in Catalonia." *Disability & Society* 7599 (June): 1–20. doi:10.1080/09687599.2017.1331835.

Radford, J., P. Bosanquet, R. Webster, and P. Blatchford. 2015. "Scaffolding Learning for Independence: Clarifying Teacher and Teaching Assistant Roles for Children with Special Educational Needs." *Learning and Instruction* 36: 1–10. doi:10.1016/j.learninstruc.2014.10.005.

Rokeach, M. 1973. *The Nature of Human Values*. New York: Free Press.

Rubie-Davies, C. M., P. Blatchford, R. Webster, M. Koutsoubou, and P. Bassett. 2010. "Enhancing Learning? A Comparison of Teacher and Teaching Assistant Interactions with Pupils." *School Effectiveness and School Improvement* 21 (4): 429–449. doi:10.1080/09243453.2010.512800.

Sabando, D., I. Puigdellívol, and M. Torrado. 2019. "Measuring the Inclusive Profile of Public Elementary Schools in Catalonia." *International Journal of Educational Research* 96 (2019): 1–20. doi:10.1016/j.ijer.2019.05.002.

Sharma, U., and S. J. Salend. 2016. "Teaching Assistants in Inclusive Classrooms: A Systematic Analysis of the International Research." *Australian Journal of Teacher Education* 41 (8): 118–134. doi:10.14221/ajte.2016v41n8.7.

UNESCO. 2009. *Defining an Inclusive Education Agenda: Reflections around the 48th. Session of the International Conference on Education*. Geneva: International Bureau of Education.

Walker, V. L., and M. E. Snell. 2017. "Teaching Paraprofessionals to Implement Function-Based Interventions." *Focus on Autism and Other Developmental Disabilities* 32 (2): 114–123. doi:10.1177/1088357616673561.

Webster, R., P. Blatchford, P. Bassett, P. Brown, C. Martin, and A. Russell. 2011. "The Wider Pedagogical Role of Teaching Assistants." *School Leadership and Management* 31 (1): 3–20. doi:10.1080/13632434.2010.540562.

Webster-Stratton, C. 2012. *Incredible Teachers, Nurturing Children's Social, Emotional, and Academic Competence*. USA: Incredible Years.

Wilson, V., U. Schlapp, and J. Davidson. 2003. "An 'Extra Pair of Hands'? Managing Classroom Assistants in Scottish Primary Schools." *Educational Management & Administration* 31 (2): 189–258. doi:10.12968/bjon.2017.26.5.258.

9 Secondary teachers' perspectives on their work with teacher assistants

Claire Jackson, Umesh Sharma and Delphine Odier-Guedj

Introduction

Over the past 30 years Australia has followed a similar trajectory to many developed countries as the number of teacher assistants (TAs) employed in mainstream schools has increased steadily, predominantly as a means by which to support students with disability (Butt 2016; Giangreco 2013; Sharma and Salend 2016; Webster and Blatchford 2020). Currently in Australia there is no mandated formal qualification required to work as a TA (Australian Government 2021). At the time this study took place, the percentage of Australian school students receiving educational adjustments due to disability, as defined by the Disability Discrimination Act 1992 (Australian Government 1992), was 20.3%. Disaggregation of this data shows that this percentage was slightly higher in schools in the state of Victoria (21.1%), where this study took place, and marginally lower across Australian Catholic schools (19.1%) which is the sector from which the sample of teachers was selected (ACARA 2020). In this chapter, TA is used synonymously with other international terms such as 'teaching assistant', 'aide', 'learning support assistant' and 'paraprofessional'.

In many instances TAs are employed in schools to provide support for students with disability, under the assumption that these students depend on TA support to access and participate in education (Giangreco and Doyle 2007). This model has been considered an effective approach to support students with disability, with many holding the view that TAs play an essential role in supporting both students and teachers (Harris and Aprile 2015). Giangreco (2021) likens this long-standing reliance on TAs to a cognitive bias known as 'Maslow's Hammer', whereby educators tend to apply familiar solutions to problems at the exclusion of potentially more appropriate solutions. In secondary schools, teachers themselves often regard the presence of a TA in their lesson as the most appropriate tool (the Maslow's Hammer) to support inclusive practices.

Several studies indicate that teachers benefit from having TAs in their lessons due to the positive effects of reduced workload and stress (Blatchford, Russell and Webster 2012). However, having a TA present in a class does not automatically lead to improved outcomes for students. The collaborative

DOI: 10.4324/9781003265580-13

relationship between the teacher and TA is considered a key factor in promoting inclusion (Ainscow 2000). Teachers play a significant role in ensuring students gain maximum benefit from having an additional adult present in their lesson (Biggs, Gilson and Carter 2019). However, this is contingent on teachers having a clear understanding of TAs' and teachers' roles in working effectively together.

Ineffective support from TAs has been shown to impact negatively on the learning outcomes of students and may lead to students feeling isolated and stigmatised (Sharma and Salend 2016). Although students may demonstrate improvements in confidence and on-task behaviour, evidence from large-scale research indicates that the presence of a TA in a classroom can have a negative effect on student attainment, particularly for students with additional learning support needs (Blatchford, Russell and Webster 2012). When schools do not have structures in place to promote effective teacher practice in working with TAs, TAs could become a high-cost resource that has a low impact on student learning (Evidence for Learning 2020).

While often there is an assumption that teachers understand how to work effectively with TAs, there is hardly any evidence that this critical aspect is specifically addressed in pre-service teacher education programs (O'Rourke and West 2015). Australian research relating to how teachers work with TAs is scarce. Most Australian researchers have predominantly looked at the work of TAs and less so on how teachers perceive their work with TAs (Butt 2016; Gibson, Paatsch and Toe 2016; Harris and Aprile 2015; O'Rourke and West 2015). Raising awareness of the work of teachers with TAs can inform us about how best to enhance collaboration and potentially improve training programs available to pre-service and in-service teachers.

The current study was undertaken to explore teachers' perceptions of their work with TAs in order to establish whether there is scope for schools to improve collaboration between teachers and TAs. While research on this topic is limited in general, it is even more scarce within secondary schools. In this study, we examined secondary teachers' perspectives about working with TAs. The study examined how teachers and TAs collaborate in a secondary school context as well as what teachers identify as helping or hindering their work together. The following research questions were used to guide the interviews:

1. How do teachers perceive their work with teacher assistants?
2. How do teachers work with TAs and what influences their work?
3. What do teachers identify as facilitators and barriers in working with TAs?

Methods

An interpretive paradigm was used in order to understand the meaning attributed by teachers to their working reality. Open-ended questions were used to collect data. They allowed the participants to freely voice their experiences and minimised the influence of the researchers' attitudes, knowledge and experiences (Creswell 2009). This small-scale study was part of a larger mixed methods study and preceded a more comprehensive quantitative study measuring teacher self-efficacy when working with TAs. TAs were not included in this study as the focus was on the work on teachers and their perceptions regarding the manner in which they work with TAs.

Participants

A purposive sample of teachers was taken from two mainstream Catholic secondary schools in Melbourne, Australia, with ethics approval from Monash University and Melbourne Archdiocese Catholic Schools (MACS). The schools were nominated by MACS as they employed at least three TAs. An expression of interest was sought through an email sent to the principals from the selected schools. The teachers who volunteered to be involved in the research ($N = 16$) participated in discussions centred around their experiences working with TAs.

Two focus groups, lasting one hour, were conducted at the participants' schools on a student-free day in December 2019. Participants included seven classroom teachers at School One and eight at School Two. Participation in the discussions provided the teachers with the opportunity to discuss what worked well in their daily interactions with TAs and what hindered their work. The guiding questions related to the way the teachers worked with TAs, who supervised their work, and the challenges they experienced in their work together. For example:

1. What type of work do the TAs in this school do?
2. How is the work of the TAs determined?
3. Who decides how the TA will be used in lessons?
4. What does it typically look like in classrooms when a TA is present?
5. Who does the TA work with when in class?
6. What are some of the positives about having a TA in class?
7. What are some of the challenges faced by teachers when working with TAs?

In addition to the teachers who participated in the focus group at School One, the Inclusion Leader (IL) participated in a semi-structured interview, guided by similar questions. This option was made available due to a potential power imbalance within a group where a perceived hierarchical relationship may exist. In the Australian context, the IL is a specialist teacher who holds a leadership position. It is typically a consultative, capacity building and administrative role, supporting the work of teachers and TAs in relation to the inclusion of students with disability and complex learning profiles. This position is often also referred to as the Learning Support Coordinator or Learning Diversity Leader and, although not mandated, it is desirable that teachers working in this capacity hold master's qualifications specialising in inclusive education or a similar field.

School One is a medium-sized coeducational secondary school in metropolitan Melbourne, with a student enrolment of 623. The school employs 56.4 full-time equivalent (FTE) teachers and 4.4 FTE TAs; 15.8% of students in the school receive educational adjustments due to disability. School Two is a medium-sized boys' secondary school also located in metropolitan Melbourne, with 921 students, 71.8 FTE teachers and 3 FTE TAs; 12.8% of students receive disability-related adjustments.

Data collection and analysis

The focus groups and semi-structured interview were recorded and transcribed by the first author. Participants were pseudonymised. The authors analysed data manually for themes following Braun and Clarke's (2006) six-step process, namely, (1) data familiarisation, (2) generation of initial codes, (3) searching for themes, (4) reviewing themes, (5) defining and naming themes, and (6) writing up the chapter.

This flexible approach enabled the authors to conduct a rigorous analysis of the codes identified in the data, categorise these codes and reach consensus on key patterns. We used a pre-existing coding frame determined by the themes that research on this topic has previously identified. Differing interpretations were discussed until agreement was reached according to the requirements for validity and rigour in qualitative research (Bazeley 2013).

Results

The process of thematic analysis led to the identification of nine dominant codes relating to factors that facilitate and inhibit the work of teachers with TAs. There was considerable overlap and interplay between the ideas discussed within each of the codes. The three key themes that emerged from and are linked to these codes have been labelled as follows: *clarity of roles*; *collaboration and consultation*; and *organisational structures*. Each of the themes is discussed under the headings that follow.

Clarity of roles

Two subthemes arose regarding role clarity. First, there were ambiguous beliefs regarding who should take responsibility for *leading the work of TAs*. Second, there were conflicting opinions relating to the *role of the TA*.

Leading the work of TAs

It was apparent that in each school there were inconsistencies in teachers' perceptions relating to whose responsibility it was to lead the work of the TA. One experienced teacher reflected that he didn't ever recall having a specific conversation with a TA about the way they were going to work with a student. Some participants expressed a desire for improved structure and consistency in the way teachers and TAs work together, and a need for clarity regarding TAs' responsibilities, whilst others perceived flexibility as an asset and a strength in the way students were supported. Some teachers believed the IL was responsible for determining the work of TAs; others believed TAs decided how they would work and who they would support, and a few teachers indicated they were responsible for leading the work of TAs.

Role of the TA

Confusion emerged in relation to the degree to which TAs should be involved in teaching students and adapting and modifying curriculum. Participants were equivocal in their views regarding what level of responsibility TAs should be given. Some teachers were certain that TAs should not take on pedagogical responsibilities and should be considered as 'an extra resource in their class and (the teacher should) direct what's happening in each of those classes'. Others noted that it helped to relieve pressure when the TA sourced learning materials for them, and they valued their input regarding the suitability of work for particular students with diverse learning profiles. Several teachers expressed a desire to have TAs adjust and modify learning tasks for students. In some cases, TAs were given the responsibility of teaching students in specialist areas such as instructing students in how to play the keyboard in a music lesson. Teachers commented that matching TAs' skills to the support required was an effective way to work together and TAs enjoyed being able to show initiative and be involved in instruction. However, it was noted that in secondary schools it was often challenging for TAs to work in classes when an understanding of specific curriculum content was required that was unfamiliar to the TA. Some teachers suggested that providing learning materials prior to the lesson helped TAs improve their subject knowledge. Others made time to discuss content together prior to lessons; however, a recurring concern raised by most was that in a busy secondary school, it was a challenge to find time to meet with TAs.

TAs in both schools were given a level of responsibility for supervising students; however, it was not clear whether TAs were given the same supervisory responsibilities as teachers, nor was it clear who held the duty of care for students and whether this was tailored to their qualifications or experience. Some teachers noted that TAs were general 'go-to' people when students needed additional help in many aspects of their learning, with the role extending to providing counselling to students. TAs who held teaching qualifications were well regarded by the participants, but it was apparent that this may have led teachers to abrogate certain responsibilities beyond those expected of a TA, given their previous experience as a teacher.

It was apparent that the role of TAs was fluid and required a level of adaptability depending on the highest need on any particular day. TAs were often required to deviate from their original timetable to respond to situations where they were needed most, such as to provide supervision on excursions, in examinations or to accompany students on placements at courses with external providers. It was also noted that within the classroom, there were different ways TAs could work. For example, one teacher stated:

> In Year 9 English we teach classes in the flexible working space, so you have essentially three classes running at the one time. So, our (TA) would not only help those students with needs but be wandering around the whole open learning area and would be a very familiar face to all the students so that she basically would be helping everyone but then making sure that our one particular student was getting the help that she needed.

TAs in these classes were regarded as a general support for all students rather than to provide targeted support for selected students.

Ability to collaborate and consult

The second major theme to emerge from the data highlighted many of the benefits of a collaborative and consultative teacher–TA relationship. Three subthemes that emerged related to *working together, time constraints* and *valuing TA's knowledge and skills.*

Working together

Several participants discussed the dynamics of their working relationships, explaining that they valued TA input into their planned learning activities. The IL described how she managed online lessons when working with a TA. Although the collaborative relationship was teacher driven, the TA was given opportunities to work with small groups or individual students, which the IL found was an effective use of their time. Another participant observed that her relationship with TAs had changed over time and rather than directing the work of the TA, she found she had begun asking the TA their opinion about how a planned lesson might work for various students, taking into consideration TA suggestions when making adjustments. Another teacher highlighted the benefits of online collaborative documents to facilitate collaborative planning:

> When I'm planning a unit, I will share it on Google Docs to my [TAs] and then they can cast their eyes over it. We'll talk about how they'll support the students ... they can edit and they can give me feedback ... and they will give me feedback ... very honest feedback.

Time constraints

A key point raised in each discussion was that having time or processes available to plan work together in advance was considered a significant contributor to an effective working relationship, however, in secondary schools, limited time was perceived as a major barrier to effective collaborative practice. It was noted that in most instances planning occurred 'on the fly' due to teachers' heavy workloads, hectic timetables and time constraints. As two teachers explained:

> If we had time to plan and time to devise goals that would be a lot more efficient and possibly a lot more ... focused, I guess. You could get something a bit more directed. That would be really helpful.
>
> We are so rushed off our feet, that if we had that time then we would know how to work with them or how to change our professional relationship with them. Time is such a big constraint.

A third teacher at the school felt pessimistic about having time available to collaborate before lessons, explaining:

> In the dream world, we'd have time to sit and plan with them. And you just don't. There just isn't the time and so it's on the fly. Most of mine is after the class ... pre-planning would be great but it's just not going to happen.

Valuing TAs' knowledge and skills

Participants in both schools commented that TAs having prior knowledge of a topic helped with establishing a collaborative relationship, as they were familiar with learning tasks, having worked in the same subject or year level in previous years. Teachers having an awareness of TAs' unique talents and interests were also found to facilitate collaborative working relationships. In addition, participants agreed on the benefits of TA retention. Longevity of service was regarded as highly desirable and contributed to more collaborative and consultative discussions, when TAs were familiar with school structures, course content and student characteristics.

The IL observed that there was room to raise the status and profile of TAs in her school by 'seeing them as a collaborator in the classroom rather than someone who is there just to sit next to a student and help them with their work'. It was also noted that as secondary students reached their final years of schooling, they were often self-conscious about receiving additional support from a TA. One teacher suggested this stigma was reduced when she introduced the TA to the class as another adult she was collaborating with who was present to help everyone. She explained:

> I know there's always been this fear ... the kids don't want them (the TAs) in there as support because they don't want to look any different to anyone else. So, in the lesson after I've done my explicit teaching and I'm getting the students on to task-based stuff, I will actually point out to the students "we've got two adults in the room today to help you all".

Many of the teachers also commented on the benefits of TAs knowing the students. They explained that in a busy secondary school, teachers were constantly moving from class to class, but some TAs might follow one or a few students over the school day and could provide valuable feedback on how particular students were tracking. Teachers also noted that TAs' prior knowledge of students' individual needs at the commencement of a new school year was highly valued and enabled them to rapidly collaborate when TAs were able to provide input into the strategies that had previously been successful for students.

Influence of organisational structures

The final theme evident in discussions with teachers was that organisational structures had the potential to facilitate or inhibit effective working relationships between teachers and TAs. Four subthemes arose from the discussions: *school processes*, *leadership*, *capacity building* and *school funding*.

School processes

Organisational influences included small-scale factors in the classroom within the control of the teacher such as having access to TAs to help students organise themselves, colour-code their timetables and folders and set up their lockers. Larger-scale organisational influences encompassed school-wide processes that were beyond teachers' control, which typically related to timetabling and time constraints. In some cases, national-level policies and those determined by individual state and territory education departments also had the potential to impact the working relationship between teachers and TAs. For example, changes in a national school funding model for students with disability led to TAs working with broader groups of students requiring support rather than those with specific diagnoses, which was symptomatic of a previous categorical funding model.

Discussions in relation to technology highlighted its potential to support the work of teachers with TAs. For example, learning management systems providing easy access to staff timetables were described as helpful in enabling teachers to plan for the presence of TAs in their lessons. Collaborative cloud-based documents were also popular as a method to share documents with TAs and gain input into lesson plans and feedback from TAs on support provided to students. It was also noted that ensuring TAs had access to email and school communications enabled effective collaboration with teachers. This extended to TAs having ready access to school devices such as tablets and laptops.

Timetabling was recognised as driving many secondary school processes and thoughtful allocation of TAs made a significant difference to the continuity of support for students. For example, teachers in School One were critical of a previous model of support whereby TAs were allocated to classes on an ad hoc basis. They expressed a preference for the reviewed organisational structure where TAs were allocated in a consistent and transparent manner, regularly attending the same lessons with the same students and teachers. They commented that working with fewer TAs made a positive difference to the support provided to students, as TAs were familiar with what had been covered in previous lessons and could track student progress more effectively. A further benefit of careful timetabling was that TAs' skills were better matched to the subjects where they provided support. It was noted, though, that one-to-one allocation of TAs to students was avoided where possible, so students had the opportunity to develop relationships with peers rather than become overly dependent on adult support. For example, one teacher described the approach a TA in her lesson took to encourage independence:

> (TAs) were really good at setting boundaries of "I will help you for ten minutes but then I need to go and help this person" and that was a really important skill that those students needed to learn because they needed to move away from that one-to-one help all the time and develop some ability … to work independently.

TAs who demonstrated flexibility and the ability to show initiative were highly valued. When teachers provided learning materials to TAs in advance, they observed that those who read through the materials prior to lessons were much better prepared for what was going to be covered, were able to participate more fully and provide more quality support. Teachers found that there were times when they did not need TA support in their class, and they were able to suggest that TAs could find alternative classes to support. In these instances, other teachers and students were the beneficiaries of additional support. This rapid deployment was facilitated by accessible timetable systems whereby TAs were able to locate students, teachers and classrooms efficiently, and maximise support available for all students.

Leadership

Supportive leadership structures were regarded as a factor that facilitated the collaboration between teachers and TAs. In secondary schools this leadership of TAs is typically multifaceted, extending from the principal and sometimes the business manager, to middle leadership positions, through to the IL and classroom teachers, with each layer of leadership playing a role in leading the work of TAs. In School One, recent changes in principalship and the appointment of an IL in a role that had undergone review were seen as contributing factors to improved support for all students. Teachers were positive regarding the support available to them from the IL and felt that regular meetings between the IL and TAs helped with planning effective support for teachers and students. Teachers reported that the profiles of TAs had been raised and their roles celebrated due to the restructure of the department.

They also appreciated greater access to professional reading materials through regular newsletters from the IL, although they regretted not having the time to read through all of the information shared.

Capacity building

Feedback from teachers was unanimous when asked if they had received any professional learning in how to work with TAs. All participants denied receiving any formal or informal training in this regard. They also noted that it was not required to be covered in any formal pre- or in-service teacher education programs or as part of their teacher registration requirements. The IL expressed surprise that her master's degree specialising in learning intervention did not include any focus on the work of teachers with TAs. All teachers expressed a desire to learn more about how they could improve their practice in this respect, particularly in a secondary school setting.

Funding

At a national level, teachers described a new Australian funding model for students with disability, introduced in 2018, as having a positive impact on their work with TAs, despite the additional administrative demands it placed on them. This new model, the Nationally Consistent Collection of Data on School Students with Disability (NCCD), requires schools to maintain evidence of the adjustments provided for students, which includes the support provided by TAs. It was noted that this increased the level of accountability required when TAs worked with students and it also raised the profile of the work of TAs, as the support they provided to specific students was recognised and documented. Although the new model encourages school teams to consider investing funding into a variety of adjustments to support the inclusion of students with disability, it was apparent that teachers in this research still regarded TAs as the 'Maslow's Hammer' solution at the expense of considering alternative adjustments. The NCCD also adds an additional layer of complexity to the role of the IL who highlighted the significant demands of the role in ensuring the school met its requirements in relation to the NCCD. The IL in School One expressed gratitude about her principal's decision to allocate her TA time for NCCD administrative support one day per week.

Discussion

The aim of this study was to gain greater insight into secondary teachers' perspectives regarding their work with TAs, and to better understand teacher practices that had the potential to facilitate or hinder collaborative relationships with TAs. The findings demonstrated that teachers were mostly aware of factors that contributed to positive working relationships with TAs and were readily able to discuss what was not working well in their contexts.

However, what was most apparent from the discussions in both schools was that there were inconsistencies in the way teachers worked with TAs, leading to confusion regarding what could be considered some of the 'best' ways to maximise their professional partnership. A second unanimous and clear concern was that time constraints in a busy secondary school impacted on teachers' ability to effectively collaborate with TAs. Organisational structures were highlighted as the third factor influencing teachers' work with TAs. A final observation from this research is that the findings mirror concerns raised by Giangreco (2021); that TAs are viewed as the Maslow's Hammer, with no mention made of alternative tools to support inclusive practice or of alternative approaches to using funding for students with disability.

Teachers' perceptions identified in this research, combined with existing literature previously systematically reviewed by the authors, allow us to make several propositions for schools and universities regarding the way secondary teachers are prepared and supported in developing and maintaining effective partnerships with TAs.

Clarity of roles

First, there is an urgent need for TAs' roles to be clearly defined to avoid confusion and misunderstandings regarding their responsibilities. None of the participants referred to TAs' role descriptions nor indicated they were aware of an organisational structure where reporting lines were clear. To facilitate an effective working relationship, teachers need to understand the delineation between their role and the TA so they can make informed decisions about how they plan to work together. This is supported by recurrent international studies highlighting the need for schools to ensure there is a consistent understanding amongst staff regarding the duties TAs should perform (Webster and De Boer 2021). Furthermore, lack of clarity and school-wide agreement in relation to role expectations for TAs leads to a significant reduction in effective inclusive practice (Webster, Blatchford and Russell 2013).

In clarifying the role of TAs, it is imperative that their pedagogical responsibilities are commensurate with their level of training and the role for which they are employed, even if the TA holds teaching qualifications. This is particularly pertinent in the secondary context, where teachers have attained a high level of subject-specific knowledge and teaching competency that the TA may not have. Literature consistently shows that there is confusion amongst teachers regarding the role of the TA (Gibson, Paatsch and Toe 2016). The consensus is that teachers should have responsibility for overseeing the learning needs of all students and TAs should not have the sole charge of those students they work with (Butt 2016). Whilst the presence of TAs is intended to support students' learning and social outcomes, students may be placed at a disadvantage if they are taught by an untrained adult performing tasks beyond their level of expertise (Gibson, Paatsch and Toe 2016). However, more recent research indicates a more effective and precise deployment of TAs that avoids the bluntness of Maslow's Hammer (Giangreco 2021) is for TAs to deliver specific targeted interventions (Sharples 2016).

Finally, all students should have fair access to teachers, and this is more likely to occur if the roles and responsibilities of TAs are clearly understood by teachers. In examining teacher–student interactions, Cameron (2014) identified that teachers often transfer the responsibility of educating students with disability to TAs, resulting in teachers having reduced contact with these students. This is due to teachers' perceptions that the TA is responsible for students with disability, and that if the teacher gives individual support to these students, the remaining students in the class are disadvantaged by having less contact with the teacher. Similarly, Butt (2016) found when teachers have a clear understanding of the role of TAs, they spend more time working with students with disability when TAs are present in the lesson, rather than abrogating their teaching responsibilities to TAs.

Ability to consult and collaborate

A further proposition that can be made is that support for students is improved when there are opportunities for teachers and TAs to consult and collaborate. For example, including TAs in planning, monitoring and reviewing students' personalised goals can help to clarify the differing roles both the teacher and TA play in supporting the student. This research highlighted a tension between what teachers perceived was effective practice and what they felt they were able to realistically execute in a busy secondary school environment. These findings mirror previous research emphasising that effective communication with TAs is a key competency of teachers when working with TAs (Ashbaker and Morgan 2012; Sobeck et al. 2021). Furthermore, teachers' organisational skills influence relationships with TAs. For example, TA practice is enhanced when teachers are well prepared and organise lessons in advance so this information can be shared with TAs ahead of time (Biggs, Gilson and Carter 2019). This is especially helpful in secondary schools when TAs work with a range of teachers, across a variety of classrooms and subject areas (Gibson, Paatsch and Toe 2016). Similarly, TAs benefit from teachers providing detailed lesson plans and materials in advance of lessons as it makes teachers' expectations explicit and avoids TAs going into lessons 'blind'.

Second, teachers perceive that the time needed for teacher–TA communication regarding planning and feedback presents challenges, particularly in secondary settings, due to TAs' contracts restricting the time available to meet outside of scheduled class time (Webster, Blatchford and Russell 2013). Providing opportunities for TAs to attend staff meetings and providing ready access to pigeonholes and emails enhance teacher–TA collaboration (Douglas, Chapin and Nolan 2016). Research emphasises the benefits of teachers discussing planned approaches to supporting students prior to lessons so TAs can anticipate their role in advance.

Influence of organisational structures

The final propositions relate to internal and external organisational structures that have the potential to facilitate effective working relationships between teachers and TAs. Literature indicates that the leadership of TAs is multi-tiered. Biggs, Gilson and Carter (2019) note that TAs should receive ongoing support, direction, training and feedback from highly qualified ILs. In addition, classroom teachers need to have appropriate leadership skills in order to foster collegial relationships with TAs. Sobeck et al. (2021) summarise literature from the past 20 years identifying core teacher competencies when leading TAs as being: (a) knowledge of roles and responsibilities of TAs related to instruction, intervention and direct services; (b) delegation of specific tasks based on the legitimate role of TAs; (c) developing instructional plans for TAs; (d) conducting planning meetings; (e) providing on-the-job training and coaching; (f) monitoring day-to-day activities and (g) providing feedback.

A major barrier to teachers being effective leaders of TAs is that they do not necessarily identify themselves as leaders. This may be a result of not having received training in how to work with and lead TAs. Typically, this falls under the role of the IL in Australian schools, and it is mostly assumed that this is a skill that comes naturally to teachers, yet international research indicates pre-service and in-service teacher training does not address leadership of support staff as a core and essential skill (Douglas, Chapin and Nolan 2016; Sobeck et al. 2021). Furthermore, if TAs run specific interventions for students, they require training in how to facilitate these programs with fidelity. Teachers would therefore benefit from completing training in how to train TAs, which could be included in their pre-service studies (Brock and Carter 2016). International research clearly demonstrates there is scope for the work of TAs to be enhanced through access to further training by teachers, and teachers would benefit from learning how to provide this effectively to TAs (Sobeck et al. 2021).

Internal organisational structures have the potential to influence the dynamic between teachers and TAs. Clear reporting structures prevent murkiness regarding who guides the work of TAs. Reflecting on internal structures and practices encourages schools and teachers to consider how support structures and lesson planning could be organised more effectively to ensure students receive equal allocation of teacher time. Research highlights the benefits of undergoing internal reviews and action planning processes to assess the efficacy of support structures (Webster, Blatchford and Russell 2013) with reflection helping teachers to develop a better understanding of the role of TAs (Giangreco, Edelman and Broer 2003). Furthermore, when schools create effective support teams, including ILs, teachers, TAs and school leadership personnel, and when all parties have clearly defined, but flexible, roles and responsibilities, inclusive practices improve (Douglas, Chapin and Nolan 2016). In Australia, the recent inception of the NCCD as a funding model has influenced schools in this regard, with its focus on the professional judgement of school teams when providing adjustments to students.

Limitations and further research

This study involved only two schools and a small sample of teachers. Care should be taken when interpreting the data as the results of the study may not be generalisable to a wider population and other education providers in Australia. However, data from this study do provide useful insights that have implications for the preparation of pre-service and in-service teachers. Discussions provided valuable insights into teachers' perspectives regarding their work with TAs. Further research involving larger sample sizes and input from teachers from independent and government schools would add to the richness of the discussions that took place.

This research focuses on teachers' perspectives and does not take into consideration the perceptions of TAs in relation to the way teachers work with them. Further research could provide insight into TAs' perceptions about how teachers collaborate with them and may also provide an indication as to what the training needs of teachers are to improve this collaborative partnership. Contrasting the perceptions of primary and secondary teachers and TAs in their experiences working together would also provide greater insight into differences in their training needs.

Conclusion

This study provided further insight into the training needs of secondary teachers, aligning it with previous research indicating that schools and universities should consider whether teachers are fully prepared to work effectively with TAs. When considering the findings in light of the Maslow's Hammer effect (Giangreco 2021), there is a tendency for secondary schools to continue to resort to the same approaches that have been in place for decades, relying heavily on TA support to include students with disability. This is potentially at the expense of considering alternative approaches that might be more effective in secondary schools. This may include considering whether funding received by schools for students with disability might be better invested in other complementary supports alongside TAs.

Several opportunities for improvement can be taken from this study. At the school level there are implications for teacher training. If schools invest in TAs as an additional resource, teachers must be aware of how to make the most of this collaboration so as to avoid the Maslow's Hammer effect. Assuming teachers have not received pre-service training in how to work effectively with TAs, this could be a focus of schools' strategic planning, whereby the international research spanning decades could inform the approach schools take to their support models. Teachers would benefit from learning how to lead the work of TAs, and schools also have a responsibility to ensure TAs are sufficiently trained to fulfil their roles. Beyond this, schools may need to reconsider their support structures through a review process to determine whether their current model effectively meets the needs of all students and offers a fully inclusive educational experience. Importantly, schools should consider how time can be made available for teachers and TAs to collaborate, which is a considerable challenge in secondary schools.

There is also the opportunity for universities to consider whether preservice teachers are fully prepared in how to work with TAs. Ideally, preservice teachers should learn how to lead support staff, how to collaborate effectively and be given the opportunity to work with TAs in their practicum placements when completing teacher training. This crucial aspect of teaching appears to be neglected in pre-service training and should feature prominently in inclusive education units. By universities and policymakers prioritising adequate training of pre-service and in-service educators to work with TAs, it is likely to lead to improved outcomes for educators, resulting in better educational and social outcomes for students they support.

References

ACARA. 2020. "School Students with Disability: Distribution of Students with Disability." Accessed 15 January 2021. https://www.acara.edu.au/reporting/national-report-on-schooling-in-australia/national-report-on-schooling-in-australia-data-portal/school-students-with-disability#view1

Ainscow, Mel. 2000. "The Next Step for Special Education: Supporting the Development of Inclusive Practices." *British Journal of Special Education* 27 (2): 76–80.

Ashbaker, Betty, and Jill Morgan. 2012. "Team Players and Team Managers: Special Educators Working with Paraeducators to Support Inclusive Classrooms." *Creative Education* 3 (3): 322–327. doi:10.4236/ce.2012.33051.

Australian Government. 1992. *Disability Discrimination Act 1992*.

Australian Government. 2021. "Education Aides." Accessed January 15, 2021. https://joboutlook.gov.au/occupations/education-aides?occupationCode=4221

Bazeley, Patricia. 2013. *Qualitative Data Analysis: Practical Strategies*. London: SAGE.

Biggs, Elizabeth E., Carly B. Gilson, and Erik W. Carter. 2019. ""Developing that Balance": Preparing and Supporting Special Education Teachers to Work with Paraprofessionals." *Teacher Education and Special Education*. 42 (2): 117–131. doi:10.1177/0888406418765611.

Blatchford, P., A. Russell, and R. Webster. 2012. *Reassessing the Impact of Teaching Assistants: How Research Challenges Practice and Policy*. Oxon: Routledge.

Braun, Virginia, and Victoria Clarke. 2006. "Using Thematic Analysis in Psychology." *Qualitative Research in Psychology* 3 (2): 77–101. doi:10.1191/1478088706qp063oa.

Brock, Matthew E., and Erik W. Carter. 2016. "Efficacy of Teachers Training Paraprofessionals to Implement Peer Support Arrangements." *Exceptional Children* 82 (3): 354–371. doi:10.1177/0014402915585564.

Butt, Rosemary. 2016. "Teacher Assistant Support and Deployment in Mainstream Schools." *International Journal of Inclusive Education* 20 (9): 995–1007. doi:10.1080/13603116.2016.1145260.

Cameron, David Lansing. 2014. "An Examination of Teacher–student Interactions in Inclusive Classrooms: Teacher Interviews and Classroom Observations." *Journal of Research in Special Educational Needs* 14 (4): 264–273. doi:10.1111/1471-3802.12021.

Creswell, John W. 2009. *Research Design: Qualitative, Quantitative, and Mixed Methods Approaches*. 3rd ed. Thousand Oaks, CA: Sage Publications.

Douglas, Sarah N., Shelley E. Chapin, and James F. Nolan. 2016. "Special Education Teachers' Experiences Supporting and Supervising Paraeducators: Implications for Special and General Education Settings." *Teacher Education and Special Education* 39 (1): 60–74. doi:10.1177/0888406415616443.

Evidence for Learning. 2020. *Teaching and Learning Toolkit*. http://evidence-forlearning.org.au/the-toolkit/

Giangreco, Michael F. 2013. "Teacher Assistant Supports in Inclusive Schools: Research, Practices and Alternatives." *Australasian Journal of Special Education* 37 (2): 93–106. doi:10.1017/jse.2013.1.

Giangreco, Michael F. 2021. "Maslow's Hammer: Teacher Assistant Research and Inclusive Practices at a Crossroads." *European Journal of Special Needs Education* 36 (2): 278–293. doi:10.1080/08856257.2021.1901377.

Giangreco, Michael F., Susan W. Edelman, and Stephen M. Broer. 2003. "Schoolwide Planning to Improve Paraeducator Supports." *Exceptional Children* 70 (1): 63–78. doi:10.1177/001440290307000104.

Giangreco, Michael F., and Mary Beth Doyle. 2007. "Teacher Assistants in Inclusive Schools." In The Sage Handbook of Special Education, edited by Lani Florian, 429–439. 1st ed. London: SAGE.

Gibson, Dianne, Louise Paatsch, and Dianne Toe. 2016. "An Analysis of the Role of Teachers' Aides in a State Secondary School: Perceptions of Teaching Staff and Teachers' Aides." *Australasian Journal of Special Education* 40 (1): 1–20. doi:10.1017/jse.2015.11.

Harris, Lois Ruth, and Kerry Therese Aprile. 2015. "'I Can Sort of Slot into Many Different Roles': Examining Teacher Aide Roles and Their Implications for Practice." *School Leadership & Management* 35 (2): 140–162. doi:10.1080/13632434.2014.992774.

O'Rourke, John, and John West. 2015. "Education Assistant Support in Inclusive Western Australian Classrooms: Trialling a Screening Tool in an Australian Context." *International Journal of Disability, Development and Education* 62 (5): 531–546. doi:10.1080/1034912X.2015.1052376.

Sharma, Umesh, and Spencer J. Salend. 2016. "Teaching Assistants in Inclusive Classrooms: A Systematic Analysis of the International Research." *Australian Journal of Teacher Education* 41 (8): 118–134. doi:10.14221/ajte.2016v41n8.7.

Sharples, Jonathan. 2016. "EEF Blog: Six of the Best – How Our Latest Reports Can Help You Support Teaching Assistants to Get Results." March 2. Accessed 30 June 2021. https://educationendowmentfoundation.org.uk/news/six-of-the-best-how-our-latest-reports-can-help-yousupport-teaching-assist/

Sobeck, Emily, Sarah Douglas, Ritu Chopra, and Stephanie Morano. 2021. "Paraeducator Supervision in Pre-service Teacher Preparation Programs: Results of a National Survey." *Psychology in the Schools* 58 (4): 669–685. doi:10.1002/pits.22383.

Webster, Rob, and Peter Blatchford. 2020. "Rethinking the Use of Teacher Aides." In *Inclusive Education for the 21st Century*, edited by Linda Graham, 383–400. Sydney: Taylor and Francis.

Webster, Rob, Peter Blatchford, and Anthony Russell. 2013. "Challenging and Changing How Schools Use Teaching Assistants: Findings from the Effective Deployment of Teaching Assistants Project." *School Leadership & Management* 33 (1): 78–96. doi:10.1080/13632434.2012.724672.

Webster, Rob, and Anke A. de Boer. 2021. "Where Next for Research on Teaching Assistants: The Case for an International Response." *European Journal of Special Needs Education* 36 (2): 294–305. doi:10.1080/08856257.2021.1901368.

Part IV
The past, present and future of research on teaching assistants

10 Maslow's Hammer

Teacher assistant research and inclusive practices at a crossroads

Michael F. Giangreco

Introduction

Over the past few decades schools have employed teacher assistants (TAs; known by a variety of names internationally) with increasing frequency to play evermore prominent roles in educating students with non-standard support needs, such as those with disabilities, economic disadvantages, who speak a non-dominant language or who are otherwise considered at-risk (Blatchford, Russell and Webster 2012; Chopra and Giangreco 2019; Sharma and Salend 2016). TAs have been woven deeply into the fabric of many schools; yet in too many situations that tapestry presents as a ragged, confusing, disorganised and unfinished work, that to date has not been elevated to a coherent, beautiful design sought by so many families and educators on behalf of their students. This phenomenon has occurred primarily in global northern countries who have the economic resources to hire TAs, yet has implications for a much wider range of nations at various stages of development in terms of universal availability of education for all students.

As a former special education teacher and administrator, I have benefitted from the dedicated and creative efforts of TAs with whom I have worked. As a researcher and provider of professional development related to inclusive education, I have observed and interacted with TAs and their colleagues continuously for over 40 years, mostly in the US, but also in a dozen other countries. This combination of experiences has led me to have enormous respect for TAs. Simultaneously, many of the core issues I have encountered seem remarkably similar across settings and over time, giving me concern about the duties TAs have been asked to undertake, the circumstances under which they have been asked to function, and serious questions about our future direction as a field in terms of inclusive service delivery and equitable educational opportunities and supports. The challenges we persistently face operationalising inclusive education are not the fault or responsibility of TAs and will not likely be solved by remedies limited to TA supports (e.g., hiring, role clarification, training, supervision).

I feel compelled to preface my upcoming comments with a clear statement of positionality, lest my points be misunderstood, taken out of context or

DOI: 10.4324/9781003265580-15

misapplied. First, I am an unapologetic advocate for extending supported inclusive education for students with the full range of disabilities. My intention here is to facilitate the progress made towards more and better equitable access to appropriately supported inclusive educational opportunities for all students – especially for students who historically have been most likely to be educationally segregated. Students with remarkably similar characteristics can be found successfully included in general education class as well as segregated in special education classes or schools. This observation has long led me to conclude that whether students are appropriately supported in inclusive classrooms has as much, probably more, to do with characteristics (e.g., attitudes towards disability, professional socialisation, curricular/instructional conceptualisations/skills) of the adults responsible for education (e.g., teachers, administrators, policymakers) as it has to do with student characteristics (Giangreco 2009).

Second, I acknowledge the potential value of TAs in schools when utilised wisely and envision appropriate roles for them supporting teachers (Chopra and Giangreco 2019). Far too often it seems to me that TAs are not utilised wisely. Despite the best intentions of hardworking school personnel, a variety of systems-level stressors and constraints too often result in schools operating from a reactive posture, where the assignment of TAs has become a readily available path-of-least-resistance to stabilise situations or have an analgesic effect that teachers and parents may find soothing. Yet these same TA supports that team members appreciate may be simultaneously delaying attention to root issues in schools that are in need of attention and improvement (Giangreco and Broer 2005).

Therefore, I am *not* calling for the elimination of, or even necessarily the reduction of, TAs in schools. In cases where reductions might be considered prudent by local teams (e.g., where problems have been identified resulting from there being substantially more TAs than special education/support teachers), I have long advocated that any potential reductions in TA staffing be offset by better alternatives that improve access to high-quality instruction (Giangreco, Broer and Suter 2011a; Giangreco et al. 2004). I doubt reduction of the TA workforce without putting in place some combination of thoughtful alternatives would yield positive outcomes.

Other than in purposely broad strokes, I will not endeavour to repeat much of what has been summarised in the literature about the current state of affairs (Brock and Carter 2013; Chopra and Giangreco 2019; Farrell et al. 2010; Giangreco, Suter and Doyle 2010; Sharma and Salend 2016; Walker and Smith 2015). Rather, I plan to focus on ideas that have received less attention in the TA literature. In doing so, I intend to push back against much of what I consider to be status quo thinking that I fear has restricted our collective progress in supporting inclusive educational opportunities for students with a wider range of disabilities.

How have so many schools ended up extensively and potentially overreliant on TAs? How have such practices been perpetuated? What might we do about it? I invite you to ask yourself whether the ideas presented resonate with your own experiences. Whether you find yourself agreeing or disagreeing with my points, I hope the following perspectives encourage you to consider the path schools are on and whether it is beneficial and sustainable. The purpose of this chapter will be to offer: (a) reasons why relying extensively on TAs as a central feature of inclusive educational service delivery can be problematic, (b) suggestions for what school leaders, educators, and parents can do when either considering the use of TAs or more effective utilisation of those currently employed; and (c) recommendations for future research that hold the potential to improve educational access, quality and support.

Why over-relying on teacher assistants can be problematic

Over the past 30 years I have researched and written about a series of concerns related to over-reliance on TAs, especially those assigned one-to-one or who are frequently in close proximity to individual students. The primary concerns include: (a) the lowest-paid, least qualified, often insufficiently supervised personnel have been assigned to support the students with the most challenging learning and behavioural characteristics, often based on questionable and ambiguous roles; (b) a host of inadvertent detrimental effects have been documented (e.g., interference with teacher engagement, separation within the classroom, interference with peer interactions, fostering dependence, stigmatisation, insufficient access to competent instruction, loss of personal control or gender identity); (c) the *training trap* that occurs when educators unadvisedly relinquish evermore instructional responsibility for students with disabilities to TAs based on those assistants receiving virtually any, even a scant, amount or level of training and then reasoning, 'Now they are trained!' and assuming this means they are now fully capable and prepared to support students in a manner similar to a qualified educator; (d) the double standard, whereby supports offered to students with disabilities (e.g., receiving the bulk of their primary instruction from TAs) would be considered unacceptable if suggested for students without disabilities; (e) the lack of alternatives to over-reliance on TAs; (f) misguided justification-based decision-making tools about TA utilisation that are rooted in an assessment of student characteristics, deficits and needs, while typically ignoring an assessment of corresponding characteristics, deficits and needs in classroom and school practices; and (g) the TA *conundrum* that explores the varying combinations of TAs preparedness for instruction, instructional roles and compensation commensurate with teacher-type instructional roles, where all combinations result in unfavourable outcomes (e.g., TA feelings of ambivalence, exploitation, frustration, disrespect; legal and ethical concerns; questionable resource utilisation; Giangreco 2013). Many of these concerns have been discussed in literature by scholars in several countries (e.g., Australia, Canada, Cyprus, England, Iceland, Ireland, Finland, New Zealand; Angelides, Constantinou and Leigh 2009; Butt 2016; Egilson and Traustadottir 2009; Rose and Shevlin 2019; Rubie-Davies et al. 2010; Rutherford 2012; Takala 2007; Tews & Lupart, 2008; Webster, Blatchford and Russell 2013; Webster et al. 2010). With these concerns acknowledged, the remainder of this section focuses on potential reasons why we may be stuck.

Maslow's Hammer

'I suppose it is tempting, if the only tool you have is a hammer, to treat everything as if it were a nail' (Maslow 1966, pp. 15–16). This human tendency to be over-reliant on a familiar tool to the exclusion of other potentially more appropriate tools (known as *Maslow's Hammer*) interferes with generating new and better solutions to important problems – yet we persist. In inclusive educational contexts, often TAs are the hammer – an effective tool well matched to certain functions, yet not suited to others. In schools where TAs are treated as Maslow's Hammer, they are a primary, sometimes nearly exclusive, tool to educationally and socially include students with certain disabilities. A student needs more instructional time or support – assign a TA. A new student with a disability (e.g., intellectual disability, autism) will be attending the school – assign a TA. A student exhibits behavioural challenges – assign a TA. A teacher expresses the need for support, a parent wants to ensure their child is not lost in the shuffle, a team wants to protect a student from bullying or facilitate peer interactions – assign a TA (see Figure 10.1).

Figure 10.1 On the brink. (Reprinted with permission, Giangreco 2010).

Compounding this problem, decades of literature suggests the research community has perseverated on a small set of the same issues related to TAs, especially role clarification, training (including planning time with teachers) and supervision. It is not that these topics are unimportant – quite the contrary – they are central to effective personnel utilisation. Rather, it is the relative narrowness and frequency with which these repeated topics have been discussed that has reinforced TAs as a prime exemplar of Maslow's Hammer. Implicit in much of the literature seems to be the suggestion that TAs are *the answer*, and that if we simply do a better job clarifying their roles, training and supervising them that a multitude of problems will be solved. I challenge this assumption as fundamentally flawed. Maslow's Hammer also is found in the justification-based decision-making approaches referred to earlier, since they tend to restrict the outcomes to the assignment of: (a) a full-time TA, (b) a part-time or shared TA, or (c) no TA (Giangreco, Doyle and Suter 2012). Again, the flawed assumption being the solution rests exclusively with the use of TAs and without sufficient consideration of other potential solutions.

When researchers address these common issues (e.g., roles, training, supervision) without conceptually situating the research in a broader context related to the well-established drawbacks associated with TA utilisation, they feed into the aforementioned *training trap* and perpetuate double standards that unintentionally hamper consideration of other, potentially more helpful, combinations of alternatives (e.g., resource reallocation, building teacher engagement and capacity, peer supports, self-determination in support service decision-making, changes in special educator/support teacher working conditions, fading/independence plans; see Giangreco et al. 2004). I am not sure we needed research to convince us, yet we have studies indicating that TAs are capable of learning and applying knowledge and skills if they receive competent instruction and ongoing coaching/supervision, and that TAs who receive competent training and supervision function more effectively than those without such foundational supports. Yet, if we persistently continue to focus on these types of studies, we are missing opportunities to tackle potentially more important and creative research questions.

How we may have gotten here: A cautionary tale

I am venturing forward to offer a generalised explanation of what I have seen happen repeatedly in my home state of Vermont, nationally in the US, and internationally. As an experiential and data-based generalisation for the purpose of illustration, I am not suggesting the scenario I present here is universal. However, it has happened with sufficient frequency to serve as a cautionary tale.

In the 1980s some progressive school leaders in Vermont were among the earliest adopters of inclusive education in the US. Students with intensive support needs, such as those with intellectual disability, multiple disabilities and autism, who had previously been educated in regional (segregated) special education classrooms, were transitioned back to chronologically age-appropriate classrooms in the schools they would have attended if not disabled. A cadre of faculty members from the University of Vermont developed a collaborative teamwork model, named *Homecoming* (Thousand et al. 1986), designed to facilitate these efforts based on best practices of that era, many of which remain relevant today.

In the years following the initial implementation of *Homecoming*, while some schools adhered to several of the model's elements, others were selective in which elements they implemented, or waned in their adherence over time. Enthusiasm for including previously segregated students was not universally shared by all school personnel. Busy teachers, who expressed feeling stressed by their existing duties, were not necessarily eager to take on additional roles and questioned how students with more severe disabilities would benefit from regular class placement when they functioned substantially below the level of their classmates. Since physical placement was necessary, but insufficient, to be included, in an effort to get a 'foot in the door' well-intended advocates offered sceptical or reluctant school personnel a combination of unhelpful explicit or implied messages (that were inconsistent with the *Homecoming* model). Some of the most problematic messages were:

- We are looking for volunteers.
- Students will be included primarily for social reasons, rather than academic learning.
- As a teacher, we are not asking you to change your practices to include this student. You are more of a host, not actually expected to function as the student's teacher.
- To support teachers, a full-time, TA will be provided along with access to a special/support educator and related services providers (e.g., physical therapist, speech-language pathologist).
- If you accept this student in your classroom, your life as a teacher will go ahead virtually unchanged because someone else is actually responsible for instruction and support – the most frequently available person being the full-time TA.

These messages were unhelpful because the voluntary nature suggested that teachers had the option to reject a student based on disability characteristics – something that would be unacceptable if applied to any other student diversity characteristic (e.g., race, ethnicity, economic status, gender identity). Emphasising the social aspect of inclusion perpetuated low expectations for student learning and was inconsistent with what is known about the importance of building social relationships via shared educational experiences. The hosting posture ran counter to the importance of teacher engagement/ownership as an essential element of quality inclusive education and preserved instructional double-standards. Some teachers who cautiously accepted the placement of students with intensive support needs did so based on their tacit agreement with these unhelpful messages. Such tepid forays allowed a host of incongruent practices to be mislabelled as inclusive (Davern et al. 1997). I suggest that students who ended up placed in these regular education classrooms, but who were isolated within the classroom, doing different work, with TAs as their de facto teachers, were not actually included – they were the proverbial, 'Island in the Mainstream' (Biklen 1985; see Figure 10.2) – this phenomenon persists today.

Figure 10.2 Island in the mainstream. (Reprinted with permission from Giangreco 1998).

As other schools sought to enact progressive policies and practices related to inclusive education, it was natural to look towards existing exemplars. So, many schools in Vermont and beyond its borders looked to these earlier adopters. A prominent feature they saw were heavily TA-reliant models that readily spread, in part, because they were relatively easy to implement (e.g., hire low-wage TAs) and continued to imply, without criticism or challenge, the attractive notion to teachers and principals/heads that the general education system could continue on its current path without any fundamental need to change its practices to include students with a wider array of characteristics and learning support needs. Vermont emerged as, and remains, among the heaviest users of TA supports in the US. More than 30 years later, having recognised the problems inherent in a TA-reliant model, many Vermont schools are exploring alternative service delivery models while seeking to maintain and extend inclusive educational opportunities and supports (Giangreco, Smith and Pinckney 2006; Giangreco and Suter 2015).

In terms of why anyone ever thought those unhelpful messages were acceptable and were so readily perpetuated and maintained, we may not need to look much further than the most parsimonious possibilities: societal ableism (Hehir 2006) and pity/charity mentalities to disability (Rapp and Arndt 2012). There are still pervasively low expectations for students with developmental disabilities. There remains an ableist mentality that seems to make the double standards regarding limited access to highly qualified teachers seem acceptable, especially for students with severe or multiple disabilities. Whether it is explicit or not, there is an undercurrent whispering, 'Does this student with severe disabilities really need a highly qualified teacher? Isn't a dedicated TA enough?' Worse yet is the insidious notion that somehow schools are doing students and families *a favour* by providing them with a one-to-one TA and/or *allowing* them access to the typical environments, personnel and experiences available to all other students without disabilities. Ableist notions erode the human and civil rights of students with disabilities. The lesson of this cautionary tale is that just because earlier adopters chose a certain path to pursue inclusive education does not mean it was the most appropriate or sustainable approach. Findings from the UK's large-scale *Deployment and Impact of Support Staff* (DISS) project demonstrated that high levels of support from TAs for students with learning difficulties were associated with a negative impact on their learning and development of non-cognitive attributes, such as independence (Blatchford, Russell and Webster 2012). While this effect was attributed to decision-making factors beyond the control of TAs, it nonetheless provides empirical evidence that a well-intentioned and long-standing model designed both to facilitate the inclusion of such students and to support their learning and development fails on its own terms (Webster et al. 2010). By assuming that earlier service delivery models were effective, and therefore worthy of replication, we inadvertently perpetuate the Maslow's Hammer effect.

Suggestions for school teams

In the absence of conclusive data on the most effective service delivery models to support inclusive education, capable of countering the aforementioned DISS project findings, we can support each other within team structures that include school personnel, families and students, by applying principles and practices to help us position ourselves for learning and exploration.

Self-examination

As we consider decisions about the deployment of TAs to support students with disabilities, it is time we shift our assessment and analysis from exclusively examining student characteristics (especially perceived student deficits and needs that we think warrant TA support) to a self-examination of our own attitudes and practices. In part, this starts with attempting to raise our critical consciousness about our attitudes and actions towards individuals with disabilities (Shin et al. 2018). Well-meaning people may hold ableist beliefs without being aware of them or without recognising how they may unintentionally contribute to harm. Virtually all of us have been raised in ableist societies that have socialised us to think of individuals with disabilities in 'less than' ways that contribute to the low expectations, double standards and inequitable access – all of which interfere with a myriad of opportunities for individuals with disabilities to pursue self-determined lives.

We can each move towards a better understanding of our own implicit biases by taking the online *Disability Implicit Association Test* (implicit.harvard.edu/implicit/takeatest.html) or any of the other *Project Implicit* bias association tests online. Another simple self-check that can be done anytime we propose a support or practice be applied to a student with a disability is to ask, *Would this situation be acceptable if the student didn't have a disability?* (Giangreco 2003). A common practice, such as a student with disabilities receiving the bulk of their instruction from a TA, rather a qualified teacher, is a prime an example of how asking this simple question holds the potential to interrupt an inequitable practice. Schools can self-assess their practices using tools such as the *Essential Best Practices in Inclusive Schools* (Jorgenson et al. 2012) or *Index for Inclusion* (Booth and Ainscow 2011), and online resources (e.g., SWIFT Center, www.swiftschools.org; TIES Center, www.tiescenter.org).

Conceptualise curricular inclusion

Skilful teachers already contribute to educating students with various disabilities who are functioning at, or near, grade-level of their classmates, such as those who have relatively mild learning challenges that require instructional adjustments or those who require access accommodations associated with orthopaedic or sensory disabilities. Teachers have legitimate questions and deserve sound conceptualisations about how to include students with more severe disabilities when they function substantially below the level of their classmates academically and socially. Ironically, when faced with such situations, it is not uncommon for some teachers to explain they are not qualified or prepared for this challenge, without critically considering that they may be deferring to an even less qualified TA.

Inclusive curricular conceptualisations start with the understanding that students can have different, individually appropriate, learning outcomes within shared educational experiences. Although beyond the scope of this chapter to describe in detail, (a) multi-level curriculum/instruction and (b) curriculum overlapping offer ways to conceptualise and plan for students of varying functioning levels to pursue different, individually appropriate, learning outcomes within shared educational experiences (Giangreco, Shogren and Dymond 2020). When educational teams have these types of tools at their disposal, they may be less likely to defer instructional responsibilities to TAs.

Match supports to needs and consider natural supports

Rather than assuming that TAs are the appropriate response to any particular issue, match the support to the need. For example, if a student with dyscalculia needs extra support in maths, who are the school personnel most qualified to support the student? Is it: (a) a TA who reports being unskilled in and uncomfortable with maths, (b) the Special Education/Support Teacher, who may not have a strong background in maths, or (c) the maths teacher or specialist? If a high school student needs support transitioning between classes, is that need best met by a TA, or a classmate who is transitioning between the same classes? By considering natural supports and challenging ourselves with questions about what support most appropriately, least intrusively and most inclusively meets a particular need, we can identify the potential risks of double standards and attempt to mitigate them. Parents are shifting their advocacy away from requesting one-to-one TAs to requests that ensure their child has access to highly qualified general education teachers with curricular content knowledge and instructional skill who collaborates with a skilled special/support educator (Giangreco et al. 2005).

Listen to self-advocates and involve them in determining their own supports

One of the simplest and most powerful steps we can all do more frequently is to listen to our students' voices in an effort to better understand their perspectives (Ainscow and Messiou 2018; Broer, Doyle and Giangreco 2005; De Leeuw, De Boer and Minnaert 2018; Tews and Lupart 2008). If our public education systems are meant to launch our students with disabilities into personally meaningful, self-determined young adulthood, sadly this important outcome remains unrealised for far too many students with developmental disabilities. Yet, positive exemplars continue to emerge;

where they do exist, a key element is self-determination (Wehmeyer and Shogren 2018).

We can take an important step forward by involving self-advocates in making decisions about their own supports, in culturally and age-appropriate ways throughout their school career. As this pertains to the utilisation of TAs, this may range from student voice in determining whether or not a TA is utilised, to getting clarification from students about what they find helpful, and what they find intrusive or stigmatising. Conceptualisations and tools to facilitate self-advocacy, specifically related TA supports, remain largely absent from the professional literature. We would be well advised to operationalise a slogan adopted by many marginalised groups, 'Nothing about us without us'.

Assign TAs to teachers, not to individual students

In situations where schools and teams have agreed that TA utilisation is appropriate, consider assigning TAs to teachers, not to individual students. This allows teachers to establish predictable partnerships with TAs that can develop over time. The scant amount of research on this subject suggests that teachers are more engaged with their students who have disabilities when the TA is assigned to the classroom, rather than an individual student (Giangreco, Broer and Edelman 2001).

Parents and school personnel want to know about the pros and cons of having a TA follow a student from grade-to-grade, yet no research or literature exists on this topic. Those who favour having TAs follow students from grade-to-grade argue that it facilitates the transition because the TA knows the student well, it adds stability for the student and family, and serves as a knowledgeable support to the receiving teacher. Those opposed to having TAs follow students worry that it may exacerbate student dependencies, interfere with teacher ownership and delay attention to needed changes in schools.

In an extreme (but nonetheless illustrative) example, a national news programme recounted a story about a young woman with Down syndrome graduating from high school who had been paired with the same, one-to-one, TA every year since kindergarten. It was one of those end-of-the-newscast stories; after 95% of the time was spent reporting on climate change, war, corruption, scandals, government gridlock, disease, corporate hijinks and alike, the final two minutes were devoted to a 'feel good' moment. The story emphasised the close and loving relationship between this student and her TA. While I do not doubt the authenticity and value of their close relationship, the story did not leave me with the intended 'feel good' sensation – quite the contrary. Would we ever allow, or celebrate, a neurotypical student being assigned the same teacher for their entire school career when everyone else has access to many? I am purposely equating the TA to a teacher because research indicates that when students are assigned a one-to-one TA, that person often provides the majority of instruction and functions as the de facto teacher (Giangreco and Broer 2005). How many other positive adult and peer relationships, experiences and interactions might this young woman have had if she had been allowed to follow a more typical pattern of adult interaction?

While individualisation remains a hallmark of special education, when it comes to the issue of whether or not a TA should follow a student to the next grade, the least dangerous default starting position would be to follow the same patterns available to all other students. When concerns are raised by those who wish to have the TA follow the student to the next grade, it presents an opportunity to ask questions that can interrupt the Maslow's Hammer effect. Rather than asking questions in ways likely to retain the TA focus (e.g., Does this student need the TA to follow along to the next grade?), we can reframe our questions in ways that open us to consider new possibilities (e.g., In what ways might we ensure that James has a successful transition to the next grade in ways that support essential teacher engagement and ownership?). Rather than assuming that the TA is *the answer*, we may need to devote attention to our next-grade transition processes. Assigning a TA may delay attention to this type of need and interfere with teacher engagement at the next level.

Determine educator roles before TA roles

One of the simplest and most powerful steps schools can take to interrupt the Maslow's Hammer effect related to TAs is found in the sequence in which we consider issues. Professional literature about TA roles almost universally ignores one of the most foundational conceptual considerations if TAs are to be used wisely to support and supplement (not supplant) the work of teachers and special/support educators – namely first articulating the roles of the teachers and special/support educators related to students with disabilities in inclusive classrooms. We cannot appropriately determine the roles of TAs in isolation or before the roles of these accountable educators have been determined. A role clarification tool is available that first establishes the basic roles of teachers and special/support educators and then, only after those roles have been established, frames a series of TA roles that '…help create opportunities for classroom teachers and special educators to spend time instructing students with disabilities and collaborating with each other' (Giangreco, Suter and Graf 2011b).

Future research and conclusions

Beyond quality writing and methodological soundness, one of the most foundational questions journal editors and reviewers ask about scholarship submitted for publication is whether it fills an important gap in the literature that substantially extends our understanding and holds the potential to improve practice. Collectively, can we stop perseverating on TA roles, training and supervision, or at least shift the ways this information has been commonly reported in the professional literature? Findings from much of the research on roles, training and supervision repeatedly confirm what we have long known and rarely tell us much new or compelling. For researchers who understandably remain interested in these core issues, framing of the research in ways that puts these issues in a fuller context is a logical step, since they do not exist in a vacuum. If a study asserts the value of utilising TAs, it should also mention the drawbacks to their utilisation. If a study examines TA roles, it should also explain the intersection with teacher and special/support educator roles. If a study reports the effectiveness of training TAs to offer instruction, it should also explain how students with disabilities are accessing primary instruction from highly qualified teachers. It is not enough to say, 'We found an effective way to improve training of TAs' when the implementation of that effective training may inadvertently exacerbate double standards, increase stigmatisation, interfere with teacher engagement, extend the training trap and other known concerns.

Future research can be enhanced by providing typically absent data in the Setting subsections of future studies. Knowing the status of a variety service delivery variables associated with inclusive service delivery can help readers better understand the context in ways that may contribute to replication. Examples of these setting variables include: (a) percentage of student on various special needs plans, (b) average class size, (c) average special educator caseload size, (d) range of grades and number of teachers supported by special/support educators, (e) special educator school density (number of special educators per total enrolment), (f) special services concentration (the number of TAs per special educator) and (f) the percentage of a school's TAs assigned one-to-one (Suter and Giangreco 2009; Suter, Giangreco and Bruhl, 2019; Giangreco, Suter and Hurley 2013).

There are talented practitioners and scholars around the world interested in intersection of inclusive education service delivery and TAs. While I rely on them to generate the palate of future research, I have my own modest wish list. Future researchers might investigate: (a) effective alternatives to over-reliance on TAs, (b) inclusive service delivery models (e.g., school and classroom staffing patterns; secondary/high school models where special educators and TAs are assigned to subject areas versus across multiple subject areas), (c) student and family perspectives, (d) pros and cons of TAs transitioning with students to the next grade, (e) processes for involving students in decisions about their own supports, (f) utilisation of TAs that contribute to teacher engagement and instruction, (g) inclusive exemplars from countries or schools that do not presently rely on TAs for instruction, (h) independence plans to fade one-to-one TA supports, (i) peer perspectives and supports, and (j) practices that explore the impact of school self-assessment on improved access to quality inclusive educational opportunities. This is not a comprehensive list, merely some initial suggestions where gaps exist in the literature.

Despite a roughly 40-year history, we are too early in the development of inclusive educational service models to say which are most effective; we have a better idea of what does not work (e.g., heavy reliance on TAs). No single model will be appropriate internationally across the range of cultural, economic and organisational contexts. We are at a crossroads, so now is not the time to limit our options to just hammers. If your school, system or country is seeking to become more educationally inclusive, be open to support solutions beyond utilisation of TAs. Avoid the tempting path taken by others before you, by not going directly to TAs as the solution. Rather, explore new possibilities, challenge the status quo and conventional thinking, learn from each other, and share. Collectively, we hold the power to interrupt the Maslow's Hammer effect related to TAs that seems to have us stuck in a research whirlpool. As we break free and explore new directions, let us remain mindful of the ongoing and significant contributions of our dedicated TA colleagues and stay focused on filling important gaps in the research literature that hold the potential to improve the outcomes for our students with disabilities.

Acknowledgements

The author acknowledges and thanks Dr Jesse Suter for his constructive feedback that contributed to the development of this chapter.

Originally published as Michael F. Giangreco (2021) Maslow's Hammer: teacher assistant research and inclusive practices at a crossroads, European Journal of Special Needs Education, 36:2, 278-293, DOI: 10.1080/08856257.2021.1901377.

© Taylor & Francis Ltd (2021), reprinted by permission of the publisher.

References

Ainscow, M., and K. Messiou. 2018. "Engaging with the Views of Students to Promote Inclusion in Education." *Journal of Educational Change* 19 (1): 1–17. doi:10.1007/s10833-017-9312-1.

Angelides, P., C. Constantinou, and J. Leigh. 2009. "The Role of Paraprofessionals in Developing Inclusive Education in Cyprus." *European Journal of Special Needs Education* 24 (1): 75–89. doi:10.1080/08856250802596741.

Biklen, D. 1985. *Achieving the Complete School: Strategies for Effective Mainstreaming*. New York: Teachers College Press.

Blatchford, P., A. Russell, and R. Webster. 2012. *Reassessing the Impact of Teaching Assistants: How Research Challenges Practice and Policy*. London: Routledge.

Booth, T., and M. Ainscow. 2011. *Index for Inclusion: Developing Learning and Participation in Schools*, 3rd ed. Bristol: Centre for Studies on Inclusive Education.

Brock, M. E., and E. W. Carter. 2013. "A Systematic Review of Paraprofessional-delivered Educational Practices to Improve Outcomes for Students with Intellectual and Developmental Disabilities." *Research and Practice for Persons with Severe Disabilities* 38 (4): 211–221. doi:10.1177/154079691303800401.

Broer, S. M., M. B. Doyle, and M. F. Giangreco. 2005. "Perspectives of Students with Intellectual Disabilities about Their Experiences with Paraprofessional Support." *Exceptional Children* 71 (4): 415–430.

Butt, R. 2016. "Teacher Assistant Support and Deployment in Mainstream Schools." *International Journal of Inclusive Education* 20 (9): 995–1007. doi:10.1080/13603116.2016.1145260.

Chopra, R. V., and M. F. Giangreco. 2019. "Effective Use of Teacher Assistants in Inclusive Classrooms." In *The SAGE Handbook on Inclusion and Diversity in Education*, edited by M. Schuelka, C. Johnstone, G. Thomas, and A. Artiles, 193–207. London: Sage. doi:10.4135/9781526470430.n18.

Davern, L., M. Sapon-Shevin, M. D'Aquanni, M. Fisher, M. Larson, J. Black, and S. Minondo. 1997. "Drawing the Distinction between Coherent and Fragmented Efforts at Building Inclusive Schools." *Equity and Excellence in Education* 30 (3): 31–39. doi:10.1080/1066568970300306.

De Leeuw, R., A. De Boer, and A. Minnaert. 2018. "Student Voices on Social Exclusion in General Primary Schools." *European Journal of Special Needs Education* 33 (2): 166–186. doi:10.1080/08856257.2018.1424783.

Egilson, S. T., and R. Traustadottir. 2009. "Assistance to Pupils with Physical Disabilities in Regular Schools: Promoting Inclusion or Creating Dependency?." *European Journal of Special Needs Education* 24 (1): 21–36. doi:10.1080/08856250802596766.

Farrell, P., A. Alborz, A. Howes, and D. Pearson. 2010. "The Impact of Teaching Assistants on Improving Pupils' Academic Achievement in Mainstream Schools: A Review of the Literature." *Educational Review* 62 (4): 435–448. doi:10.1080/00131911.2010.486476.

Giangreco, M. F. 1998. *Ants in His Pants: Absurdities and Realities of Special Education*. Thousand Oaks, CA: Corwin.

Giangreco, M. F. 2003. "Working with Paraprofessionals." *Educational Leadership* 61 (2): 50–53.

Giangreco, M. F. 2009. "Opportunities for Children and Youth with Intellectual Developmental Disabilities: Beyond Genetics." *Life Span and Disability: An Interdisciplinary Journal (Ciclo Evolutivo E Disabilitá)* 12 (2): 129–139.

Giangreco, M. F. 2010. *On the Brink* (Cartoon). University of Vermont, Center for Digital Initiatives. https://cdi.uvm.edu/collection/giangrecocartoons.

Giangreco, M. F. 2013. "Teacher Assistant Supports in Inclusive Schools: Research, Practices and Alternatives." *Australasian Journal of Special Education* 37 (2): 93–106. doi:10.1017/jse.2013.1.

Giangreco, M. F., and S. M. Broer. 2005. "Questionable Utilization of Paraprofessionals in Inclusive Schools: Are We Addressing Symptoms or Causes?." *Focus on Autism and Other Developmental Disabilities* 20 (1): 10–26. doi:10.1177/10883576050200010201.

Giangreco, M. F., S. M. Broer, and S. W. Edelman. 2001. "Teacher Engagement with Students with Disabilities: Differences between Paraprofessional Service Delivery Models." *Journal of the Association for Persons with Severe Handicaps* 26 (2): 75–86. doi:10.2511/rpsd.26.2.75.

Giangreco, M. F., S. M. Broer, and J. C. Suter. 2011a. "Guidelines for Selecting Alternatives to Overreliance on Paraprofessionals: Field-testing in Inclusion-oriented Schools." *Remedial and Special Education* 32 (1): 22–38. doi:10.1177/0741932509355951.

Giangreco, M. F., M. B. Doyle, and J. C. Suter. 2012. "Constructively Responding to Requests for Paraprofessionals: We Keep Asking the Wrong Questions." *Remedial and Special Education* 33 (6): 362–373. doi:10.1177/0741932511413472.

Giangreco, M. F., A. T. Halvorsen, M. B. Doyle, and S. M. Broer. 2004. "Alternatives to Overreliance on Paraprofessionals in Inclusive Schools." *Journal of Special Education Leadership* 17 (2): 82–90.

Giangreco, M. F., K. A. Shogren, and S. K. Dymond. 2020. "Educating Students with Severe Disabilities: Foundational Concepts and Practices." In *Instruction of Students with Severe Disabilities: Meeting the Needs of Children and Youth with Intellectual Disabilities, Multiple Disabilities, and Autism Spectrum Disorders*, edited by F. Brown, J. McDonnell, and M. E. Snell, 9th ed., 1–27. Upper Saddle River, NJ: Pearson.

Giangreco, M. F., C. S. Smith, and E. Pinckney. 2006. "Addressing the Paraprofessional Dilemma in an Inclusive School: A Program Description." *Research and Practice for Persons with Severe Disabilities* 31 (3): 215–229. doi:10.1177/154079690603100302.

Giangreco, M. F., and J. C. Suter. 2015. "Precarious or Purposeful? Proactively Building Inclusive Special Education Service Delivery on Solid Ground." *Inclusion* 3 (3): 112–131. doi:10.1352/2326-6988-3.3.112.

Giangreco, M. F., J. C. Suter, and M. B. Doyle. 2010. "Paraprofessionals in Inclusive Schools: A Review of Recent Research." *Journal of Educational and Psychological Consultation* 20 (1): 41–57. doi:10.1080/10474410903535356.

Giangreco, M. F., J. C. Suter, and V. Graf. 2011b. "Roles of Team Members Supporting Students with Disabilities in Inclusive Classrooms." In *Choosing Outcomes and Accommodations for Children: A Guide to Educational Planning for Students with Disabilities*, edited by M. F. Giangreco, C. J. Cloninger, and V. S. Iverson, 3rd ed., 197–204. Baltimore: Paul H. Brookes.

Giangreco, M. F., J. C. Suter, and S. M. Hurley. 2013. "Revisiting Personnel Utilization in Inclusion-oriented Schools." *Journal of Special Education* 47 (2): 121–132. doi:10.1177/0022466911419015.

Giangreco, M. F., S. Yuan, B. McKenzie, P. Cameron, and J. Fialka. 2005. ""Be Careful What You Wish for…": Five Reasons to Be Concerned about the Assignment of Individual Paraprofessionals." *Teaching Exceptional Children* 37 (5): 28–34. doi:10.1177/004005990503700504.

Hehir, T. 2006. *New Directions in Special Education: Eliminating Ableism in Policy and Practice*. Cambridge, MA: Harvard Education Press.

Jorgenson, C. M., M. McSheehan, M. Shuh, and R. M. Sonnenmier. 2012. Essential Best Practices in Inclusive Schools. National Center on Inclusive Education, Institute on Disability, University of New Hampshire. http://www.tash.org/wp-content/uploads/2011/03/Essential-Best-Practices-070312-FULL-Jorgensen.pdf

Maslow, A. H. 1966. *The Psychology of Science: A Reconnaissance*. New York: Harper & Row.

Rapp, W. H., and K. L. Arndt. 2012. *Teaching Everyone: An Introduction to Inclusive Education*. Baltimore: Paul H. Brookes.

Rose, R., and M. Shevlin. 2019. "Support Provision for Students with Special Educational Needs in Irish Primary Schools." *Journal of Research in Special Educational Needs* (2). Advance online publication. doi:10.1111/1471-3802.12465.

Rubie-Davies, C. M., P. Blatchford, R. Webster, M. Koutsoubou, and P. Bassett. 2010. "Enhancing Learning? A Comparison of Teacher and Teaching Assistant Interactions with Pupils." *School Effectiveness and School Improvement* 21 (4): 429–449. doi:10.1080/09243453.2010.512800.

Rutherford, G. 2012. "In, Out or Somewhere in Between: Disabled Students' and Teacher Aides' Experiences of School." *International Journal of Inclusive Education* 16 (8): 757–774. doi:10.1080/13603116.2010.509818.

Sharma, U., and S. Salend. 2016. "Teaching Assistants in Inclusive Classrooms: A Systematic Analysis of International Research." *Australian Journal of Teacher Education* 41 (8): 118–134. doi:10.14221/ajte.2016v41n8.7.

Shin, R. Q., L. C. Smith, Y. Lu, J. C. Welch, R. Sharma, C. N. Vernay, and S. Yee. 2018. "The Development and Validation of the Contemporary Critical Consciousness Measure II." *Journal of Counseling Psychology* 65 (5): 539–555. doi:10.1037/cou0000302.

Suter, J. C., and M. F. Giangreco. 2009. "Numbers that Count: Exploring Special Education and Paraprofessional Service Delivery in Inclusion-oriented Schools." *Journal of Special Education* 43 (2): 81–93. doi:10.1177/0022466907313353.

Suter, J. C., M. F. Giangreco, and S. A. D. Bruhl. 2019. "Special Education Personnel Absences in Inclusion-oriented Schools: Implications for Building Effective Service Delivery Models." *Remedial and Special Education*. Advance online publication. doi:10.1177/0741932519865617.

Takala, M. 2007. "The Work of Classroom Assistants in Special and Mainstream Education in Finland." *British Journal of Special Education* 34 (1): 50–57. doi:10.1111/j.1467-8578.2007.00453.x.

Tews, L., and J. Lupart. 2008. "Students with Disabilities' Perspectives of the Role and Impact of Paraprofessionals in Inclusive Education Settings." *Journal of Policy and Practice in Intellectual Disabilities* 5 (1): 39–46. doi:10.1111/j.1741-1130.2007.00138.x.

Thousand, J. S., T. J. Fox, R. Reid, J. Godek, W. Williams, and W. L. Fox. 1986. "Homecoming Model: Educating Students Who Present Intensive Educational Challenges within Regular Education Environments." In *A Guide for Establishing Shared Responsibility among Teachers, Administrators and Parents for the Education of Students Who Present Intensive Educational Challenges*. Burlington, VT: University of Vermont, Center for Developmental Disabilities. ERIC Document Reproduction: ED 284 406.

Walker, V. L., and C. G. Smith. 2015. "Training Paraprofessionals to Support Students with Disabilities: A Literature Review." *Exceptionality* 23 (3): 170–191. doi:10.1080/09362835.2014.986606.

Webster, R., P. Blatchford, P. Bassett, P. Brown, C. Martin, and A. Russell. 2010. "Double Standards and First Principles: Framing Teaching Assistant Support for Pupils with Special Educational Needs." *European Journal of Special Needs Education* 25 (4): 319–336. doi:10.1080/08856257.2010.513533.

Webster, R., P. Blatchford, and A. Russell. 2013. "Challenging and Changing How Schools Use Teaching Assistants: Findings from the Effective Deployment of Teaching Assistants Project." *School Leadership & Management* 33 (1): 78–96. doi:10.1080/13632434.2012.724672.

Wehmeyer, M. L., and K. A. Shogren. 2018. "Life Design and Career Counseling: Self-determination and Autonomous Motivation." In *Counseling and Coaching in Times of Crisis and Transitions: From Research to Practice*, edited by L. Nota and S. Soresi, 113–124, London: Routledge.

11 Conclusion

Researching teaching assistants: What have we learned and where do we go next?

Rob Webster

The final chapter of this book considers three aspects of the scope and impact of the research on and involving teaching assistants (TAs). Firstly, I revisit the point made by Michael Giangreco in the previous chapter about the research community's preoccupation with a narrow and recurring set of interests, and consider why these topics endure in the literature. Secondly, I reflect on what these contributions add to, and can be said about, one of these topics: role clarification. Rather than relitigate the arguments and issues about role clarity and ambiguity, I instead draw on the empirical studies and the collaborative work with schools featured in this book to address the two practical questions posed in the introductory chapter: (i) how might we refine and usefully describe the "support" that TAs provide; and (ii) what alternative approaches might we introduce *alongside* TAs in order to better include and educate pupils with special educational needs (SEN) in mainstream schools, and thus reduce schools' reliance on TAs? Thirdly, I shall look to the future of research in this field, by identifying a persistent and urgent research gap: the shortage of international data on TAs. Given the pre-eminence of TA deployment as a means to facilitate pupils with SEN's access to and participation in mainstream education, I argue that the continued lack of large-scale data on TAs' characteristics, experiences, practices, and impact poses a risk to advancing the global inclusion agenda.

Why has research "perseverated on a small set of the same issues related to TAs"?

In his contribution to this book, one of the long-time researchers on paraprofessional issues, Michael Giangreco, appeals for greater diversity in the corpus of empirical and theoretical work on TAs and inclusion. As he makes clear, it is an entreaty rooted in a concern that "decades of literature suggests the research community has perseverated on a small set of the same issues related to TAs". He identifies "role clarification, training (including planning time with teachers), and supervision" as the most commonly researched themes that appear in the literature.

As the reader will have observed, these themes are represented in this volume. To be clear, nobody is suggesting that these themes are not important

DOI: 10.4324/9781003265580-16

areas of investigation, thought, and development. But the point Giangreco raises is whether research on these topics – especially from jurisdictions where TAs are an established part of the school workforce – offer diminishing returns. While we cannot say that we have learned everything we are ever likely to learn about TA role clarity, preparation, etc., we have arguably learned *enough* to justify tilling this patch of the field with a lot less intensity hereon, and (as Giangreco urges) to move on to new and valuable lines of enquiry. So, how might we reconcile Giangreco's concern over perseveration with the fact that these very topics concerning the TA role and inclusion attract, and will very likely continue to attract, a disproportionate amount of researchers' attention?

For a start, a reasonable and practical distinction about value might be made on the basis of research provenance. As more jurisdictions worldwide instigate programmes to create and expand a TA workforce – driven, at least in part, in many places by parents advocating for the use of TAs (Sharma and Salend 2016) – data on issues pertaining to these themes will remain essential if policymakers are to avoid the kinds of latent issues that were unintentionally baked into the US and UK systems at the point of inception, decades ago. Done well, informed by, and building on existing work, such new research is potentially useful, as it might produce examples of innovative solutions to persistent problems. While there is no guarantee that new territories will avoid making the same missteps and miscalculations in implementation, there is sufficient variation across educational jurisdictions and cultures to justify maintaining an empirical record of how TA role clarity, preparation, etc. are addressed in the fledgling stages, and to capture emergent insights that might challenge the status quo.

It is worth dwelling on why the recurring topics Giangreco identifies continue to attract researchers' attention. It is not because the field lacks talented or creative researchers. Instead, one plausible reason is that much of the research that composes the field's evidence base (as it currently stands) is built to no small degree on work by postgraduates and PhD students. Indeed, several contributions to this book are based on work carried out as part of a master's- or doctoral-level thesis. It is worth noting too that some of the under-researched topics on and involving TAs are also those that are more difficult to undertake by one (often less experienced) researcher. A good example of this is research on the over-reliance on TAs, be it on the part of pupils, parents, schools, or entire education systems. Addressing research questions that explore individuals' intentions and values, or risk implying something questionable about their competency or the quality of their decision-making, is potentially emotive. As school-based research relies on building and maintaining cordial relationships with schools and staff, postgraduate students may understandably veer away from research topics that they perceive as carrying a higher risk to success. Add to this the fact that the focus of such inquiries are TAs – the practitioners with perhaps the least amount of authority and agency within the education system – and there are more than enough elements to blow a dissertation project off course.

In this reading, perhaps what we see is a function of early career researchers sticking to 'safe' topics, which can be researched in schools without causing disruption, division or disquiet.

Scale is also an issue here. That many of the papers on TAs submitted to journals stem from postgraduate or doctoral research directly or indirectly about TAs arguably connects to Sharma and Salend's (2016) observation that the evidence base is "characterized by the use of qualitative research designs, relatively small sample sizes, and self-reports that focus on the perceptions of participants, who are mostly TAs" (p. 127). I say this from the position of an academic who is often invited to review such papers. So, while my observations are drawn from extensive professional experience, they remain necessarily speculative.

To reiterate, I do not assume or ascribe either the fixation on the recurring issues, nor the methodological tilt, to researchers' lack of imagination or skill. Indeed, the reasons why certain issues and topics relating to TAs remain under-researched, under-represented – even unaddressed – in the literature may have more to do with factors that we might *perceive* to be beyond the control of researchers; that is, that the research agenda as it relates to TAs is decided by actors (e.g. governments and research councils) outside of our influence. Later in this chapter, I set out a case for addressing a particular data gap that, even while encompassing the familiar topics, does so with renewed purpose and on a more meaningful scale and scope.

Revisiting the role clarity/ambiguity dilemma

Of course, another reason why these commonly researched issues endure is because, in practical terms, there are key aspects to them that remain largely unresolved and unreconciled. Role clarification is perhaps the best example of such an issue. Throughout this book, contributors have discussed the persistent problem of role clarity and role ambiguity. Indeed, it was a clear undercurrent to the first three chapters by Zhao, Rose, and Shevlin; Östlund, Barow, Dahlbergb, and Johansson; and Lübeck and Demmer. In each case, the authors describe the TA role in their respective context as "complex". Whenever the issue of role clarity/ambiguity is raised, it is typically in relation to an overlap and/or a lack of distinction between the TA's role and the teacher's role (Vivash and Morgan 2019). It is worth noting that Östlund and colleagues remind us that there is potential for ambiguity *within* paraprofessional roles that focus on instruction and caregiving.

As noted in the introductory chapter, the absence of common agreement and clarity about the specific purpose of TAs means that teachers and school leaders not only often overlook and undervalue their contributions, but they do not know how to deploy TAs in potentially more effective ways. In fact, the increased number of and sustained use of TAs has provided a cover for fully engaging with and resolving role ambiguity, as well as staving off wider debates about how we effectively include and educate pupils with SEN in mainstream settings. As Slee (2012) argues, where SEN policy has majored on mechanisms of individual support, it has given teachers "permission to withdraw, while specialists or hired aides get on with the task of inclusion". A continual flow of new TAs into schools may, on the surface, *look* like a successful policy response to demand or need, but it quietly contributes to the brewing of other dilemmas that require more nuanced thought and radical fixes.

Perhaps its intractability is a reason why Giangreco lists role clarification as one of the topics "that seems to have us stuck in a research whirlpool". And at risk of getting pulled into the whirlpool's orbit, we cannot conclude this book without rehearsing the role clarity/ambiguity dilemma in the context of what we have now learned from the research reported in it. To that end, let us return to the two questions posed in the introduction. Firstly, on the basis of the contributions to this book and work from elsewhere in the field, what can we now say about what effective TA support should or could look like? And, secondly, how might the range of options and alternative approaches to including and educating pupils with SEN in mainstream settings be expanded in ways that – as well as reducing the dependency of TAs – have intrinsic value in terms offering pupils more inclusive and potentially more impactful experiences of school?

Characterising effective TA support

In order to address the first question about effective TA support, let us first take a look at how the TA role has been characterised in the previous chapters. A key theme – indeed, a tension – running through these contributions is that while the TA role is not intended to be pedagogical in nature, in reality, it is. In this sense, the evidence presented in this book is not only consistent with the confusion expressed in the wider literature, but it is also emblematic of a nebulous conceptualisation of "TA support". It is difficult to differentiate the role of the TA from that of the teacher if it is unclear and uncertain what at least one of these roles (in this case, the one allotted to the TA) looks like, independently of the other. Failure to address this, from the policy level downward, leads to an "operational confusion", which largely explains the ambiguity problem at the level of the classroom and even the individual pupil (Webster 2022).

The chapters in this collection suggest that the empirical work on which they report was carried out in contexts in which the TA role is ostensibly non-pedagogical in nature. Griffin and Blatchford and Zhao et al. (both Ireland) and Östlund et al. (Sweden) describe paraprofessionals as having a *"non-teaching care* remit" (Griffin and Blatchford), carrying out "personal care support" (Zhao et al.) and "social, medical and nursing tasks" (Östlund et al.) as a "prerequisite" for meaningful participation in mainstream classrooms and the proper functioning of the teaching environment. As part of the welfare system rather than the school system, Lübeck and Demmer describe how, in Germany, legal definitions of the paraprofessional role preclude "pedagogical work". Meanwhile, Vogt, Koechlin, Truniger, and

Zumwald inform us that "Swiss policy documents states that TAs should neither take on the role of teachers nor provide instruction, but solely assist". Where operative functions such as 'assist' and 'support' are not further defined, confusion is very likely to persist – as we saw in the interviews with secondary teachers conducted by Jackson, Sharma, and Odier-Guedj (Australia). Their study found inconsistencies and differences in "the degree to which TAs should be involved in teaching students and adapting and modifying curriculum".

Yet in all of these cases – and sometimes in spite of a legal or policy steer – there had been an unchecked drift to TAs performing 'teacher-like', instructional tasks, because "paraprofessionals are inevitably confronted with pedagogical requirements... due to their proximity to the child" (Lübeck and Demmer). In a similar fashion, the study by Jardí, Puigdellívol, Petreñas, and Sabando found that while teachers in Catalan schools are "legally the main professional responsible for managing student behaviour", in practice, there was "excessive delegation" of "responsibility for behaviour management" to TAs.

In order to navigate policy red lines in the Irish context, Griffin and Blatchford propose a reimagining of the TA role as an "edu-carer". This formulation swerves anything that resembles teaching and construes the TA's function in terms of "a scaffolding role, operating between the pupil's receipt of direct teaching input from a trained teacher and the pupil's independent functioning". Pinkard and Haakma, de Boer, Van Esch, Minnaert, and Van Der Puttena extend this conceptualisation of non-pedagogical support to the facilitation of interactions with their typically developing peers. Their research in the UK and the Netherlands (respectively) suggests a potentially useful role for TAs with regard to helping pupils with SEN to feel more included, and supporting problem-solving around a shared activity. Haakma et al. remind us that the variability of practice means that training and support for TAs are vital to ensuring positive experiences and outcomes, as "TAs may intend to foster interaction, while unintentionally hampering it".

The 'scaffolding role' is based on the work of Bosanquet, Radford, and Webster (2021), which seeks to optimise TAs' proximity to pupils (often, though not exclusively, those with SEN) and to repurpose their everyday opportunities for extended interaction with them to foster independence. Instead of replacing the teacher in an instructional capacity, TAs should be recast as scaffolding experts, supporting pupils to engage in learning and to develop the skills to manage their own learning independently. It is a deliberate inversion of the ineffective 'complete and correct' practices that have been found to define TAs' practice and their talk to pupils (Radford et al. 2011; Rubie-Davies et al. 2010).

What is significant about Bosanquet et al.'s alternative approach to the TA role is how it shifts the purpose and prioritisation of the support function. The starting point is to acknowledge – as some national policies do – the teacher as the pedagogical expert in the classroom, and to recognise that both TAs' skills and pupil outcomes are maximised when TAs support problem-solving *alongside* the mainstream curriculum. A randomised trial in which TAs were trained in the Bosanquet et al. approach found not only that TAs' talk behaviours improved sharply, but that it had a positive impact on pupil engagement (Dimova et al. 2021). Furthermore, data from the same study found evidence of a change from what was found in the landmark Deployment and Impact of Support Staff (DISS) project, where the tendency to deploy TAs as proxy teachers for lower-attaining pupils and those with SEN resulted in those pupils who most needed high-quality teacher input actually receiving the least input, as well as having fewer opportunities to work independently (Blatchford, Russell and Webster 2012).

As noted above, the contributions to this book and the broader evidence indicate that at least part of the function that TAs absorb is pedagogical in nature, regardless of what policy, legislation or unspoken convention intend or demand. Even if schools angle TA support towards scaffolding and fostering pupil independence, it remains realistic to assume that their role will retain a residual element of instruction. And as Lübeck and Demmer argue, their role ought to be formally acknowledged in our shared vocabulary of teaching, learning, and support.

That being so, it is worth reiterating the point made in the introduction, that the most consistent and compelling evidence of TAs having a positive, sometimes rapid, impact on learning outcomes is to train and deploy them to deliver curriculum intervention programmes to small groups or on a one-to-one basis (Alborz et al. 2009; Sharples 2016; Slavin 2016, 2018; Nickow, Oreopoulos and Quan 2020). As interventions tend to be delivered away from the classroom, a key organising principle of this approach is to ensure that the coverage and input pupils with SEN receive in this context must more than compensate for the time they spend away from mainstream lessons and teacher-led teaching. One way to achieve this is for teachers and TAs to provide a bridge between the two learning contexts, by making explicit and relatable connections for pupils between what they have covered outside the classroom with what is happening back inside the classroom (Webster, Bosanquet, Franklin and Parker 2021).

Broadening the palette of provisions and support

Warnock (2005) reminds us that "inclusion should mean being involved in a common enterprise of learning, rather than being necessarily under the same roof". Primary-aged pupils with SEN in UK schools, for example, have been shown to be simultaneously present in, but estranged, from mainstream lessons; they are in the class, but not *of* the class (Webster 2022). Educating children with a wide range of needs, some of them quite complex, is challenging. And while TAs are a crucial organisational fact of school life when it comes to their inclusion in mainstream schools, Giangreco's invocation of Maslow's Hammer is vivid reminder that TAs should not be – indeed, they are not – the only tool at our disposal for ensuring their effective participation and education.

Being part of the "common enterprise" and receiving personalised input from TAs are both important, but this volume may have convinced the reader that education systems and schools need to reduce the way in which inclusion relies so heavily on them. To be clear, nobody is saying that schools should get rid of or replace TAs, but that they must broaden their palette of provisions and support. There are alternative approaches that have intrinsic or additive value in terms offering pupils a more authentic inclusive experience and may contribute to improved outcomes. Giangreco lists a number of contenders in his chapter. A full appraisal of the alternatives is outside the scope of this chapter, but it is worth considering several other factors that ought to be weighed into these deliberations.

Firstly, schools could deliver some lessons in some curriculum areas to smaller classes of pupils with SEN, taught by highly skilled, specialised teachers, and blend this with mainstream mixed attainment teaching. Secondly, the judicious use of smaller teaching and learning contexts for and including pupils with SEN is also connected to the need to improve the social mix in lessons. Compared with classes organised on the basis of the problematic notion of 'ability', mixed attainment teaching has greater potential to improve outcomes for all pupils (Kutnick et al. 2005; Taylor et al. 2016). To increase opportunities for peer support, secondary schools could, for example, take the bold step of mixed attainment teaching, for at least some subjects. As a minimum, schools should adopt grouping strategies that mitigate the more harmful effects of streaming or 'hard' setting (Francis et al. 2017; Mazenod et al. 2018). In lessons, teachers should ensure that pupils with SEN are not routinely grouped together for paired or group work, but have opportunities to interact, work with, and learn from a broader range of their peers. The trio of chapters by Haakma et al., Griffin and Blatchford, and Pinkard provide indications of how TAs might facilitate peer interactions.

Finally, broadening the palette of provisions and support necessarily means ensuring that all teachers are confident and competent in relation to SEN. That SEN should be a staple of initial teacher education and a recurrent topic in teachers' in-service training should hardly need saying, but there are cases of historical failure, for example in the UK, that show teachers' knowledge deficit on SEN goes back decades. In his skilful assessments of the landscape, Hodkinson (2009, 2019) concludes that the adequacy, quality, and amount of training in SEN offered to pre-service teachers in England has been one of repeated missed opportunities, with the rhetoric from successive governments on the value and status of SEN in teacher training coming to sound "like a scratched record".

The international data shortage on TAs

Having considered the scope and impact of research related to TAs to date, this chapter turns finally to future directions. Giangreco is right when he says that the research community needs to extend the topics and areas of enquiry that will compose the "palate of future research", and the "wish list" he provides in his chapter – together with the ideas from our other contributors, based on their research – offers inspiration. Similarly, in their analysis of the international, empirical studies of TAs in inclusive classrooms (published between 2005 and 2015), Sharma and Salend (2016) identify areas for future research on which there are either a very limited number of studies or none at all. These include: parents' perspectives on the use of TAs; perceptions of pupils with disabilities regarding their experiences with TAs (including any differences between those with high incidence disabilities and low incidence disabilities); how pupils without disabilities "view the roles, efficacy, and presence of TAs in their classrooms"; and "research to develop and validate alternatives to the use of TAs".

As well as broadening the range of research topics, we must show a greater degree of ambition in our methodological approaches and scale of operation. It is remarkable that, despite their increasing prevalence in schools across the world, and the very clear way in which inclusion in many developed education systems has become reliant on the employment and deployment of TAs, there are virtually no international data on the characteristics, role, and contribution of TAs, and their relationship to and impact on inclusion. There are a limited number of studies involving large sample sizes, or more varied sets of participants and stakeholders, or multi-method, longitudinal efforts. And while there are some econometric analyses, which attempt to divine a causal relationship between the presence of TAs and academic outcomes, they take no account of school and classroom processes (see, e.g., Andersen et al. 2018; Hemelt, Ladd, and Clifton 2021). Though often favoured by policy-makers, such analyses are voguish and reductive, and offer hardly anything of value by way of transmutability; the findings have little practical use at the classroom level. Thirteen years on from the publication of findings from the pioneering UK-based DISS project (Blatchford et al. 2009), we have yet to see anything that approaches its scale and scope, or that aspires to its influence and real-world impact.

The literature is devoid of heavyweight, international comparative studies of TAs. The most influential international study on schools and classrooms, the Organisation for Economic Co-operation and Development's (OECD) Teaching and Learning International Survey (TALIS), is lauded by policy-makers and researchers of advanced nations for the richness of its data and the detailed insights it provides; however, it has vanishingly little say about TAs. The third and most recent wave of TALIS from 2018 – which involved over 275,000 respondents from 31 countries (Organisation for Economic Co-operation and Development 2021a) – stated that "teacher aides [and] pedagogical support staff ... were not considered to be teachers and, thus, not part of the TALIS international target population" (Organisation for Economic Co-operation and Development 2021b).

Leaving aside whether there is, or there ought to be, an equivalence between TAs and teachers in this regard, the decision to exclude TAs from TALIS matters. Not just, I would argue, in and of itself, but because other high-level analyses of education rely on the data TALIS collects, such as the authoritative Global Education Monitoring (GEM) annual report (which is hosted and published by the United Nations Educational, Scientific and Cultural Organisation). The focus of the 2020 GEM report was inclusion, yet its authors were unable to report much at all about TAs because "comparable international data on inclusion-related use of support personnel are not generally available" (United Nations Educational, Scientific and Cultural Organisation 2020, p. 306). Its recommendations relating to TAs were, therefore, limited to a familiar recycling of what we already know from the (mainly small-scale and qualitative) research base.

Elsewhere, a rare international survey, commissioned by Education International (the global union federation of teacher trade unions), of the characteristics, employment, and working conditions of just over 3,000 'education support personnel' [ESP] – a group among which TAs are prominent – concluded: "there are significant gaps in the knowledge and understanding of ESP: who they are, what they do, and what they need to do their jobs effectively" (Butler 2019, p. 1).

A particular challenge concerns the way "definitions and labels in data collection instruments vary across countries and education levels" (United Nations Educational, Scientific and Cultural Organisation 2020, p. 305), and how, in the aggregate, it becomes difficult to explicitly differentiate between qualified/certified teachers and TAs. The GEM report cites the example of the South African government, which collects data on "educators", who are defined as "any person who teaches, educates or trains other persons or who provides professional education services" (Department of Basic Education 2018, p. 34). However, resolving such seemingly theological questions about definitions should not be beyond the conceptual and methodological capabilities of the international education research community.

As the drive towards inclusion continues, all the indications are that governments across the world are prepared to spend large amounts of public money on employing more and more TAs to facilitate it. Yet, "data on teaching assistants is limited, even in high-income countries" (United Nations Educational, Scientific and Cultural Organisation 2020, p. 300) in terms of what this costs, or to what extent it represents value for taxpayers' money. Such questions can, of course, be both reductive and a rather blunt way of quantifying TAs' highly nuanced contributions to education. Nonetheless, these are the kinds of questions that motivate policymakers and imply a prima facia case for national governments to show as much interest in the working lives, practices, and perspectives of TAs as they do in those of teachers.

So, to address the dearth of macro-level data on TAs, we need an ambitious, ongoing programme of international data collection and evidence building, which reflects, and is proportionate to, the known global trends concerning inclusion and TAs. It makes sense, then, to extend TALIS – an existing data collection effort that is funded by, and maps education labour force trends in, the most world's advanced economies.

But what should such a research programme include? To start with, many of the themes selected for inclusion in the 2018 TALIS survey are relatable to the lives of TAs:

- instructional practices
- professional practices
- initial preparation for the role
- school climate
- job satisfaction
- human resource issues
- stakeholder relations
- career opportunities
- professional responsibility and autonomy.

At the more basic, but nonetheless essential, descriptive level, such a survey would be able to track demographic trends relating to equality, diversity, and representation. Essential, you would think, for a role synonymous with inclusion.

The GEM report points to how a broader "shortage of data on teachers" from countries that are not included in TALIS represents one of three "data gaps remain[ing] in key areas of the SDG 4 [the fourth Sustainable Development Goal on education] monitoring framework" (United Nations Educational, Scientific and Cultural Organisation 2020, p. 198). The macro data gap relating to TAs can be seen as part of the same issue. Providing and sharing the robust evidence needed to underpin policymaking and practice, and to hold world leaders to account, are essential if we are to achieve SDG 4. Progress will be all the slower, if not unworkable, without a coordinated and consolidated data collection effort that incorporates and reflects the role and contribution of TAs.

Perhaps a future cycle of TALIS could be expanded to include a pilot survey of TAs in a select number of territories where they are a well-established part of the school workforce. Survey items could be limited to questions drawn from several of the most relatable themes from the teacher survey (see above), and trialled in countries such as the US, the UK, Norway, and Finland; countries that are not only above the OECD average in terms of TA-pupil ratio (7.3 TAs per 1,000 pupils) (Masdeu Navarro 2015), but also have large enough numbers of TAs from which a meaningful sample can be drawn. The pilot might extend to Brazil, Chile, France, the Netherlands, and Sweden, which an interrogation of the most recent OECD data from 2018 suggests also have sufficiently sizable and sampleable TA populations across both primary and secondary education (Organisation for Economic Co-operation and Development 2021c).

Though, as noted, it will not be without its conceptual challenges, taking the time to characterise and crystallise a limited set of descriptive categories that capture the core functions of TAs across jurisdictions is foundational to producing the data that, within a couple of TALIS cycles, are capable of producing the kind of data that have – impressively, and in relatively short order – transformed and enhanced our understanding of teachers and teaching.

Final thoughts

There is, I believe, an interesting parallel between the ideas expressed here concerning the future of TA-related research and the TA role and experience itself. It is a parallel that will be recognisable to, and resonate with, many researchers familiar with the field. A common refrain voiced not just by researchers, but also by TAs, other educators, and the groups that represent TAs' interests, such as trade unions, is that TAs should be treated with greater respect and value. In education systems where TAs are an established presence, researchers and advocates rightly maintain that the contribution of TAs is habitually and too easily overlooked, and that a higher esteeming of their role is long overdue. I think we researchers should be arguing for a similar kind of recognition and for a greater valuing of *our* field of inquiry within the arenas of policy, practice, and academia.

Researchers conclude, again correctly, that it is the power imbalances within schools and education systems overall that maintain the status quo: TAs are limited in terms of the influence they have over instigating change in their context. But here there is a crucial difference. Unlike TAs, in *their* context, researchers and academics are relatively more agentic. If we are to move our field on, there are things we can do right away. We can start by agreeing to apply Giangreco's 'Maslow's Hammer' test to *all* aspects of the research process, in our own endeavours and supportively as part of collegiate activities, such as peer review and student supervision (see also Webster and de Boer 2021). We can shape and set a new and exciting research agenda. We can expand and develop our suite of methodological approaches, making our research more innovative and responsive to the rapidly evolving education landscape. And crucially, we can focus more resources on actually addressing, in collaboration with schools, some of the persistent real-world problems caused by and connected to an over-reliance on TAs, instead of trying to mitigate their worst effects. As Giangreco notes in his contribution to this book, none of this runs counter to the view we all hold about the value of "the ongoing and significant contributions of our TA colleagues". What is key here is thinking more expansively, creatively and collaboratively about the bigger picture: improving the participation of and outcomes for pupils with learning difficulties and disabilities.

Given TAs' lack of agency, researchers perhaps understandably target the messages from their work to policymakers and education leaders. As we consider the shape of the post-pandemic world, and identify and address the problems exacerbated and caused by national lockdowns (time out of school; lack of access to specialist and peripatetic services, such as physiotherapy, for those with SEN), we have – dispiritingly, but not unsurprisingly – little reason to think that after decades of sidelining TAs, policymakers are about to listen to us or to act on our evidence immediately. Encouragingly though, as the empirical work included in this volume attests, it is perhaps the dialogic, collaborative work between researchers and practitioners and pupils in schools that offers us the best, most direct, expedient to change.

The final appeal left to make is to researchers: to capitalise on this potential, and assert ourselves in this reimagined space, so that *we* might use *our* work to catalyse real change on the ground, in schools.

References

Alborz, A., Pearson, D., Farrell, P., and Howes, A. 2009. *The Impact of Adult Support Staff on Pupils and Mainstream Schools*. London: EPPI-Centre, Social Science Research Unit, Institute of Education. Accessed 25 October 2021. http://eppi.ioe.ac.uk/cms/Portals/0/PDF%20reviews%20and%20summaries/Support%20staff%20Rpt.pdf?ver=2009-05-05-165528-197

Andersen, S. C., Beuchert, L., Nielsen, H. S., and Thomsen, M. K.. 2018. "The Effect of Teacher's Aides in the Classroom: Evidence from a Randomized Trial." *Journal of the European Economic Association* 18 (1): 469–505. doi:10.1093/jeea/jvy048.

Blatchford, P., Bassett, P., Brown, P., Koutsoubou, M., Martin, C., Russell, A., and Webster, R., and Rubie-Davies, C. 2009. *Deployment and Impact of Support Staff in Schools. Results from Strand 2, Wave 2*. London: Department for Children, Schools and Families.

Blatchford, P., Russell, A., and Webster, R. 2012. *Reassessing the Impact of Teaching Assistants: How Research Challenges Practice and Policy*. Oxon: Routledge.

Bosanquet, P., Radford, J., and Webster, R.. 2021. *The Teaching Assistant's Guide to Effective Interaction: How to Maximise Your Practice*. 2nd ed. Oxon: Routledge.

Butler, P. 2019. "Understanding the Invisible Workforce. Education Support Personnel's Roles, Needs and the Challenges They Face." Brussels: Education International. Accessed 4 February 2021. https://issuu.com/educationinternational/docs/research_esp_final_report

Department of Basic Education. 2018. *Education Statistics in South Africa 2016*. Accessed 4 February 2021. https://www.education.gov.za/Portals/0/Documents/Publications/Education%20Statistic%20SA%202016.pdf?ver=2018-11-01-095102-947.

Dimova, S., Culora, A., Brown, E.R., Ilie, S., Sutherland, A., and Curran, S. 2021. *Maximising the Impact of Teaching Assistants. Evaluation Report*. London: Education Endowment Foundation. Accessed 7 October 2021. https://educationendowmentfoundation.org.uk/projects-and-evaluation/projects/maximising-the-impact-of-teaching-assistants.

Francis, B., Archer, L., Hodgen, J., Pepper, D., Taylor, B., and Travers, M-C. 2017. "Exploring the Relative Lack of Impact of Research on 'Ability Grouping' in England: A Discourse Analytic Account." *Cambridge Journal of Education* 47 (1): 1–17. https://doi.org/10.1080/0305764X.2015.1093095

Hemelt, S. W., Ladd, H. F., and Clifton, C. R.. 2021. "Do Teacher Assistants Improve Student Outcomes? Evidence from School Funding Cutbacks in North Carolina." *Educational Evaluation and Policy Analysis* 016237372199036. https://doi.org/10.3102/0162373721990361

Hodkinson, A. 2009. "Pre-Service Teacher Training and Special Educational Needs in England 1970–2008: Is Government Learning the Lessons of the Past or is it Experiencing a Groundhog Day?" *European Journal of Special Needs Education* 24 (3): 277–289. https://doi.org/10.1080/08856250903016847

Hodkinson, A. 2019. "Pre-Service Teacher Training and Special Educational Needs in England, 1978–2018: Looking Back and Moving Forward?" In *Including Children and Young People with Special Educational Needs and Disabilities in Learning and Life. How Far Have We Come Since the Warnock Enquiry – and Where Do We Go Next?* edited by R. Webster, 36–41. Oxon: Routledge.

Kutnick, P., Sebba, J., Blatchford, P., Galton, M., Thorpe, J., MacIntyre, H., and Berdondini, L. 2005. *The Effects of Pupil Grouping: Literature Review. Research Report 688.* London: DfES. Accessed 31 March 2021. https://dera.ioe.ac.uk/18143/1/RR688.pdf

Masdeu Navarro, F. 2015. Learning Support Staff: A Literature Review. OECD Education Working Papers. No. 125. Paris: OECD. https://doi.org/10.1787/19939019

Mazenod, A., Francis, B., Archer, L., Hodgen, J., Taylor, B., Treshchenko, A., and Pepper, D.. 2018. "Nurturing Learning or Encouraging Dependency? Teacher Constructions of Students in Lower Attainment Groups in English Secondary Schools." *Cambridge Journal of Education* 49 (1): 53–68. https://doi.org/10.1080/0305764X.2018.1441372

Nickow, A., Oreopoulos, P., and Quan, V. 2020. The Impressive Effects of Tutoring on PreK–12 Learning: A Systematic Review and Meta-Analysis of the Experimental Evidence. NBER Working Paper No. 27476. Accessed 1 August 2020. https://www.nber.org/papers/w27476

Organisation for Economic Co-operation and Development. (2021a). "Talis Faq." Accessed 4 February 2021. https://www.oecd.org/education/talis/talisfaq/

Organisation for Economic Co-operation and Development. (2021b). "Annex A. Technical Notes on Sampling Procedures, Response Rates and Adjudication for TALIS 2018." Accessed 4 February 2021. https://www.oecd-ilibrary.org/sites/1d0bc92a-en/1/3/1/index.html?itemId=/content/publication/1d0bc92a-en&_csp_=1418ec5a16ddb9919c5bc207486a271c&itemIGO=oecd&itemContentType=book

Organisation for Economic Co-operation and Development (2021c). "Education Database: Management educational personnel and teacher aides (Edition 2020)." OECD Education Statistics (database) Accessed 16 March 2021. https://doi.org/10.1787/04c5a18d-en

Radford, J., Blatchford, P., and Webster, R. 2011. "Opening Up and Closing Down: Comparing Teacher and TA Talk in Mathematics Lessons." *Learning and Instruction* 21 (5): 625–635. https://doi.org/10.1016/j.learninstruc.2011.01.004

Rubie-Davies, C., Blatchford, P., Webster, R., Koutsoubou, M., and Bassett, P. 2010. "Enhancing Learning?: A Comparison of Teacher and Teaching Assistant Interactions with Pupils." *School Effectiveness and School Improvement* 21 (4): 429–449. https://doi.org/10.1080/09243453.2010.512800

Sharma, U., and Salend, S.J. 2016. "Teaching Assistants in Inclusive Classrooms: A Systematic Analysis of the International Research." *Australian Journal of Teacher Education* 41 (8): 118–134. Accessed 11 February 2021. http://ro.ecu.edu.au/ajte/vol41/iss8/7

Sharples, J. 2016. *EEF Blog: Six of the Best – How our latest Reports Can Help You Support Teaching Assistants to Get Results.* Accessed 17 April 2020. https://educationendowmentfoundation.org.uk/news/six-of-the-best-how-our-latest-reports-can-help-you-support-teaching-assist/

Slavin, R. 2016. *Trans-Atlantic Concord: Tutoring by Paraprofessionals Works.* Accessed 17 April 2020. https://robertslavinsblog.wordpress.com/2016/03/03/trans-atlantic-concord-tutoring-by-paraprofessionals-works/

Slavin, R. 2018. *New Findings on Tutoring: Four Shockers.* Accessed 17 April 2020. https://robertslavinsblog.wordpress.com/2018/04/05/new-findings-on-tutoring-four-shockers/

Slee, R. 2012. "Inclusion in Schools: What is the task?" In *What Works in Inclusion?*, edited by C. Boyle and K. Topping, 41–55. Maidenhead: Open University Press.

Taylor, B., Francis, B., Archer, L., Hodgen, J., Pepper, D., Tereshchenko A., and Travers, M.-C. 2016. "Factors Deterring Schools from Mixed Attainment Teaching Practice." *Pedagogy, Culture and Society* 25 (3): 327–345. https://doi.org/10.1080/14681366.2016.1256908

United Nations Educational, Scientific and Cultural Organisation (2020) *Global Education Monitoring Report 2020: Inclusion and Education: All Means All.* Paris: UNES. Accessed 4 February 2021. https://en.unesco.org/gem-report/report/2020/inclusion

Vivash, J., and Morgan, G. 2019. "The Role of Educational Psychologists in Fuelling the Narrative of the 'Velcro TA'." *Frontiers in Education* 4: 66. https://doi.org/10.3389/feduc.2019.00066

Warnock, M. 2005. *Special Educational Needs: A New Look.* London: Continuum.

Webster, R. 2022. *The Inclusion Illusion: How Children with Special Educational Needs Experience Mainstream Schools.* London: UCL Press.

Webster, R. Bosanquet, P., Franklin, S., and Parker, M. 2021. *Maximising the Impact of Teaching Assistants in Primary Schools: Guidance for School Leaders.* Oxon: Routledge.

Webster, R., and de Boer, A. (2021) "Where next for research on teaching assistants: The case for an international response." *European Journal of Special Needs Education*, 36 (2): 294–305. https://doi.org/10.1080/08856257.2021.1901368

Index

Page numbers in **Bold** refer to tables; and page numbers in *italics* refer to figures.

Abbott, L. 144
ability to collaborate and consult: time constraints 163–164; valuing knowledge and skills 164–165; working together 163
Alborz, A. 30, 105, 118
Almqvist, L. 29
ambiguous role in inclusive schooling: Grammar of Schooling 46, 51–55; implications 54–55; paraprofessionals *vs.* inclusive school development 48–50; role confusion in everyday interaction 50–51
Anderson, L. 29, 31, 40
Aprile, K. T. 144

Barow, T. 5, 29–43, 196, 197
Bassett, P. 105, 128, 131–132, 143–144
behaviour management, TAs: attention to diversity committees 152; Catalan context 145, 152; codes and sub-codes **147**; coordination in 149–150; data analysis 147; participants 145–146, **153**; planning and designing teaching sessions 153; procedures 146, 150–151; roles 147–148; semi-structured interviews 146; student behaviour 145; systematic review 144
Bengtsson, K. 29
Biggs, E. E. 170
Blatchford, P. 79, 85–100, 104–105, 127–128, 131–132, 143–144, 200
Bosanquet, P. 127, 131, 144, 198
Braun, V. 109, 161
Broer, S. M. 106

Brown, P. 128, 143
Brown, S. 30, 41
Bruhn, A. L. 145
Butler, C. 95
Butt, R. 143, 169

Cable, C. 108
Cameron, P. 169
Carter, E. W. 170
Casserly, A. M. 25
Causton-Theoharis, J. 128
Chapman, S. 30, 41
Chopra, R. 170
clarity of roles 161–163, 168–169; characterising effective TA support 197–199; palette of provisions and support 199–200
Clarke, V. 109, 161
Clunies-Ross, P. 144

Dahlberg, K. 5, 29–43, 196–197
Davidson, J. 152
Deacy, E. 25
de Boer, A. 1–7, 5, 61–82, 198, 200
Demmer, C. 5, 46–55, 196–197, 199
Deployment and Impact of Support Staff (DISS) project 86, 88, 105, 116, 184, 185, 199, 201
Der Puttena, V. 5
disability implicit association test 185
Douglas, S. 170
Doveston, M. 106
Doyle, M. B. 106

European Journal of Special Needs Education 5–6
Eyres, I. 108

Farrell, P. 118
Flyybjerg, B. 15
Fraser, C. 106, 117

Giangreco, M. F. 3, 6, 97, 106, 145, 158, 168, 177–190, 194–195, 197, 199, 200, 204
Gibson, D. 144–145
Gilson, C. B. 170
Global Education Monitoring (GEM) annual report 202–203
Göransson, K. 29
Gould, M. 95
Grammar of Schooling: changing the established role structure 53–54; concept of 46; paraprofessionals as a transitional phenomenon 53; paraprofessionals challenge 52; paraprofessionals into existing role structure 52–53; rewriting 55
Griffin, C. 85–100, 197, 200
Groom, B. 105

Haakma, I. 5, 61–82, 198, 200
Hancock, R. 108
Hansson, S. 29
Harris, L. R. 144
Harvey, D. 25
Hedegaard-Sørensen, L. 31
Heinrich, M. 136
Hendrix, N. M. 145
Hodkinson, A. 200
Homecoming model 182
Howes, A. 118

Inclusive Research in Irish Schools (IRIS) 13
intellectual disability (ID) 2, 29, 64, 180–181
interactions initiated: by peers 70, *73*, *74*, *75*; by student 70, *71–72*; by teaching assistants 70, *71–72*

Jackson, C. 6, 158–172
Jardí, A. 6, 143–154, 198
Johansson, A. 5, 29–43, 196–197

Kamstra, A. 63
Kang, S. 145
Keating, S. 13
Kenny, M. 86
Kerins, P. 13, 25
Kienhuis, M. 144
Klang, N. 29

Klassen, R. 105
Koechlin, A. 6, 125–139, 197
Koster, M. 62
Koutsoubou, M. 105, 128, 131–132, 144
Krammer, K. 131–132

Lamb, B. 104
Langager, S. 31
Lindqvist, G. 29
Lipsky, M. 32, 41
Little, E. 144
Loxley, A. 86
Lübeck, A. 5, 46–55, 48, 196–197, 199
Lupart, J. 106

Madden, L. O. B. 144
Maes, B. 63, 79
Making a Statement (MaSt) project 86, 88, 95, 97
Malmgren, K. W. 128
Martin, C. 128, 143
Martin, T. 30
Maslow, A. H. 2, 180–181
Maslow's Hammer effect 2, 158, 168–169, 180–181, 184, 188, 199, 204
MAXQDA tool 131–132
McConkey, R. 144
McDonagh, D. 13, 25
Meadows, S. 106, 117
Minnaert, A. 5, 61–82, 198, 200
Mitchell, D. 30
Morano, S. 170
Morris, J. 96
Muijs, D. 105

Nakken, H. 62
Newton, C. 108
Nijs, S. 63, 79
Nilholm, C. 29

O'Connor, U. 13
Odier-Guedj, D. 6, 158–172
O'Donnell, M. 95
O'Kane, C. 108
Oliver, M. 96
O'Neill, A. 13
organisational structures 170–171; capacity building 167; funding 167; leadership 166–167; school processes 165–166
Östlund, D. 5, 29–43, 31, 40, 196–197

Paatsch, L. 144
Palm, E. 96
paraprofessionals: ambiguous role in inclusive schooling 46–55; claims 36; curriculum implementation 30; deployment and employment in Germany 47–48; experiences 40; *vs.* inclusive school development 48–50; informal responsibility 41; interviewees 35; participation and influence 41–42; point of view 41; research questions 31; self-reported knowledge *35–37*; transitional phenomenon 53; working in teams 30–32; working with students with ID 30
parent-helper model 1
Patton, M. Q. 15
Pauli, C. 131
Pearson, D. 118
Penne, A. 79
perspectives and experiences of children, SEN: data analysis 109; design 107; impacts of TA support 105; mosaic approach 108; participant information **107**; procedures 108; pupil voice 105–106; purpose of study 106–107; semi-structured interviews 108; TA developments 104–105; thematic analysis process 109, *110*, 111–115
Petreñas, C. 6, 143–154, 198
Pijl, S. J. 62
Pinkard, H. 104–120, 198, 200
Planning and Assessing for Independence model 98
policymakers claim 4
profound intellectual and multiple disabilities (PIMD): coding schemes 65–66, **66**; communication modes 78; data analysis 66–67; data collection 65; day care centres for children 63; direct support professionals 61, 63; findings 78; inclusion moments 62, 64, 67, **68–69**, 70; interactions initiated by peers 70, *73*, 74, *75*; interactions initiated by student 70, *71–72*; interactions initiated by teaching assistants 70, *71–72*; mainstream classrooms 61; participants 64; procedure 64–65; research implications 81; strengths and limitations 80; students' characteristics 65; students perception behaviours 78; TA's roles 79–80; 'To School Together' project 61–64, 67, 74
promoting independence, SNA: collaboration between SNAs and teachers 20; primary school 19–20; school professionals' perspectives 20–21
Puigdellívol, I. 6, 143–154, 198

Radford, J. 127, 131, 144, 198
Reusser, K. 131
Reynolds, D. 105
Robertson, C. 95
Rose, R. 5, 11–26, 13, 105–106, 196–197
Rubie-Davies, C. M. 105, 128, 131–132, 144
Russell, A. 128, 143

Sabando, D. 6, 143–154, 198
Salend, S. 144, 196, 201
Scaffolding Framework 98
Schlapp, U. 152
Schnebel, S. 132
Senior, J. 144
Sharma, U. 6, 144, 158–172, 196, 201
Shevlin, M. 5, 11–26, 86, 196–197
Slee, R. 196
Sobeck, E. 170
special educational needs (SEN): EHCPs 115–116; impacts of TA support 105; inclusive classrooms 62; learning difficulties 115; mainstream schools 1, 2, 6; perspectives and experiences of children 104–120
Special Educational Needs in Secondary Education (SENSE) study 86, 88
special needs assistant (SNA) scheme: academic tasks 91–92, **92**; evidence-based practice and frameworks 97–98; Irish policy context 85; non-teaching care 85; OPTIC schedule data 91, **92**; procedure 89; pupil assignment 93; pupil proximity 93–94, 97; pupils' independence/dependence 95–96; pupil support strategies 94; qualitative data 89; quantitative data 89; renewed thinking 98–99; research design and participants 88; research in field 86–87; research rationale and focus 86; school leadership 96–97; significant care needs 85; systematic observation schedule 88–89; total classroom context 90, **90**; total interaction data 90–91, **91**

special needs assistants (SNA) provision: coding and analysis 17; core elements of 24; emotional reassurance 23–24; findings 17–18, 24, 25; identifying research questions 14–15; in Ireland 11–12; Irish research 13; managing behaviour 19; mixed methods approach 14; organisational support 18–19; parents' attitude 22–23; physical caretaking 18; project IRIS 13; promoting independence 19–21; pupils' attitudes 21–22; school professionals 25; semi-structured interviews 15–16, **16**; teachers acknowledgement 26

special needs teachers (SNT): being an educator and caregiver 36–39; cooperation between paraprofessionals and SNTs 34–36; educational planning for a school week *35*; instruction and formative assessment 40; interviewed paraprofessionals 34; knowledge-oriented tasks 42; lack of supervision for professional development 39–40; mixed methods approach 32–33; paraprofessionals working in teams 30–32; paraprofessionals working with students with ID 30; self-contained classrooms 29; street-level bureaucrats 32, 41

street-level bureaucrats 32, 41–42

TALIS survey 201–203

TAs' instructional support and effects on pupils, SEN: co-constructivist theory of learning 127; constructivist teaching 127; inclusion for pupils 128; individual seatwork 127; research questions 128–129

Teacher Assistant As Facilitator (TAAF) model 143

teachers' perceptions: capacity building 167; collaborative and consultative teacher 163–165, 169; data collection and analysis 161; full-time equivalent (FTE) teachers 161; funding 167; Inclusion Leader (IL) participants 160; leadership 166–167; limitations and further research 171; organisational structures 170–171; researchers' attitudes 160; role clarity 161–163, 168–169; school processes 165–166

teaching assistants (TAs): behaviour management 143–154; Covid pandemic 2; curricular inclusion 185–186; curriculum access 115; developments 104–105; educator roles 188; employment and deployment 7; essentialness of 2; everyday role 3; future research 188–190; GEM report 202–203; impact support 105; individual students 187–188; international data shortage 200–204; Island in the Mainstream 183, *183*; key stakeholders perceive 105; listen to self-advocates 186–187; mainstream schools in Switzerland 125–126; match supports to needs 186; over-relying on 179; participant's experiences 116–117; peer interactions 62; peer-review process 5; prevalence and prominence of 3; pupil voice research 105–106, 118; reliant model 184; research on 2–5, 194–196; role of 64; self-examination 185; social-emotional benefits 119; social-emotional support 118; social participation of students 62; special educational needs (SEN) 2; specific pupil with SEN 126, 137; TALIS survey 201–203

teaching assistants and teachers: coding schemes 131–132, **132–133**; data analysis 131; individual seatwork 131, 134, **134**, 136; observational data 138; pupils with SEN during individual seatwork 134–135, **135**; research design 129–130; statistical analysis 132; TAs employed as general aide 135–136, **136**, 137; thirty-one classes 130; types of individual support 131–132, **132**; video observation 130–131

Tews, L. 106, 128

thematic analysis process: logistics of my TA support 109, *110*; positive impact of TA support *110*, 114–115; teacher *vs.* TA comparisons *110*, 113; what is my ideal TA like *110*, 113, *114*; what is my TA like *110–111*, 111–113, *112*

Thomas, N. 108

Tiernan, B. 25

Tobin, W. 51

Toe, D. 144

'To School Together' project 61–64, 67, 74

Truniger, A. 6, 125–139, 197

Turner, J. 108
Tyack, D. 51

UN Convention on the Rights of Persons with Disabilities (UN-CRPD) 46, 48–49

Vancel, S. M. 145
Van Der Putten, A. A. J. 61–82, 198, 200
Van Esch, S. 5, 61–82, 198, 200
Van Houten, E. 62
Vlaskamp, C. 63, 79
Vogt, F. 6, 125–139, 197
voluntary arrangements 1

Wagner, S. 132
Ware, J. 95
Warnock, M. 199
Webster, R. 1–7, 79, 104–105, 127–128, 131–132, 143–144, 194–205
Wetso, G.-M. 29
Whitchurch, C. 98
Wilson, D. 108
Wilson, V. 152
Wise, S. 145

Zhao, Yu 5, 11–26, 196–197
Zumwald, B. 6, 125–139, 198